TELLING WOMEN'S LIVES

feminist educational thinking

Series Editors:
Kathleen Weiler, Tufts University, USA
Gaby Weiner, Umea University, Sweden
Lyn Yates, La Trobe University, Australia

This authoritative series explores how theory/practice and the development of advanced ideas within feminism and education can be fused. The series aims to address the specific theoretical issues that confront feminist educators and to encourage both practitioner and academic debate.

Published titles:

Jill Blackmore: *Troubling Women: Feminism, Leadership and Educational Change*
Jacky Brine: under*Educating Women: Globalizing Inequality*
Kaye Haw: *Educating Muslim Girls: Shifting Discourses*
Petra Munro: *Subject to Fiction: Women Teachers' Life History Narratives and the Cultural Politics of Resistance*
Kathleen Weiler and Sue Middleton (eds): *Telling Women's Lives: Narrative Inquiries in the History of Women's Education*

Titles in preparation include:

Pen Dalton: *Dismantling Art Education*
Bob Lingard and Peter Douglas: *Men Engaging Feminisms: Pro-Feminism, Backlashes and Schooling*
Georgina Tsolidis: *Feminist Pedagogies of Difference*

TELLING WOMEN'S LIVES

Narrative inquiries in the history of women's education

edited by
KATHLEEN WEILER
and
SUE MIDDLETON

OPEN UNIVERSITY PRESS
Buckingham · Philadelphia

Open University Press
Celtic Court
22 Ballmoor
Buckingham
MK18 1XW

email: enquiries@openup.co.uk
world wide web: http://www.openup.co.uk

and
325 Chestnut Street
Philadelphia, PA 19106, USA

First Published 1999

A catalogue record of this book is available from the British Library

ISBN   0 335 20173 3 (pb)   0 335 20174 1 (hb)

Library of Congress Cataloging-in-Publication Data
Telling women's lives: narrative inquiries in the history of women's
    education / edited by Kathleen Weiler and Sue Middleton.
        p.   cm. – (Feminist educational thinking series)
    Includes bibliographical references and index.
    ISBN 0-335-20174-1 (hardcover). – ISBN 0-335-20173-3 (pbk.)
    1. Women–Education–History–Cross-cultural studies.   2. Feminism
and education.   3. Feminist theory.   4. Poststructuralism.
    I. Weiler, Kathleen.   II. Middleton, Sue, 1947–   . III. Series.
    LC1481.T45   1999
    371.822–dc21
                                                                              98-20780
                                                                                    CIP

Typeset by Type Study, Scarborough
Printed in Great Britain by Biddles Ltd, Guildford and King's Lynn

Contents

Notes on contributors

Helena C. Araújo is Associate Professor at the Faculty of Psychology and Education, University of Porto, Portugal where she lectures in the Sociology of Education and Gender Studies. Her main areas of interest are women and education, citizenship, the teaching profession and gender, mass schooling and the state.

Valinda W. Littlefield is a Staff Associate at the Afro-American Studies and Research Program and an ABD History student at the University of Illinois, Urbana-Champaign. She is currently writing a dissertation entitled ' "I am only one, But I am one": Southern African-American Women Schoolteachers, 1884–1954'.

Helen May is the Professor of Early Childhood Teacher Education at the Institute for Early Childhood Studies, Victoria University and Wellington College of Education. Her previous publications include *Discovery of Early Childhood*, *Minding Children, Managing Men*, and *Mind That Child*. Her research and teaching interests are early childhood policy, curriculum and history.

Sue Middleton is a Professor and Assistant Dean (Graduate Studies) in the School of Education at the University of Waikato in Hamilton, New Zealand. She has published widely on the themes of feminist educational theory, education policy, life-history methods, sexuality and the body. Her recent books are *Educating Feminists: Life Histories and Pedagogy*, *Disciplining Sexuality: Foucault, Life Histories and Education* and (with Helen May) *Teachers Talk Teaching 1915–1995: Early Childhood, Schools and Teachers' Colleges*.

Alison Oram is Reader in Women's Studies at Nene University College, Northampton, UK. She has researched and published on women's politicization, women teachers, and spinsterhood in the context of twentieth-century feminism, and on lesbian history. Recent publications include *Women Teachers and Feminist Politics 1900–39* (Manchester University

Press, 1996). She is currently working on a sourcebook of British lesbian history in the nineteenth and twentieth centuries for Routledge.

Alison Prentice taught at the Ontario Institute for Studies in Education of the University of Toronto. She retired in the spring of 1998 and is now an adjunct professor at the University of Victoria in British Columbia. Her early research in the history of education focused on elementary schooling and teachers; more recently she has explored the history of women's work in higher education. She has published articles and books in the fields of educational and women's history, most recently the second edition of a co-authored text *Canadian Women: A History* (1996) and a co-edited volume entitled *Creating Historical Memory: English-Canadian Women and the Work of History* (1997).

Kate Rousmaniere teaches in the Department of Educational Leadership, Miami University, Oxford, Ohio. She is the author of *City Teachers: Teaching and School Reform in Historical Perspective* (Teachers College Press, 1997), and co-editor of *Discipline, Moral Regulation, and Schooling: A Social History* (Garland, 1997). She teaches and writes about the history of American teachers and teacher unions, gender issues in education, and methodological questions in the social history of schooling. She is currently working on a biography of Margaret Haley.

Linda Tuhiwai Smith is an Associate Professor in the School of Education and Director of the International Research Institute for Maori and Indigenous Education at the University of Auckland, New Zealand. She has a background in Maori and indigenous education. She has helped establish alternative Maori language schools in New Zealand and an alternative tribal university. She teaches a range of undergraduate and graduate classes but specializes in the development of Maori and indigenous researchers. Her book, *Decolonizing Methodology: Research and Indigenous Peoples* is soon to be released.

Marjorie Theobald is an Associate Professor and Reader in the Faculty of Education at the University of Melbourne. She taught for many years in secondary schools. She has written extensively in the area of history of women's education. Her latest book, *Knowing Women: Origins of Women's Education in Nineteenth-century Australia*, was published by Cambridge University Press in 1996. She is currently writing a history of women teaching in Australia.

Kathleen Weiler has written widely in the area of women and education. Her most recent book is *Country Schoolwomen: Teaching in Rural California 1850–1950* (Stanford University Press, 1998). She is an Associate Professor of Education at Tufts University, where she teaches courses in the history and sociology of education, women's education, and peace and justice studies.

Series editors' preface

At the end of the twentieth century it is not a new idea to have a series on feminist educational thinking – feminist perspectives on educational theory, research, policy and practice have made a notable impact on these fields in the final decades of the century. But theory and practice have evolved, and educational and political contexts have changed. In contemporary educational policy debates, economic efficiency rather than social inequality is a key concern; what happens to boys is drawing more interest than what happens to girls; issues about cultural difference interrupt questions about gender; and new forms of theory challenge older frameworks of analysis. This series represents feminist educational thinking as it takes up these developments now.

Feminist educational thinking views the intersection of education and gender through a variety of lenses: it examines schools and universities as sites for the enacting of gender; it explores the ways in which conceptions of gender shape the provision of state-supported education; it highlights the resistances subordinated groups have developed around ideas of knowledge, power and learning; and it seeks to understand the relationship of education to gendered conceptions of citizenship, the family and the economy. Thus feminist educational thinking is fundamentally political; it fuses theory and practice in seeking to understand contemporary education with the aim of building a more just world for women and men. In so doing, it acknowledges the reality of multiple 'feminisms' and the intertwining of ethnicity, race and gender.

Feminist educational thinking is influenced both by developments in feminist theory more broadly and by the changing global educational landscape. In terms of theory, both poststructuralist and postcolonial theories have profoundly influenced what is conceived of as 'feminist'. As is true elsewhere, current feminist educational thinking takes as central the intersecting forces that shape the educational experiences of women and men. This emphasis on the construction and performance of gender through both discourses and material practices leads to an attitude of openness and questioning of accepted assumptions – including the underlying assumptions of the various strands of feminism.

In terms of the sites in which we work, feminist educational thinking increasingly addresses the impact of 'globalization' – the impact of neo-laissez-faire theories on education. As each of us knows all too well, the schools and universities in which we work have been profoundly affected by the growing dominance of ideas of social efficiency, market choice, and competition. In a rapidly changing world in which an ideology of profit has come to define all relationships, the question of gender is often lost, but in fact it is central to the way power is enacted in education as in society as a whole.

The books in this series thus seek to explore the ways in which theory and practice are interrelated. They introduce a third wave of feminist thinking in education, one that takes account of both global changes to the economy and politics, and changes in theorizing about that world. It is important to emphasize that feminist educational thinking not only shapes how we think about education but what we do *in* education – as teachers, academics, and citizens. Thus books within the series not only address the impact of global, national and local changes of education but what specific space is available for feminists within education to mount a challenge to educational practices which encourage gendered and other forms of discriminatory practice.

Kathleen Weiler
Gaby Weiner
Lyn Yates

1 Introduction

Sue Middleton and Kathleen Weiler

Since the early 1970s, feminist educational theorizing and research has taken root and flourished within and across the various disciplines, fields and methods of inquiry that make up the complex academic subject of 'education studies'. This rapid growth is evident in the reading lists for the many courses on women, gender and/or sexuality and education that have been developed since the early 1980s or from a casual glance through a library catalogue or visit to a good educational book store. The 1980s and 1990s saw many single-authored feminist studies in education; a number of multi-authored texts that have brought together feminist writings from a single country or region; and – more recently – several multi-authored collections of feminist writings in education by writers from a range of disciplinary and theoretical perspectives and geographical settings.[1] As is true in the broader field of education studies, within feminist education studies, historical research has been somewhat overshadowed by sociology, psychology, philosophy, curriculum theory, policy studies and education administration. In part, it is in response to this lack that we have compiled this collection by scholars who are engaged in an exploration of the history of women in education in a wide range of geographical, cultural, institutional and temporal settings.

From another perspective, this collection can be viewed as a continuation of a conversation about the history of women in education begun in 1991 with the publication of *Women Who Taught*, edited by Alison Prentice and Marjorie Theobald. In that collection, Prentice and Theobald brought together key essays from the 1980s from the international community of educational historians exploring the meaning of education for women that was emerging in the English-speaking metropolitan countries. Prentice and Theobald saw the study of women in education as an opportunity to explore broader questions of the relationship of gender and power. As they argued in their essay, 'The historiography of women teachers', writing the history of women teachers 'is to confront a central theoretical problem in understanding the past: how to evoke the oppressive structures that maintained a patriarchal order while at the same time affirming that women were not the passive victims of that oppression'.[2] As impressive as the essays in *Women Who Taught* were, they also made clear the need for further research, both studies uncovering previously unexamined lives of women in educational settings and those analysing the complex location of women teachers, not only as they were disciplined by institutions, but also as they asserted a certain autonomy and agency. Moreover, the essays in *Women Who Taught* were written between the late 1970s and late 1980s and thus did not reflect the impact of poststructural and postcolonial theory that influences much feminist educational research in the late 1990s. *Telling Women's Lives* takes up the challenge of *Women Who Taught* to continue the exploration of the meaning of the lives of women in education; employing a wider range of theoretical approaches, these chapters consider both the way that women teachers are constructed by dominant institutions and discourses and the way they construct themselves.

The connections among the chapters in this collection reveal more than a shared concern with the history of women's education, for there are some more specific common theoretical and methodological concerns among these writers. Underlying all of these chapters is the recognition that education has always been framed by assumptions about gender, assumptions which have sometimes been articulated but more often left silent. As in the wider field of women's studies, feminist historians of education have explored these assumptions as they are revealed in the discursive practices – the personal narratives, scholarly studies and policy statements – of women as historical actors. Gender, these historians have argued, must be attended to both when it is the focus of debate and when it is implicit and unremarked. Influenced by poststructuralist theory (the work of Foucault in particular), feminist historians such as those whose work is published here, like other feminist social theorists, have emphasized that gender is an unstable and constantly shifting construct, always being recreated through the process and language through which we understand and define ourselves. Yet gender is not studied in isolation. These writers agree that since the late nineteenth century – in many countries and regions – mass state schooling has constructed and stratified both students and teachers in terms of gender, racial and class characteristics. This focus is evident also in the contributors' shared methodological concerns as they engage in reflections on the process of history writing and consider the impact of various theoretical debates on their own history making. Their work reflects the influence of not only feminist theory and poststructuralism, but also postcolonial theory and theories of the educational state. In their chapters, they address such important issues as the nature of historical evidence, the need to uncover the forgotten stories of women as teachers, the material conditions of teaching as work for women, and the ways that the framing of gender and sexuality has shaped women's and men's experiences in the educational state.

This book includes chapters by scholars who have completed major studies and who are now reflecting on the theoretical implications of their work and scholars beginning new studies and exploring new directions. It is organized into two parts. The chapters in the first, 'Reflections on memory and historical truth', address various aspects of what has been called 'the crisis of representation' in feminist and social theory – a rethinking both of the question of authorship and of ways of representing the subjects of research. The second, 'Narrative Inquiries', consists of more empirical studies that employ the theoretical and methodological concerns of the chapters in the first part to explore specific educational settings.

The first part comprises contributions from feminist scholars who are reflecting on the theoretical issues raised by their own research into the lives of women in education. They consider the ways in which the historian as author is implicated in the choice of what is represented, the uses of evidence, the various representations of 'the educated woman' or 'the woman teacher' that are brought forth in scholarly studies, and the historian's own position in relation to her 'subjects'. Like other contemporary feminist theorists, these authors are concerned with both the representation of the writer/theorist/scholar and the representation of others/subjects of research in contemporary social theory. Of course there is a potential danger in this concern with representations, that it can lead to a kind of confessional approach, in which the scholar writes more about herself than she does about that outside of herself which she is trying to know. But a self-conscious consideration of the power and location of the author can also highlight the processes of meaning making and consciousness, and as Leslie Bloom comments, can 'increase our curiosity about the ways that identity and subjectivity are actively produced both in the lives of researchers and respondents and in the field as part of the research process'.[3] The focus on the ways that women are represented in discourse is essential precisely because of the patriarchal nature of ideology and language. All of these authors are concerned with capturing the contested nature of gendered and raced identities. They use the concepts of gender and race cautiously precisely because the unproblematic use of these terms as givens can gloss over and obscure the heavy historical baggage these words carry. An emphasis on gender and race as they are constructed through language highlights the 'bad fit' of competing representations, the grating inconsistencies – all natural in a power-laden discursive system which attempts to fix people in place – with the effect of giving some privilege and others oppression.

In Chapter 2, 'Teachers, memories and oral history', Marjorie Theobald raises a set of related personal and theoretical problems that she encountered in the process of writing a feminist history of Australian women teachers in the twentieth century. She uses the literature on the history of women teachers in the United States and Australia to argue that historians of the nineteenth century have tended to construct the lady-teacher as hero, as pioneer, and as exemplar of emerging feminist consciousness. But, she argues, when we turn to the twentieth century, these tropes function as road blocks to conceptual advances; finally, she speculates about ways that might lead out of this impasse. Alison Prentice explores her career as a historian of teachers in the multiple and shifting personal locations in which she found herself over time in Toronto. In 'Workers, professionals, pilgrims: tracing Canadian women teachers' histories', she explores the development of her own understanding of teaching as women's work as an exemplar of changing paradigms of a wider community of feminist educational historians. In 'Reflections on writing a history of women teachers', US researcher Kathleen Weiler considers the theoretical debates over language, subjectivity and experience that have been of concern to poststructuralist historians in the context of her study of California rural teachers. In 'Connecting pieces: finding the indigenous presence in the history of women's education', Linda Tuhiwai Smith reflects on her teaching and research on the education of Maori girls and women in Aotearoa New Zealand. Using the experience of teaching her graduate class 'Tikanga Rangahau: the issues of research by Maori, with Maori, and for Maori', Tuhiwai Smith discusses the process of uncovering the indigenous presence in educational history and the complex relationship of student, researcher and subject of research that develops in that process.

The more empirical studies in the second part illustrate these concerns, but do so by means of fine-grained analyses of a variety of narrative sources. From its beginnings, feminist scholarship has been concerned with recovering what has been lost, with telling stories. In fact, feminist scholarship has been largely defined by its political stance – its attempt to know the world differently, to recover what has been hidden and lost, in order to contribute to the building of a more just world for women and men. The dichotomy between poststructuralist suspicions of all claims to truth on the one hand and the political and ethical ground of feminist scholarship on the other has produced a creative and productive tension and has been the stimulus for original and powerful new scholarship. Part II includes chapters that seek to recover lost histories – the narratives of women in education whose lives have been ignored or overlooked as insignificant in the authoritative histories that have dominated educational studies in the past. While the contributors remain sensitive to the theoretically complex questions of the representation of historical figures highlighted in the earlier chapters, they are primarily concerned with substantive issues. Some focus primarily on presenting stories that have been silenced – both through oral histories that they have collected and through archival research. Others use multiple narratives from oral sources as a springboard to more general theoretical and political questions. Sensitive to the need to avoid what Chandra Mohanty calls 'cultural reductionism'[4] – the process of fixing women in place because of their ethnicity or class as well as gender – these chapters discuss, in the course of uncovering 'ordinary' and extraordinary women's lives, the workings of both gender and race as systems of privilege and oppression that work alongside and in interaction and contradiction with those of sexuality and gender.

In 'Disciplining the teaching body 1968–78: progressive education and feminism in New Zealand', Sue Middleton and Helen May draw on a small segment of the life history narratives they collected for a wider oral history of educational ideas in New Zealand in the twentieth century; they pose questions about the relationship – the consistencies and contradictions – between progressive education and feminism in New Zealand state schools in the 1970s. Next, Alison Oram uses the example of the lives of women primary and secondary school teachers in England and Wales to explore how dominant discourses of femininity and sexuality shifted between the wars in her chapter, ' "To cook dinners with love in them?" Sexuality, marital status and women teachers in England and Wales, 1920–39'. Here, women's stories about marriage and sexuality are placed in the wider context of a falling birthrate, consequent eugenic fears, the increasing popularization of new psychology and sexology and associated government policies on education and sexuality during the interwar years. In Chapter 8, Helena Araújo analyses Portuguese women teachers' subjectivities on the basis of the accounts of five women who lived and worked under the fascist regime of Salazar. In their life histories, their resistances and accommodations to this regime are revealed, as well as the ways they addressed the changing legal situation of women, their views of feminism, and the ways they contended with the renewed emphasis on their role in the patriarchal family in the Estado Novo. The approach here is similar to C. Wright Mills's 'sociological imagination' which, in his well known words, 'enables us to grasp history and biography and the relations between the two within society'.[5] In 'To do the next needed thing: Jeanes teachers in the southern United States 1908–34', Valinda Littlefield investigates the work of the Jeanes teachers, who worked in the segregated African-American schools of the American South. She argues that these African-American teachers, predominantly women and themselves from rural communities, subverted expectations that they simply teach conformity to a racist social structure to encourage self-sufficiency and cooperation in African-American rural communities. Finally, Kate Rousmaniere builds upon ongoing questions about the nature of women teachers' work and broader questions of the intersection of class and gender in women's labour history in 'Where Haley stood: Margaret Haley, teachers' work, and the problem of teacher identity'. In this she pursues the argument that teachers have never fit into categories of the American left, particularly in the tumultuous period in which Haley worked and organized. Workers were conceived of as white, male and often ethnic while feminists were defined as white middle class social reformers, and women teachers were imagined as politically neutral individuals. The life of Chicago activist Margaret Haley, she argues, challenges all of these assumptions.

Taken as a group, the chapters in this collection locate women teachers within a more complex understanding of the rise of the educational state, shifts in the global economy, and continuing patterns of racial and western privilege. As is true for many historians and social theorists, these authors are conscious of the ways in which history very often rests on first person narratives, on representations and claims to truth that are laden with assumptions of power, privilege and subordination that underlie social relationships. While these authors are all conscious of these dynamics of meaning making, at the same time, they remain committed to a scholarly project of reclaiming but also rethinking women's lives in education. The writers of these chapters, themselves both scholars and teachers, thus explore the ways they are implicated in the very subject of their research – the educated woman who is also an educator. Their tellings of women's lives are put forward more as inquiries and explorations than they are as final truths. It is our hope that these studies will inspire others to uncover or tell new stories of women's lives in education.

Notes

1 Examples include M. Arnot and G. Weiner (eds) (1987) *Gender and the Politics of Schooling*. London: Hutchison; M. Arnot and K. Weiler (eds) (1993) *Feminism and Social Justice in Education: International Perspectives*. London: Falmer Press; L. Stone (ed.) (1994) *Education Feminism*. New York: Routledge; G. Weiner and M. Arnot (eds) (1987) *Gender under Scrutiny*. London: Hutchison.
2 A. Prentice and M. Theobald (1991) The historiography of women teachers: a retrospect, in A. Prentice and M. Theobald (eds) *Women Who Taught*. Toronto: University of Toronto Press, p.9.
3 L. Bloom (1996) Stories of one's own: nonunitary subjectivity in narrative representation. *Qualitative Inquiry* 2(2): 178.
4 Chandra Mohanty (1988) Under western eyes: feminist scholarship and colonial discourses. *Feminist Review* 30: 61–88.
5 C. Wright Mills (1959) *The Sociological Imagination*. Middlesex: Penguin, p.12.

Part I

REFLECTIONS ON MEMORY AND HISTORICAL TRUTH

2 Teachers, memory and oral history

Marjorie Theobald

Some time ago I received an Australian Research Council grant to support an ambitious study of women teaching for the state in the years 1920–60. The third phase is to be an oral history project, encompassing women who taught for a lifetime, women who taught only briefly before marriage, and women who left teaching to enter other occupations. I chose the decades 1920–60 for several reasons. In comparison with the nineteenth century the period is seriously under researched and under theorized. Australian historians have looked at the legislative 'defeat' of female teachers by male bureaucracies in the nineteenth century, but we have tended to assume that nothing much happened until the reluctant decision of state education departments to recover the teaching labour of married women as the systems expanded in the period following the Second World War.[1] Yet the period affords the opportunity to study the profession when the marriage bars were in place and spinsterhood was increasingly constructed as pathological. The decades 1920–60 are also marked by an absence of the militant feminism which won the vote for women in Australia before the First World War. As the vast majority of highly educated women became secondary teachers, their professional and private lives are potentially important in understanding the nature of organized feminism between the wars. As I am a historian of the nineteenth century the project was something of a departure for me, but with the publication in 1996 of a major book on my research for the previous ten years, it was time to move on.[2] The research grant was a matter for celebration and an affirmation of the importance of feminist history and of women teachers in Australian history. Moreover, I began with an unexamined belief in oral history's 'extraordinary potential as a tool of feminist scholarship'.[3]

I was therefore taken by surprise when my initial explorations precipitated a personal and professional crisis about the project I had committed myself to. I am now convinced that the ubiquitous presence of memory and oral testimony in any history of women teaching in the twentieth century is deeply implicated in this personal crisis. This chapter is an attempt to work through this personal crisis and to clear some theoretical ground on which to build a feminist history of women teaching in the twentieth century.

I will try to reconstruct my initial research agenda as faithfully as I can. I began the research process in the long summer vacation of 1994–5 by reading at home from my own research library three types of literature, collected over the years with just such a project in mind. The first category consisted of autobiographies or novels by writers who had once been teachers. If I am pressed to endow this pleasurable armchair activity with the dignity of a research question, I wanted to know what wells up from the creative writer's subconscious once the persona of the teacher is discarded, a catharsis not available to those who remained in teaching. In the second category were my collections of other people's interviews with women teachers and scholarly works which purported to be based on such interviews. The third category consisted of feminist theoretical writings on oral history, memory and personal narratives.

I began my reading in the first category with Christina Stead's Australian novel, *For Love Alone*.[4] Stead herself attended Sydney Teachers' College in the early 1920s and taught unenthusiastically for a few years.[5] In this passage Teresa, the reluctant school teacher heroine, describes a typical day at her school.

> The day was like all days. The frantic old woman with bird's nest hair who taught Lower Third slashed the boys' legs with a ruler, although it was against the law, and no one told on her because she had gone queer. The young brunette with Upper Third said the life was rotten and if any woman could get out of it by marriage, she ought to, no matter what the man was like; she'd take anybody herself. The jolly married teacher of fourth, ungraded, and on the lowest pay because she was a married woman, an old hand, did her embroidery, slapped her brats with her open hand and chuckled at Teresa's crowd . . . The woman of thirty-five with faded fair hair grumbled incessantly about her feet, about not sleeping with her 'arthuritis', the inspectors, new methods which they expected to see, and the notes mothers sent her by the children. Sitting blowsily in the teachers' room, standing dully in the playground, patronizing, wretched, dull, deaf to hope and with no thought of a way out, they groused helplessly, in their own minds condemned to servitude for life – till sixty-five – and they might go queer before, like the old woman in Lower third, especially if they remained, as desired by the Department, unmarried.[6]

After Christina Stead I read New Zealand novelist Janet Frame's autobiography, *An Angel at my Table*, in which we learn that she attempted suicide by swallowing aspirin on the day the inspector was due in her classroom.[7] Next came Dymphna Cusack's autobiographical account of her 20 years as a secondary teacher in New South Wales, in which she constructs herself as a disorderly teacher. The tone of the book is set by the title, *A Window in the Dark*, a metaphor she used for the act of teaching.[8] With Janet Frame, Cusack tells us that she loved teaching but hated the circumstances under which she was obliged to teach – exacerbated in her case by official disapproval of her political radicalism and the unseemly realism of her novels. Here is teacher-turned-novelist Sylvia Ashton-Warner in *Spinster*, her subtle psychological study of women teaching in mid-twentieth century New Zealand.

> Yet I teach well enough on brandy. Once it has fired my stomach and arteries I don't feel Guilt. It supplies me with a top layer to my mind so that I may meet my fifty Maori infants as people rather than as the origin of the Inspectors' displeasure; and whereas I am so often concerned on their account with the worst in children, I now see only the best. Never do I understand them more, and never is more creative work done . . . Indeed the only thing that seriously upsets me is this unpardonable loss of precision in my bastard art and the damage done to my nylons when I walk too inaccurately between the stove and the easel. Which means another fifteen-and-six [shillings and pence] . . . fifteen-and-six further away from that boat steaming out through the Wellington Heads. Fifteen-and-six more of this bell, or hell or whatever I mean . . . Intoxicating.[9]

I will not labour the point. The Gothic imagination of the novelist need not necessarily trouble us as historians; writing in the interwar years, for example, Stead's purpose in *For Love Alone* was to launch herself, in the guise of Teresa, on that myth encrusted journey from Sydney to London and the Promised Land. Her caricature could more easily be dismissed than Ashton-Warner's sensitive exploration of women, sexuality and teaching. Yet these professional understandings did nothing to quell the sense of foreboding which began to rob me of my voice as a historian of women and teaching.

In the strongest possible contrast was the literature in the second category, the testimonies of women who taught, and remained in teaching, in the decades 1920–60; indeed it is difficult to believe that they inhabited the same universe as Stead, Frame and Ashton-Warner. The bulk of my present collection was obtained by the simple expedient of writing to each State Department of Education which supports a history service and three – those of Queensland, New South Wales and Victoria – obliged. At this stage in my research I make no spurious claims to total coverage, nor have I commenced my own schedule of interviewing. My reaction can best be described as a pervasive sense of disappointment and a guilty conviction that I did not want to be complicit in the production (and reproduction) of these 'goody two shoes' narratives of the teacher. I did not expect the high drama of the teacher narratives produced in the period after the second women's movement transformed dramatically the way women speak about their profession;[10] but I expected different metaphors for similar concerns. Instead I encountered what Dea Birkett and Julie Wheelwright refer to as 'examples of a potential heroine's behaviour which was anything but exemplary'.[11]

Vivia Flannery was interviewed at the age of 82 as part of an oral history project to document the role played by women in the Queensland Teachers' Union. Her photograph in the published collection exacerbates my guilt about speaking in this way.[12] Flannery is by no means typical of women teachers in the first half of the twentieth century, though she is more typical of teachers sought out for interview: she remained in teaching for a lifetime when the generality of Australian women were ejected by the marriage bars; she also had a lifetime commitment to teacher unionism at a time when she herself testifies that the majority of women did not. She does not eschew a 'commitment to women's rights' when this is raised by the interviewer. Flannery is even mentioned in the official history of the Queensland Teachers' Union.[13]

I am not suggesting that Flannery's oral testimony is in any way 'false'. I am inclined to agree with Luisa Passerini that, deliberate deception aside, 'the guiding principle could be that all autobiographical memory is true; it is up to the interpreter to discover in which sense, where, for what purpose'.[14] And I am in agreement with Katherine Borland that 'For feminists, the issue of interpretive authority is particularly problematic, for our work often involves a contradiction.' On the one hand, she argues, we seek to 'empower the women we work with by revaluing their perspective, their lives, and their art'; on the other, we map out political and structural dimensions of women's lives which those we interview might not hold to be valid.[15] Nevertheless, there are aspects of the Flannery transcript which are extremely problematical for a feminist historian in the late twentieth century.

Much feminist theorizing about oral testimony, about the relationship between researcher and researched, is predicated on 'researching down', often across cultural divides, and among women who have been confined to the private sphere.[16] A different dynamic is at work here. Flannery's narratives are the obverse of those characterized by Kristina Minister as typically female, that is, 'narrators' stories and descriptions [which] exhibit an unfinished or incomplete quality . . . not conform[ing] to the plot and action structures of publicly performed pieces.'[17] In Minister's terms, Flannery's stories are in the masculine mode, 'attention-getting monologic narratives . . . well polished from repeated rehearsal . . . featuring the narrator as the central character'. One such narrative is proffered in support of Flannery's claim for the essential goodness of all children (a twentieth century, not a nineteenth century trope among those who taught). In response to the question 'Have there ever been children that you have not liked or have not found a way to get on with?',[18] Flannery tells a well rehearsed story about reclaiming a difficult girl by the simple expedient of putting her in charge of the sports material. At one point in the interview she interpolates: 'These . . . incidents, together with others over the years, convinced me that children, even at a young age, size up situations to establish their behaviour . . . hence my respect for them.'[19] Flannery prides herself on having mastered what Minister characterizes as the sociocommunication modes of the male world.

> I always prepared well . . . I went to a lot of bother preparing because I felt that far too many teachers were ill-informed and that included men who came to Conference without the desirable preparation . . . In presenting a motion, I endeavoured to be logical and concise, both in regard to my argument and to its linguistic presentation. I do not think my manner was aggressive or insulting.[20]

Yet Flannery's unshakeable belief in the masculinist chivalry of the state, the Queensland Education Department, its officers and her fellow unionists sits oddly with her protracted and unsuccessful battle for equal pay. The interviewer persists: 'Have you ever felt in conflict with men; you have never had any problems?' – 'No, I have not. I found that the men seemed to have confidence in me. They knew that I would speak for the benefit of all teachers regardless of whether they were head teachers or staff teachers, male or female.'[21] Her 'rebellious self-image' (again following Passerini) is mapped on to legitimate union activity, in turn legitimized by her father's and uncle's prominence in the union. For Vivia, union work is a respectable, not a radical or consciousness raising activity.

The teacher-as-public-woman also mitigates against those revelations of the self which are the life blood of feminist 'life histories'. In Flannery's narrative, revelations of the self and of sexuality are displaced onto familiar 'travel' and 'accommodation' narratives collectively formed by the policy of Australian education departments to send all beginning teachers to remote one teacher schools. Through her narratives of travel to her first schools and the circumstances in which she was obliged to live Flannery sets up a muted melodrama of sexual danger, once again produced coterminously with the chivalry of the local men, train drivers, landlords, inspectors, the men who shared her hotel accommodation, even the local drunk, 'Micky Drippin':

> I found the men respected me and I respected them. One day, one of the men who . . . ran the barber's shop at the Hotel . . . said, 'What do you do when you have finished your laundry on Saturday?' I said, 'I just go upstairs'. He said, 'How about coming into the billiard room and scoring for us?' Which I did. That just showed me that they thought I might be a bit lonely up there on my own.[22]

When we interview teachers, we not only 'ask about the inner life . . . in the context of the public sphere', a burden of guilt which we share with all feminist interviewers;[23] we expect revelations of a personal nature from women whose lives have been led in the public sphere. Flannery does not oblige and there is no reason why she should. But this is not the kind of history of teaching I want to write.

I should stress that I am talking here about the problems inherent in interviewing the *generality* of women teachers. There is, for example, a genre of teacher narratives exemplified by the work of Kathleen Weiler, Kathleen Casey and Sue Middleton, which stands out from these sanitized versions of the teaching life precisely because they eschew the generality of teachers and choose women in their own image, radical women who see teaching as a way to change the world.[24] Studies around specific cohorts of women with bitter memories, such as Donna Dwyer's oral history work with married women teachers in the Victorian Education Department between the wars, also elicit narratives of a different kind.[25] Perhaps I was simply unlucky in the books I had accumulated on my shelves; perhaps it is the reticence of earlier generations of women teachers who believed that it was bad manners to rain on the parade; perhaps it is a matter of authorial style – as Emily Toth has argued, academics often tinker nervously with a good yarn, intimidated by the current privileging of text over narrative.[26] Nevertheless, though I admire Vivia Flannery and women like her, my immediate reaction to these texts was that if this is exemplary oral history then for me, oral history stands squarely in the path of conceptual advance in the field.

This petulance will not do. As a historian, I was disturbed by the literature in ways which signalled that it was my professional duty to dig further. My reaction was intimately connected to my own past, to the circumstances under which I came to be reading the literature, and to the point I had reached in my agenda as a historian of women's education. My reading rekindled, rather than created, a personal foreboding about writing a history of women teaching in the twentieth century. The truth is that I am moving reluctantly into the twentieth century. I know that I will give offence to many eminent colleagues when I say that to me the twentieth century is not history; to co-opt L.P. Hartley, the past is a different country – they [should] do things differently there. The twentieth century is my mother's and my father's world. The twentieth century is me. I know too much about the twentieth century. In Ailsa Zainu'ddin's words:

> The generation most difficult for historians to understand, to appreciate and to recreate is the one which immediately precedes their own – their parents' generation. It is familiar because, to some extent, it has been shared but it is more difficult to perceive through their eyes because we have already glimpsed it as children through a glass darkly. We have acquired knowledge without necessarily understanding its significance for the actors.[27]

Yet the burden which Ailsa Zainu'ddin shares with Carolyn Steedman, Drusilla Modjeska and Germaine Greer – writing a parent into history – is not precisely my burden.[28] With Christina Stead, Dymphna Cusack and Janet Frame, I shared the fate of the lady-teacher-by-default, caught in a web of circumstance in which we sold ourselves as teachers to the educational state in exchange for tertiary education and escape, so we believed, from our mothers' world. I did not write novels, though I left teaching in 1978 without a backward glance for doctoral studies and a new career as an academic historian. My encounter with the testimonies of these teachers and teachers-turned-writer did not produce innocent knowledge. I find myself situated unhappily at the epicentre of oral history where teachers remember themselves, teachers are remembered by the taught, and I remember myself both as teacher and taught. There is a mad lady-teacher in my attic.

Most of these issues are taken up in the third category of literature which contributed to my initial loss of confidence in the project I had embarked upon; feminist theoretical works on oral history and personal narratives.[29] Paradoxically, as will be apparent in my analysis of the Flannery interview, the literature has already sharpened my perceptions in rewarding ways. It is not intended here to mount a critique of the literature and its concerns: epistemological issues, a debate shared with practitioners of oral history generally; feminist concerns about exploitation (that issue of 'researching down'); issues of 'ownership' of the narrative and the text; tensions between empowerment of the subject and the imperative of the authorial voice; the practicalities of the craft. My point here is that in all of these riches I find no direct engagement with the personal malaise which has overtaken me. These works share a characteristic which diminishes their potential to help me; they are overwhelmingly written by women who have not initially served an apprenticeship as historians working beyond the reach of memory. They are sociologists, anthropologists, literary theorists and linguists coming from the other direction.[30] As Allyson Holbrook reminds us, 'We all draw on myths, and researchers bring a layer of formal theoretical knowledge that can have its own mythic dimensions'.[31] Certainly, sociologists, anthropologists and linguists bring to the practice of oral history their own formal theoretical knowledge, but for historians like myself the baggage is of a different kind. To that discursive space where teachers remember themselves, where they are remembered, and where I remember myself-as-teacher, I must bring my baggage of feminist research on women who taught, beyond the reach of memory.

Historians who work beyond the reach of oral history depend crucially upon the exotic, that which is beyond memory; they live in romantic dependence upon a finite cache of sources which have survived. There is nobody alive to contradict them. This is not to say that historians have failed to debate the epistemological basis of the knowledge they create, or indeed the essentially intersubjective nature of their encounter with the surviving sources; it is simply to say that they do not create the sources in the first place. In contrast, as John Murphy has pointed out, 'the oral historian, or interviewer, is actually present to witness and procreate the narrative, and hence is always implicated, always an accomplice.'[32] What Murphy does not canvass is the potential of this encounter to disappoint those who make the transition from 'beyond memory' to 'within memory'.

I want to argue that it is no accident that feminist historians of women's education have been preoccupied with the nineteenth century, safe territory which is beyond the reach of memory and guilt.[33] In order to do so I need to sketch in the ways in which we have written about women teachers since the 1970s. Feminist historians who began to write the history of women's education in the 1970s shared an international dilemma which in hindsight rendered problematical the search for a 'voice' in which to open the debate. We were part of the second women's movement and the inequalities of the 1970s were part of our lives: the dearth of women at the top in educational institutions; the gendered nature of the curriculum and curriculum choices; the hidden agenda of the coeducational school, of textbooks and of teacher education programmes; the resilience of the ghetto female professions of teaching, nursing and social work. Memory and history were briefly in equipoise. It was a legitimate question to ask why educational reforms in the past had led to apparently conservative outcomes in the present. Yet at the same time, feminist history itself began in the 1970s as a political act to restore to women their own past; no matter how disturbing that past might be, feminist history was quintessentially an act of celebration. The historiography of women's education, and therefore of women teachers, has been fundamentally shaped by this uneasy juxtaposition of celebration and critique.

There were local reasons why this dilemma was exacerbated for feminist scholars contemplating the elementary school teacher in US history. In the 1970s they confronted an opus of work which was preoccupied with the rise of state systems of mass elementary education, and characterized by two warring schools of thought.[34] If I may resort to simplification: the earlier, or liberal/Whig school, as it is sometimes known, interpreted the rise of mass compulsory state systems as a story of triumphal progress – a benign project of the emerging liberal democratic state faced with the task of crafting a modern nation out of a polyglot immigrant society. The later revisionist scholars – who, like feminist historians, were grounded in the conflict politics of the 1960s and 1970s – employed a Marxist conception of the state as the creature of the bourgeoisie. They interpreted the emergence of mass systems of state schooling in the western nations as oppressive, imposing upon working class children work discipline in the developing capitalist workplace and docility in the face of new, democratic forms of government. In the United States this process of revising the history of elementary education was bitter, not only because the younger group of historians were attacking that most sacred of sacred cows, the US public school, but because they had to establish their credentials in a society recently emerged from the McCarthy era and historically lacking a legitimate left-wing/labour politics.

To return to my theme of women teachers, neither Whig historians nor revisionist historians were hospitable to a sympathetic study of the ordinary teacher, male or female. Historians who celebrated the rise of national school systems focused on 'great men' – politicians, bishops, administrators and inspectors – who apparently commanded reform to flow from a blueprint drawn up at head office. Revisionist historians turned this thesis on its head, retaining a focus on great men but ascribing to them unworthy motives. In so doing they cast teachers, by implication or neglect, as unwitting agents of oppression. Nevertheless, the computer assisted studies of educational bureaucracies characteristic of the revisionists could not overlook the fact that elementary school teachers in nineteenth century North America were increasingly women, while school administrators were increasingly men.[35] Almost by accident, this constituted the starting point for a gender analysis, if not a feminist analysis, of the teaching profession in North America. It also triggered off the 'feminization of teaching' debate – a phrase which carried overtones of disapproval – which quickly went international and rages unabated to this day.[36]

Feminist historians were the natural allies of the revisionist historians, sharing a focus on asymmetries of power, a political agenda of change and a sense of outrage at the shortcomings of education in the present. They too sought answers to present educational disadvantage by studying the past. Yet they could not share the luxury of the unrelenting condemnation characteristic of the revisionists. The central problematic for US historians writing the history of women as elementary school teachers was how to shape their own celebratory/political narrative against a backdrop of historiography hostile to the educational state and those complicit with it – by implication, the 'lady-teacher'.

My reading of the literature is that American feminist historians, from Nancy Hoffman and Polly Welts Kaufman to Sari Knopp Biklen, Linda Perkins and Geraldine Clifford, have reacted by avoiding the issue of the educational state and its contradictory relationship with women teachers, preoccupying themselves instead with the construction of the lady-teacher as hero.[37] They have set out to trawl the enviable collections of nineteenth century teachers' diaries, letters and personal papers in search of autonomy, professionalism and emerging feminism. The American lady-teacher who emerges from the literature is possessed of a quasi-missionary sense of purpose which enabled her to battle against overwhelming odds, to obtain a Normal School education at her own expense, to go west, to go south, to teach on Indian reservations, to tame the Dukhabors. The educational state remains enshrined as a dark revisionist presence, sometimes emerging in embodied form as the superintendent, sometimes providing a foil for women's superior ways of doing things, but by and large unexamined, leaving women's experiences as teachers floating free of the material and structural conditions which underpinned them.

This is not to say that the American studies lack a set of underlying feminist propositions: the effect of domestic ideology and notions of Republican motherhood on the role of the female teacher; her construction as the 'angel in the schoolhouse'; women's appropriation of Protestant evangelical religion as a means to personal empowerment; common or garden economic exploitation. And these writers have a common interest in confronting the nineteenth century stereotypes of the lady-teacher, both as angel in the schoolhouse and as horse-faced spinster who has failed in the business of life. Nor should we doubt that some teachers did and said these things. Nevertheless, it is rare to read in the American literature of a lady-teacher who taught by default, beat her students, spoke against votes for women, or married in order to escape. It is no accident that several American texts quote the turn-of-the-century immigrant child's view of the American lady-teacher:

> I have forgotten everything the schools ever taught me. But the glamour of the lady teachers, shining on the East Side World, I shall never forget. I see them now, all fused and molded into one symbolic figure, in dresses that seemed always delicate and gracefully silhouetted, in great puffed sleeves, with a neck that always seemed long and arched, with a pompadour that always seemed to make the forehead lofty and noble. The symbol sits enthroned on the dais-platform before a desk.[38]

It is important to trace these themes in the work of America's most prolific and tough minded exponent of the lady-teacher as hero, Geraldine Clifford. In her manifesto, 'Saints, sinners and people', Clifford laid out a research agenda for a 'people-centred, not a pedagogue-centred, orientation to the past'.[39] Since then she has, to quote her own words, 'examined hundreds of letters of nineteenth-century teachers – written to family, friends, other teachers, suitors [and found] rising expressions of assertiveness, self-determination, and ego'. She argues that 'prominent feminists, like teacher Lucy Stone, placed a great store on their independence. But so did quite ordinary women teachers'. As with Hoffman, Kaufman and others, Clifford's work demonstrates the strengths and weaknesses of aggregating into truth the diaries and letters of women teachers across space and time, but that is not my main focus here. Clifford's immersion in the private papers of women teachers has led her to take an important step in mapping the subjectivities of teaching women. In an influential article entitled ' "Lady teachers" and politics in the United States, 1850–1930' Clifford makes explicit what is implicit in the work of her predecessors – a direct relationship between the subjectivity of the lady-teacher and the emerging political consciousness and activism of American women.[40] Clifford argues that women teachers constituted 'a large part of the forgotten women of feminist history in the United States – the readied soil to catch the seeds of feminism'. We have all been eager to follow Clifford's lead.

It is a phenomenon so obvious as to be overlooked that the 'feminization of teaching' occurred coterminously with those emancipatory impulses across a broad spectrum of women's lives which we now refer to as first-wave feminism. Prominent among the demands of nineteenth century feminists was the reform of female education, a reform which they saw as a crucial first step in the emancipation of women. In the work of Geraldine Clifford I discern a resolution of that uneasy marriage of celebration and critique which is the lot of modern feminist historians of education – that is, to subsume the experience of teaching itself within the grand narrative of emancipation. It is time to ask whether Clifford's thesis now functions as a conceptual road block in the path of a history of women teaching in the twentieth century, a question to which I will return.

Australian feminist historians have also conferred heroic status upon the female elementary schoolteacher, but in a different way. We do not have the wealth of personal papers which underpin the work of Kaufman, Clifford and others in the United States. The discourses which worked to position American women as the 'angel in the schoolroom', assiduously promoted by Horace Mann and Catharine Beecher, were subdued in Australia's educational past, as indeed was the Evangelical fervour which inspired them. Those demographic and political episodes through which the United States' lady-teachers have been imagined (going west, going south) had their counterparts in Australia – the pastoral era, the gold rushes, the opening up of the land to selection, the achievement of nationhood – but they did not spawn a diaspora of Evangelical schoolmistresses on the move. There was indeed a tribe of lady-teachers on the move, but they were sullen, resentful and ingenious in their efforts to return to the cities and provincial towns.[41]

Australian historians have been obliged to encounter our elementary schoolmistresses through the centralized State bureaucracies which both shaped their professional lives and preserved the documentary evidence of that encounter. We have been obliged to begin with the larger structures and work inwards towards the teachers, a way of proceeding which stands the American experience on its head. And we were writing against different political and historiographical realities. While revisionist history surfaced in Australia with the New Left it did not arouse the passions which it did in the United States. The legitimacy of labour politics in Australia is reflected in the legitimacy of labour history; revisionism did not set megatrends and it did not create silences. Working within these traditions Australian historians brought gender perspectives to the hardy perennials of labour history. Inevitably, we have conceptualized the teacher as hero in the Marxist sense of 'worker-against-the-system', though I argue that our work is firmly grounded in both the narrative and in the material and structural conditions of teachers' lives.[42] Certainly, we have heard the 'voice' of the lady-teacher, but we have heard it differently. Nineteenth century teachers, we have discovered, were a disorderly lot: they wrote often to their employers – about schoolhouse and residence, about headteachers, about parents and about salaries. They pressed their case through departmental inquiries, through parliamentary committees and even through the courts.[43] Despite the opacity of everyday life in bureaucratically generated documents, historians have found in the archives of Australian education departments an astonishing amount of detail about the private lives of teachers, empirical evidence of just that interdependence of the private and the public that feminist historians have insisted upon: the demography of households; miscarriages; breastfeeding of children in school; the employment of servants; bankruptcy files.[44] And it is this potent brew of emancipatory romance, pioneering derring-do and gritty realism which renders so pallid the personal teacher narratives of the twentieth century.

Is there still a meeting place for the feminist historian and the custodians of teacher narratives in the twentieth century?[45] Can I write the history of teaching I want to write without practising that 'savage social therapy' which Chanfrault-Duchet warns us against? Shulamit Reinharz observes that feminist researchers often begin with an issue that is both 'an intellectual question and a personal trouble'.[46] I want to suggest that Reinharz's proposition cannot fully account for the personal malaise which I have explored in this chapter. I began by proposing that a personal knowledge of the mad woman in the teaching attic has proved conceptually uncomfortable for feminist historians like myself; in Reinharz's terms, this has worked to separate, not to link, the intellectual questions from the personal troubles. What happens if we admit that the history of teaching has largely been written by women who do not wish to be school teachers? Would this catharsis release us to reconceptualize a feminist history of women teaching in the twentieth century, free from the twin hazards of hagiography (in the case of elementary school teachers) and arrogant dismissal (in the case of secondary teachers)?[47]

We could begin with the proposition that any history of women teaching in the twentieth century must come to terms with the fact that teaching has become a commonplace occupation for women – Christina Stead would say a despised occupation for women. We must come to terms with the 'ordinary', a trend which I discern in collections such as Richard Altenbaugh's *The Teacher's Voice: A Social History of Teaching in Twentieth Century America*.[48] We 'know' this from our own experiences as teachers and taught. In all Australian states the historic defeat of the lady-teacher was accomplished by the turn of the century; structures were in place which confined women to the lower echelons of the teaching service, under the control of men. The marriage bars installed a revolving door which skewed the profile of women teaching into a base of young and transient women and a core of older, 'spinster' women presiding over the infant room. As Sheila Jeffries has argued, the unmarried woman was increasingly pathologized in the twentieth century.[49]

The grand romance of teaching will no longer do. A monolithic feminism, such as that organized around the suffrage campaigns, can no longer frame our assumptions about the teaching profession or pre-empt the questions which we ask. An oral history of women teaching in the twentieth century may well contribute to a new history of feminism between the wars. Public affirmations such as teacher activism and private affirmations such as woman centred households will contribute to that history, but the questions we ask teachers and the stories we tell about them can no longer sit unexamined beside a grand narrative of emancipation. Nineteenth century feminist demands for the *right* to education were indeed part of the high romance of emancipatory struggle. And the profession of secondary teaching may have been the creation of that struggle, though the profession of elementary school teaching was not. In either case, what happened to women *as teachers* – as subjectivities shaped by institutionalization, the 'everydayness' of waged labour, and the lifetime of self-censure demanded of them – may well be the antithesis of the pleasurable melodrama of emancipation experienced by nineteenth century women in the western nations. Our task as oral historians is to listen attentively for the myths, tropes and folk memory which emerged from those defeats, losses and transformations.

This is not an injunction to write ordinary history about ordinary things; I am suggesting that we must come to terms with the ordinary and the everyday in order to destabilize it – in Carolyn Steedman's disturbing words, 'to see the prisonhouse [of the classroom] in the light of history and politics, infinitely connected with the world outside, whose artefact it is'.[50] Subversion of the ordinary works to put on the research agenda new and interesting questions. A psychology of teaching, Steedman reminds us, is dangerous yet rewarding territory. By the time I packed my tools of trade and left the classroom in 1978 I was convinced that the twentieth century school was the last stronghold of nineteenth century notions of the 'feminine', that within this child's world, the woman teacher is condemned to experience over and over again the childhood of other people's children, with all the institutional indignities which that necessitates. As a mother and as a teacher I had formulated a question which as feminist historians we have chosen not to ask: if schools keep mothers sane, what do they do to women who teach? We should place on our research agenda as oral historians the possibility that women's sanity in the twentieth century classroom was achieved through a psychology of transience not entirely reducible to the marriage bars, an ironic refusal of eternal motherhood which Christina Stead caricatured so cruelly in *For Love Alone*. We know, though we have not raised our knowledge to the level of theory, that men have always been transients in the classroom, moving hierarchically through the ranks to administration or out of the profession altogether in buoyant economic times. I am suggesting that a different psychology of transience may have shaped the dynamics of the twentieth century classroom for women, in Sylvia Ashton-Warner's terms, 'a top layer to the mind'. I am suggesting that the history of teaching belongs as much to those who left as to those who stayed. As feminist historians we have been enchanted by the marriage bars which operated in most Australian states in the twentieth century; we have thrived upon the politics of exclusion, not pausing to ask whether the generality of women wanted to stay in teaching for a lifetime. The mad lady-teacher in the attic is waiting to be heard; discursive space must be cleared for her before we embark on a history of women teaching in the twentieth century. If my silence is to be broken, the first lady-teacher I must interview is myself.

Notes

1 In nineteenth-century Australia, as in most other western nations, the state moved decisively into the area of elementary schooling. All Australian colonies implemented what are colloquially known as 'free, secular and compulsory' Acts in order to get all children into school. This in turn fuelled a need for teachers and opened up the possibility of paid employment for women. By 'legislative defeat' I mean the process of confining women to the lower echelons of the teaching service on lower salaries, with men in positions of leadership at the top. Again, this process was common to the western nations. For the legislative defeat of the lady-teacher in the Australian context, see M. Theobald (1996) *Knowing Women: Origins of Women's Education in Nineteenth-Century Australia*. Melbourne: Cambridge University Press, ch.5.

2 Theobald, *Knowing Women*.

3 S.B. Gluck and D. Patai (eds) (1991) *Women's Words: The Feminist Practice of Oral History*. New York: Routledge, p.1.

4 C. Stead (1990, first published 1945) *For Love Alone*. London: Angus and Robertson.

5 H. Rowley (1993) *Christina Stead: A Biography*. Melbourne: Heinemann, pp.53–7.

6 Stead, *For Love Alone*, p.112.

7 J. Frame (1993) *An Angel at my Table*. London: HarperCollins.

8 D. Cusack (1991) *A Window in the Dark*. Canberra: National Library of Australia.

9 S. Ashton-Warner (1961) *Spinster*. Harmondsworth: Penguin, p.14. *Spinster* was made into a film starring Shirley MacLaine, Laurence Harvey and Jack Hawkins.

10 For oral history interviews collected after the second women's movement see (1986) *The Done Thing: Women Speak about their Lives in Teaching*. Melbourne: Teachers' Federation of Victoria.

11 D. Birkett and J. Wheelwright (1990) 'How could she?': unpalatable facts and feminists' heroines. *Gender and History* 2(1): 49.

12 R. Bonnin (ed.) (1988) *Dazzling Prospects: Women in the Queensland Teachers' Union Since 1945*. Brisbane: Queensland Teachers' Union.

13 A. Spaull and M. Sullivan (1989) *A History of the Queensland Teachers' Union*. Sydney: Allen and Unwin, pp.242–3.

14 L. Passerini (1989) Women's personal narratives: myths, experiences, and emotions, in Personal Narratives Group (eds) *Interpreting Women's Lives: Feminist Theory and Personal Narratives*. Bloomington, IN: Indiana University Press, p.197.

15 K. Borland (1991) 'That's not what I said': conflict in oral narrative research, in Gluck and Patai, *Women's Words*, p.64.

16 K. Olsen and L. Shopes (1991) Crossing boundaries, building bridges: doing oral history among working-class women and men, in Gluck and Patai, *Women's Words*, pp.198–9.

17 K. Minister (1991) A feminist frame for the oral history interview, in Gluck and Patai, *Women's Words*, p.37.

18 Bonnin, *Dazzling Prospects*, p.19.

19 Ibid., pp.21–2.

20 Ibid., p.24.

21 Ibid., p.16.

22 Ibid., p.18.

23 D. Patai (1991) US academics and third world women: is ethical research possible?, in Gluck and Patai, *Women's Words*, p.142.

24 K. Casey (1993) *I Answer with my Life: Life Histories of Women Teachers Working for Social Change*. New York: Routledge; K. Weiler (1988) *Women Teaching for Change: Gender, Class and Power*. New York: Bergin and Garvey; S. Middleton (1993) *Educating Feminists: Life Histories and Pedagogy*. New York: Teachers College Press.

25 D. Dwyer (1998) 'The married woman and the Victorian Education Department, 1872–1956'. PhD thesis. University of Melbourne.

26 E. Toth (1996) *Women's Review of Books* 13(5): 7.

27 A.G.T. Zainu'ddin (1990) Inheriting the 16 Club: women's continuing education 1920–1980. *History of Education Review* 19(2): 63.

28 C. Steedman (1986) *Landscape for a Good Woman: A Story of Two Lives*. London: Virago; D. Modjeska (1990) *Poppy*. Melbourne: McPhee Gribble; G. Greer (1989) *Daddy, We Hardly Knew You*. London: Hamish Hamilton.

29 Of my collection of books in this category the most influential have been: S.B. Gluck and D. Patai (eds) (1991) *Women's Words: The Feminist Practice of Oral History*. New York: Routledge; C.G. Heilbrun (1988) *Writing a Woman's Life*. New York: Ballantine Books; *Gender and History* 1990, 2(1) special edition on auto/biography; K. Darian-Smith and P. Hamilton (eds) (1994) *Memory and History in Twentieth-Century Australia*. Melbourne: Oxford University Press; S. Magarey, C. Guerin and P. Hamilton (eds) (1992) *Writing Lives: Feminist Biography and Autobiography*. Adelaide: Australian Feminist Studies Publications; Personal Narratives Group (eds) (1989) *Interpreting Women's Lives: Feminist Theory and Personal Narratives*. Bloomington, IN: Indiana University Press; M. Maynard and J. Purvis (eds) (1994) *Researching Women's Lives from a Feminist Perspective*. London: Taylor and Francis; C. Steedman (1986) *Landscape for a Good Woman: A Story of Two Lives*. London: Virago; S. Alexander (1994) *Becoming a Woman and Other Essays in 19th and 20th Century Feminist History*, Part III, Memory and History. London: Virago; S. Reinharz (1993) *Feminist Methods in Social Research*. New York: Oxford University Press; H. Roberts (ed.) (1981) *Doing Feminist Research*. London: Routledge and Kegan Paul; S. Middleton (1993) *Educating Feminists: Life Histories and Pedagogy*. New York: Teachers College Press; D. Modjeska (1990) *Poppy*. Melbourne: McPhee Gribble.

30 For example, of the sixteen contributors to Gluck and Patai, *Women's Words*, only four were trained as historians and of those four, three appear to have entered the discipline as oral historians. The same pattern is apparent in *Interpreting Women's Lives*. There is an interesting cultural difference in the Australian literature, where the percentage of historians is higher, though my thesis still holds good.

31 A. Holbrook (1995) Methodological developments in oral history: a multi-layered approach. *Australian Educational Researcher* 22(3): 38.

32 J. Murphy (1986) The voice of memory: history, autobiography and oral memory. *Historical Studies* 22(87): 84.

33 For a fuller account of this nineteenth century bias in the literature, see M. Theobald (1995) Imagining the woman teacher: an international perspective. *Australian Educational Researcher* 22(3): 87–112.

34 C.E. Kaestle (1988) Recent methodological developments in the history of American education, in R.M. Jaeger (ed.) *Contemporary Methods for Research in Education*. Washington, DC: American Educational Research Association, pp.61–71.

35 A. Prentice and M. Theobald (eds) (1991) *Women Who Taught: Perspectives on the History of Women and Teaching*. Toronto: University of Toronto Press.

36 For an overview of the 'feminization' debate, see J. Albisetti (1993) The feminization of teaching in the nineteenth century: a comparative perspective. *History of Education* 22(3): 253–63.

37 N. Hoffman (1981) *Woman's 'True' Profession: Voices from the History of Teaching*. New York: Feminist Press/McGraw-Hill; P.W. Kaufman (1984) *Women Teachers on the Frontier*. New Haven, CT: Yale University Press; L. Perkins (1989) The history of blacks in teaching: growth and decline within the profession, in D. Warren (ed.) *American Teachers: Histories of a Profession at Work*. New York: Macmillan; G. Clifford (1989) Man/woman/teacher: gender, family and career in American history, in Warren (ed.) *American Teachers*; S.K. Biklen (1995) *School Work: Gender and the Cultural Construction of Teaching*. New York: Teachers College Press.

38 Hoffman, *Woman's 'True' Profession*, pp.200–1.

39 G. Clifford (1975) Saints, sinners and people: a position paper on the historiography of American education. *History of Education Quarterly* 15(Fall): 257–72.

40 G. Clifford (1987) 'Lady teachers' and politics in the United States, 1850–1930, in M. Lawn and G. Grace (eds) *Teachers: The Culture and Politics of Work*. London: Falmer Press. The quotations are from p.10 and p.16.

41 Noeline Williamson (1982) The employment of female teachers in the small bush school of New South Wales, 1890 to 1900: a case of stay bushed or stay home. *Labour History* 43: 1–12.

42 For biographical essays on Australian teachers in this genre, see R.J.W. Selleck and M. Sullivan (eds) (1984) *Not So Eminent Victorians*. Melbourne: Melbourne University Press; M. Theobald and R.J.W. Selleck (eds) (1990) *Family School and State in Australian History*. Sydney: Allen and Unwin.

43 See, for example, my own study of 16-year-old teacher, Agnes Grant, who brought charges of breach of promise and seduction against her headmaster, precipitating two departmental inquiries, a parliamentary committee of inquiry and two court cases: M. Theobald (1984) Agnes Grant, in Selleck and Sullivan, *Not So Eminent Victorians*.

44 M. Theobald (1990) The 'everyday world' of women who taught. *History of Education Review* 19(2): 15–23.

45 M. Chanfrault-Duchet (1991) Narrative structures, social models, and symbolic representation in the life story, in Gluck and Patai, *Women's Words*, p.89.

46 S. Reinharz (1993) *Feminist Methods in Social Research*. New York: Oxford University Press, p.260.

47 I take up this point concerning secondary teachers in Theobald, Imagining the woman teacher.

48 R. Altenbaugh (ed.) (1992) *The Teacher's Voice: A Social History of Teaching in Twentieth Century America*. London: Falmer Press.

49 S. Jeffries (1985) *The Spinster and her Enemies: Feminism and Sexuality 1880–1930*. London: Pandora.

50 C. Steedman (1987) Prisonhouses, in Lawn and Grace, *Teachers*, p.120.

3 Workers, professionals, pilgrims: tracing Canadian women teachers' histories

Alison Prentice

In late October 1997, 250,000 Canadian teachers walked off the job in Ontario, my home province and the locale for most of my scholarly work on the history of Canadian teachers. They were defying a government that was already well known for its draconian measures and that now seemed bent on bringing school boards and teachers into line. In particular, the teachers' protest was designed to call attention to Bill 160, which gives the provincial government the power to bypass local boards of education and the bargaining process in a number of crucial areas, such as class size and classroom hours. Ontario's teachers kept the schools closed for two weeks, returning to work only when the dangers of increasing government by provincial regulation had been thoroughly exposed.

From my present perch overlooking the Straits of Juan de Fuca in British Columbia (BC), Ontario's teachers and their problems seem far away. But this is an illusion. There are many distancing factors, it is true: the sheer number of miles between BC and Ontario; the barriers of mountains, plains and great lakes; regional cultures that do differ enormously from one province to another in Canada; the distance created by my own imminent retirement from teaching. But the Canadian media were full of the story; and emails from friends who were on the spot arrived here, as commentaries on the protest were posted and then forwarded around the country.[1] Surprisingly, there was little comment on several features of the walkout that seemed especially significant to me. One was that all five of the teachers' associations of Ontario joined together in this historic protest. Second, in advocating the walkout, association leaders were acknowledging, at some level, teachers' identity and heritage as workers, accustomed to seeking redress of their grievances through collective action. Third, since all of Ontario's elementary and secondary teachers walked out, the majority of the protesters must have been women. The importance of women's participation was symbolized by the role played by one woman teacher. Eileen Lennon, the president of the teachers' umbrella organization, the Ontario Teachers' Federation, was leading spokesperson of the protest.[2]

At this time of writing, we cannot know what the fallout of Bill 160 will be for Ontario schools. What is fairly certain is that the protest will someday enter the books as a significant moment in the history of Ontario education.[3] We return to uncertainty, however, when we consider what this history making might mean. Will the history of the teachers' walkout be read? If read, will it be remembered in all its complexity? In particular, will women's issues and the role of gender relations in teachers' dissatisfaction be understood as part of the story?

Although the question of whether the history of education will be read is a question dear to my heart, the question of how it will be written concerns me almost more. All too easily we focus on the big event and the struggles for political power among the leading actors: presidents of teacher associations, male or female, and ministers of education. While the leaders can hardly be ignored, my own quest over the years has increasingly been to record and analyse the feelings, motivations and actions of the rank and file in educational history, especially the women who taught in Canadian classrooms. In this I have hardly been alone. Indeed, it has been inspiring to be part of a larger feminist and educational history that has increasingly valued both women's work, in education as in other parts of life, and found pleasure and instruction in the stories of ordinary women. In my case, the initial focus was on occupational structures and gender relations within those structures; this soon developed into a focus on women teachers' collective history and identity as workers; more recently, I have been attracted to the study of individual careers and journeys in the teaching profession, and the history of women's work in higher education.

Teachers simply appeared in my early scholarly work; I did not summon them. It is true that I was a former secondary school teacher with a somewhat jaundiced view of the teaching work that I had loved, despite my lack of love for the schools and school systems in which it had occurred. But by the time I embarked on a doctorate, I saw myself less as a teacher and more as a parent of two boys in school and a citizen. What I wanted to explore was the history that was behind the schooling that we parents and citizens seemed determined at all costs – and the costs were considerable – to commit our children. My own educational background had been privileged. It had taken me through progressive public schools in Toronto and an Anglican secondary school in the same city, an American women's college, a year of study in Europe, and a master's degree in history prior to my year of teacher training at the Ontario College of Education.[4] I often thought that my own interest in education had a lot to do with having experienced so many different kinds of schools and schooling. But my approach also had much to do with the fact that I began my PhD in the 1960s, when class and community differences in education were becoming burning issues. My doctoral research was thus in part designed to explore the origins of parental, class and community alienation from the schools. The focus was on the turbulent mid-nineteenth century when the basic structures of state school systems had been put in place. Ontario was the site of this research chiefly because I lived there. The Ontario Archives were nearby; research on nineteenth century Ontario educational issues could be combined, relatively easily, with family life.

As I have suggested, the teachers emerged; they were not summoned. They emerged because they were there in the archives – along with the parents and children, school trustees and superintendents and the local citizenry – wowing me with their amazing nineteenth century words. All of these people had written to the most prolific wordsmith of them all, the notorious Egerton Ryerson, Ontario's first Chief Superintendent of Schools, a man whose writings on school problems were voluminous. Ontario's present day alienation from a dictatorial educational regime is more than reminiscent of the Ryerson era in education. His notoriety stemmed not just from his enormous propaganda machine, but also from his reputation as a 'Prussian dictator', determined to ram his version of educational reform down the throats of Upper Canadians at all costs. One of the leading architects of Ontario's provincial school system, Ryerson and his fellow school promoters introduced much regulation into the lives of children, their parents and teachers. Not surprisingly, Ryerson's policies also led to protest. Indeed, the correspondence generated by the educational reforms of his era almost equalled that generated by Britain's colonial office, governing the entire British empire, during the same period.[5] Education office records reveal that our forebears – teachers included – had plenty to say to government on the subject of education.

But the teachers were also in the archives because Ryerson and his fellow school promoters, in their quest to improve the calibre of Ontario's mid-nineteenth century teaching force, made a vast and ongoing study of them. Among the characteristics of school teachers that the newly formed provincial Department of Education scrutinized, a very significant one was their sex. Was the teacher male or female? How many teachers in a particular township, county, town or city were male? How many were female? How old were these schoolmistresses and schoolmasters? How many had been to Normal School? What teaching certificates did they have? Numbers could not be resisted in the late 1960s and early 1970s, when I was writing my dissertation, any more than they could be in the mid-nineteenth century. Indeed they have much to tell us. The growing numbers of young female teachers help to explain, for example, the irate parents who wrote to Egerton Ryerson complaining that they could not send their boys to school. 'Grown-up' boys, such parents felt, could not be taught by 'mere' girls. Their numbers help to explain, as well, the anxiety manifested by people like Ryerson on the subject of professionalism. A professional teacher, according to the Chief Superintendent, was a person who was head of his own household, had a room of his own, and time to study in the evenings. The growing numbers of young women teachers who lived with their parents, or teachers who 'boarded from house to house', did not qualify.[6]

For various reasons, neither the teachers nor the problem of teachers' gender figured prominently in the book that grew out of my dissertation. The manuscript had to be shortened and the chapter on teachers was one of two from the original study that disappeared.[7] But, it was perhaps already in my mind that the teachers really deserved much more than the thesis chapter on them provided. Well before *The School Promoters* went to press, a fellow graduate student had persuaded me to expand my work on nineteenth century women teachers. I joined Harvey Graff and Wendy Bryans in putting together a session on the subject for the Canadian Association for American Studies (CAAS), which met in Ottawa in the spring of 1974.[8] Since this was one of Canada's earliest scholarly meetings devoted to women's studies, it was wonderful luck to be involved. My only regret was missing its greatest moment – the electrifying keynote address by the emerging feminist philosopher, Mary O'Brien.[9] Instead I grabbed that morning to spend in Ottawa's National Archives. With two young boys at home, and a university teaching job that had begun in 1972, getting to archives outside of Toronto was a problem and this was too good a chance to miss.

Combining motherhood and employment may have made research in other cities difficult, but it was ideal in every other respect. Life with my family balanced research and teaching; our home in Toronto was only a few blocks from the Archives of Ontario, on the one hand, and the Ontario Institute for Studies in Education (OISE) and its outstanding research library on the other. The latter contained many gems, including historical runs of the annual education department reports not only of most of the Canadian provinces, but of many American states as well. The presence of those reports and of educational periodicals from Nova Scotia, New Brunswick and Quebec, in addition to the Ontario records, made it possible for me to construct a paper for the CAAS session that went beyond my own province. This, in turn, allowed me to question a powerful paradigm most graphically displayed in Quebec educational history. In this paradigm the rapid increase, during the second half of the nineteenth century, in the proportions of teachers who were women was simply portrayed as negative. There was little explanation but much concern; the focus seemed to be on male teachers' claim to professional status, a claim undermined by women's movement into the occupation. My CAAS paper, eventually published as 'The feminization of teaching in British North America and Canada, 1845–1875',[10] took issue with this paradigm only in a footnote. But it did attempt both to explain what was going on and to examine the movement of women into public school work from the perspective of the women involved. Given the time lines for books and articles, it is not surprising that this study was in print two years before *The School Promoters* came out in 1977. By the time I left my teaching post at York University's Atkinson College in 1975 to take a job at the Ontario Institute for Studies in Education, I was already launched on the trajectory that would define my major research interests from then on.

If Canadian patriotism (Canada's centennial celebration in 1967 made a profound impression on me and my contemporaries) and the stimulus of a meeting in Ottawa were catalysts for examining the histories of teachers in provinces other than Ontario, one of my first OISE students challenged me to continue such out-of-province explorations. Most students at the Institute are forced by their circumstances to examine materials relating to Ontario; the logistics of study outside the province seem as insurmountable to them as they seemed to me. This was not true for Marta Danylewycz, a European-born doctoral student who came to OISE to complete a formal education that had begun with her schooling in Ohio and been enriched by several years of teaching and graduate study in Montreal. Marta's innovative doctoral thesis on the history of two Quebec religious orders launched her not only as a fine social historian, but also as a historian of women teachers; Quebec's famous teaching order, the Congregation of Notre Dame, was one of her subjects.[11] It was Marta who proposed that she and I should collaborate on some comparative studies of gender relations in the history of teaching. We would draw on the manuscript census, in addition to other materials, and focus on Ontario and Quebec, the two provinces we knew best. In embarking on this research, we were fortunate in having the outstanding research assistance of Beth Light, an associate with OISE's Canadian Women's History Project. Beth's work with Michael Katz, when the latter was at York University, had made her an expert quantitative historian.

Beth was a co-author of the first paper that I published with Marta. This study of the evolution of the sexual division of labour in teaching revealed how different the history of gender relations in Canadian teaching evidently was, in some respects, from that described by David Tyack, Myra Strober, Audri Lanford and others, for the United States. The influence of urban centres on the distribution of men and women teachers seemed minimal in the Ontario and Quebec counties we examined; in contrast to what may have happened elsewhere, in these places the absence of male immigrant teachers and the poverty of the frontier emerged as far more important factors in the earliest shifts towards teaching forces that were predominantly female.[12]

When funding from the Historical Atlas of Canada briefly added the geographer, Susan Laskin, to the team, our quantitative work expanded. The task of creating maps and figures to illustrate the history of education across nineteenth century Canada led us to explore all the statistical data on schools and teachers that we could find for that century – and revealed their flaws. It was difficult to compare trends from one Canadian region to another, because the statistics gathered were not necessarily comparable. Conclusions drawn from one set of statistics, moreover, sometimes disagreed with those drawn from another, for the same region.[13] Although it was exciting to participate in the creation of an atlas that would attempt to document regional similarities and differences in education across Canada, most illustrations, finally, had to focus on a single region or locality. Thus, we had maps illustrating the gendering of teaching in the Maritime provinces;[14] and from Marta's research, we created maps documenting the spread of the Congregation of Notre Dame (CND) in Quebec. Recruitment of new sisters to the teaching order, these maps showed, could be linked to the movement of CND academies into given localities and regions. This illustration joined others in a plate intended to demonstrate the continuing importance of ethnicity, class and race, but particularly of religion and gender, in the history of formal education in nineteenth century Canada.[15]

Marta and I went on to publish several other articles on our Quebec and Ontario teachers exploring these and similar themes.[16] The last essay that we wrote shifted the focus: we moved away somewhat from gender relations in teaching to a consideration of women teachers as workers, an interest that followed logically from our initial concern to understand why and in what manner common and parish school teaching forces became predominantly female in nineteenth century Ontario and Quebec. The subordination of most women teachers in state school systems was all too apparent. Urban schools, in particular, were organized hierarchically, with male principals and female assistant teachers, wherever the sexes were taught together. But even in rural schools, women taught and men supervised. Salary scales in all schools, urban or rural, single sex or mixed, favoured men over women. By the early 1980s, Marta and I had made a brief research trip to the National Archives in Quebec and read enough in the records of both provinces to get some sense of what these inequities meant to nineteenth and early twentieth century schoolmistresses, as well as some idea of the conditions under which they laboured. In contrast to much historical writing on teachers – and the protestations often of the teachers themselves – we were inclined to see women teachers less as budding professionals, than as unacknowledged workers. Our last essay on Ontario and Quebec teachers looked at typical working conditions – and teachers' protests against them – and took issue with paradigms that focus exclusively on teaching as a 'profession'. We finally argued against the professional/worker dichotomy and that teachers' work should be recognized for what, in many ways, it actually was: part of labour history.[17] The book on Quebec and Ontario teachers and gender that Marta and I planned would have developed this argument.

This book never materialized. Our collaboration ended with Marta's sudden death, in March 1985, at the hands of her demented brother. Marta was just beginning a university teaching career when her life was so tragically cut short.[18]

Although Marta's and my book was never written, several essays that I published after her death did develop aspects of its proposed central themes: gender relations in teaching, the experience of women teachers as workers and, very tenuously, the issue of professionalism. One dealt with the ideas and attitudes of the early members of the Women Teachers' Association (WTA) of Toronto. This important turn-of-the-century organization grappled with several, sometimes conflicting possibilities and agendas: affiliation with Toronto's Labour Council; professional goals and concerns; links with middle class women's reformist groups, such as Toronto's Local Council of Women; and social events. Sorting out these frequently conflicting alliances and concerns was not easy for the women of the WTA. The records reveal teachers whose needs and identities were not altogether clear either to themselves or others. Nor were these needs and identities fixed over time. Yet, if they did not easily fit into any single mould, WTA members certainly recognized the particularity of their interests as women. And many of their complaints had to do with the material conditions of their daily working lives.[19]

An essay on the early students who attended the Toronto Normal School focused on related themes. This study dealt with the segregation of male and female students, the gender issues that developed in this early coeducational experiment, and the differing experiences of the men and women, as both students and graduates. Toronto Normal's messages to budding women teachers were ambiguous. Female students were treated to powerful lessons in hierarchy, segregation and control; at the same time they could look forward to the possibility of relative autonomy in the future, especially if they got teaching jobs in cities. A strong, collective identity as women teachers may also have been forged; it is certainly to graduates of this school that we owe the founding of Toronto's WTA.[20]

A final look at elementary teachers, written collaboratively with University of Ottawa historian Ruby Heap, returned to organized teachers' quest for economic justice at the turn of the twentieth century. In the province of Quebec, Ruby and I discovered English and French speaking women teachers working together to fight for better treatment in the provincial teachers' pension schemes. Their struggles resulted in some changes for the better, although by no means full equality or justice for women in teaching.[21]

Gender relations in the teaching labour force and women teachers as workers seemed, in the late 1970s and the 1980s, important if straightforward topics. More difficult to write about were subjects that I attempted to explore in some papers that never made it into print. One of these looked at a spate of official investigations into teachers' misconduct that took place in Ontario and Quebec in the late nineteenth century.[22] These unusual 'trials' needed to be contextualized; the additional work was never done.

Another dealt with teachers' ill health, and financial problems in retirement, drawing on a fascinating set of superannuation records from Ontario.[23] A third dealt, in part, with the vexing and ever present question of teaching as a profession, as the issue unfolded in mid-nineteenth century Ontario. This proved a subject that simply needed much more thought and so I shelved it.[24] The complexity of these topics was not the only reason for abandoning them; in the 1980s I was also involved in work on two books – one a co-authored study entitled *Schooling and Scholars in Nineteenth-Century Ontario* – and the other a multi-authored text on the history of women in Canada. In the first, teachers were the focus of several chapters; in the second, we showed how prominently the occupation of teaching figured in the larger history of Canadian women's participation in the labour force.[25]

In the middle 1980s my research interests were also moving in new directions. Marta's death had followed all too quickly the death of my younger son in a car accident, in which I was also badly injured. Research and writing that focused on women like myself – especially when undertaken collaboratively with other women – had been an important part of my healing. Now 'women like myself' included college and university teachers as well as school teachers. Thus, by the time Marjorie Theobald and I were putting together our 1991 collection of essays on the history of women teachers,[26] I was gathering histories of women's work in higher education. Marjorie's early work was an important influence; her studies of the ladies' academies and private schools of Australia taught us to question many stereotypes regarding so-called lady-teachers and what they taught, as did those of her sister Australian, Ailsa Zainu'ddin.[27] Their insights and those of several American historians were revising our perceptions in many ways.[28] No longer could we accept the ladies' academies and seminaries of the nineteenth century as ephemeral or lacking in serious purpose. Indeed, they and their teachers not only were clearly in the vanguard of the movement for women's higher education but also were implicated in women's increasing search for professional employment and lifetime careers in meaningful, non-domestic work.

Research on Ontario's nineteenth century ladies' schools for *Schooling and Scholars* had whetted my appetite; a foray into the history of a particularly prominent ladies' academy mistress, Mary Electa Adams, only increased the fascination. I was also fortunate in having students and friends pursuing similar interests. We now know much more about Ontario nineteenth century private school and academy mistresses from monographs by Johanna Selles and Jane Errington, who have set women's teaching work in the context, in Johanna's case, of Methodist initiatives in higher education, and in Jane's, of early nineteenth century women's employment generally.[29] Susan Gelman has explored the history of a group of teachers who inherited the struggles of these early schoolmistresses, the late nineteenth and early twentieth century women who taught in Ontario's state secondary schools, while Elizabeth Smyth has taken up the much neglected topic of Roman Catholic convent academy and college teachers in the same province. Anna Lathrop has examined the history of a fascinating early twentieth century Toronto private school that provided several generations of Ontario women teachers with unique training in drama and physical education.[30]

My own first investigations in the field of higher education focused on the lives and careers of Mary Electa Adams and Mossie May Kirkwood. Adams was one of the few women's academy teachers for whom one could trace a more or less continuous career; a reading of the single volume of her diaries that remains to us revealed both how ambitious and how woman oriented this illustrious nineteenth century Methodist educator had been. Her career strongly supported my argument that we should include the women's colleges and academies of the nineteenth century in the history of Canadian higher education; the closing of many of them and the evolution of the remainder into private secondary schools had, until then, tended to exclude them in a history that often focused on universities alone. Mossie May Kirkwood first came to my attention because of her fascinating 1930s booklet entitled *For College Women . . . and Men*. In it, this twentieth century English professor proclaimed the importance of meaningful employment outside the home for all women – even married women with children like herself. One could not help but wonder how this extraordinary individual had managed to carve out a career both as a teacher and dean of women's residences at the University of Toronto, lasting from 1917 until well after the Second World War. The answer, I learned from oral history tapes that Kirkwood recorded in 1973, was with considerable difficulty. Mary Electa Adams and Mossie May Kirkwood became the subjects of a study that mapped the struggles of these two women for work in Canadian higher education.[31] My first foray into the biographical mode, this essay signalled a change in direction in more ways than one. Biographical studies continued – and still continue – to have a strong appeal for me.

But, as always, it seemed important to have some numbers. Digging up those numbers, with the help of several able assistants, and putting them all together in a discussion of women's work at the University of Toronto in the decades prior to 1940, laid much of the groundwork for my research and writing in the 1990s. The problems of the women faculty at Toronto, we discovered, were faced by other women throughout the university. The female labour force at the university was increasingly composed of women working in a multitude of assistantship roles: as researchers, teaching assistants, secretaries, laboratory technicians and librarians – not to mention food workers and cleaners. Not always visible in this research, moreover, was the additional and typically unpaid work of faculty wives. We were not the first to discover that the myth of the professor as individual genius, unencumbered in his solitary pursuit of knowledge, frequently obscures or denies altogether the labour of countless assistants and helpers, many of whom are women. But the data on the University of Toronto demonstrated just how important such women were to the emerging research university in the first half of the twentieth century.[32]

My most recent research has focused largely on faculty women, with special attention to two groups particularly close to my heart: historians and physicists. An essay on historians places those who penetrated university teaching prior to 1950 in the context of Canadian university and departmental cultures, as these and other women experienced them. In the introduction to the collection of essays that contains this piece, co-editor Beverly Boutilier and I grapple further with the historical profession's treatment of women. It seems all too apparent that professionalizing academics, during the first half of the twentieth century at least, defined themselves as historians, in part, by creating boundaries that excluded women and the kind of historical writing that many women did.[33] Was the situation in physics comparable? The study of women in this field attracted me because of their conspicuous absence, on faculty, in the physics department that employed my husband at the University of Toronto. There had been women once, I knew, as I had met one whose career was just ending as Jim's was beginning. Indeed research on the university revealed that almost one-quarter of Toronto's earliest PhDs in physics were granted to women and that three women had made fulltime, lifetime careers in the Toronto physics department, all beginning in the interwar years.[34] In the early stages, in fact, women seem to have been more successful in physics than they were in history, in leading Canadian universities. It was intriguing to try to figure out why.

If Mary Electa Adams and Mossie May Kirkwood attracted me to biography, the physicists and historians got me hooked on oral history. As a result, it has been my good fortune over the years to interview some wonderful Canadian women scholars. One was the physicist, Elizabeth Allin, who taught at the University of Toronto from 1931 to 1972; another was Margaret A. Ormsby, whose career unfolded for the most part in the history department of the University of British Columbia after 1945. These persistent women managed to make spaces for themselves in the Canadian academy and I was keen to tell their stories. But it was also vital to try to set these stories in context – a context which includes many highly qualified women who did not achieve professorial status, but whose collective efforts were nevertheless important both to the women who did and to the university's twentieth century work.[35]

The biographical approach, especially if one considers less prominent protagonists, leads us to look for multiple meanings in women's participation in the world of teaching. Dianne Hallman's account of her Nova Scotia mother's career in the classroom, an account constructed through interviews and correspondence long after the fact, points us in this direction. The career in question was brief; once she took on family responsibilities, Dianne's mother moved out of the classroom permanently. What she chiefly remembered and wished to focus on was less the inadequate classrooms, low pay or poor equipment she undoubtedly knew about and experienced, than the importance of her service to an appreciative community. Responsive children and parents were recalled and valued; problematic wages or teaching conditions seemed, in retrospect, less significant.[36]

Memories are coloured, in the end, by events and feelings over a lifetime; many retired women teachers prefer, perhaps, to focus on those that are positive. The interviewer's position and perspective must also alter the view. Certainly, my interviews with Elizabeth Allin and Margaret Ormsby revealed women who wished to express – to me at least – their loyalty to the institutions that had provided them both with long careers and interesting work. When queried, Allin did recall feeling that women at Toronto were not treated with quite the same equality that she was surprised to discover at Cambridge during her year of study there in 1933–4. Only in retrospect did she see the oddity of the separate entrances for women that still prevailed, evidently, in Toronto's physics laboratories during the 1930s. Allin nevertheless remembered feeling very at home in the physics department at Toronto, presumably in spite of these separate entrances and other minor irritants. About her slow progress to a full professorship, she was entirely silent; nor did I wish to probe too deeply. The one promotion she did mention was the assistant professorship granted in 1941 after almost a decade of fulltime teaching for Toronto. She shared this increased status and job security with two other women who had worked in the physics department even longer. All three, according to Allin, felt 'very lucky' to be promoted.

Margaret Ormsby was willing to explore more of her negative memories, perhaps because our interview took place the day after we had both been present at a session on the status of women in the historical profession that I organized and chaired for the Canadian Historical Association annual meeting in 1990. Ormsby commented on her isolation in the history department at the University of British Columbia (UBC), but attributed this chiefly to her lone membership in a generation which had achieved few appointments of either sex in her field. Her historian colleagues at UBC were thus either much younger or much older than she was. Yet, although she used the word 'lonely' several times in the interview, Ormsby also expressed much appreciation for her university. The received opinion when she was job hunting was that western universities were more welcoming to the idea of women on faculty than eastern ones; for Ormsby this proved her salvation. The early 1940s, at McMaster University in Hamilton, Ontario, had seen her presiding over a desk in the ladies' washroom; at UBC, at least, she enjoyed the benefit of a proper office. She also experienced fairly rapid promotion and recognition by her peers, eventually becoming head of her department and the second woman president of the Canadian Historical Association. Another significant point, for Ormsby, was what she remembered as the perfect equality that women enjoyed with men in UBC's faculty dining room. This was a major plus for UBC indeed, given that faculty clubs at eastern universities, like Toronto and McGill, were strictly off limits to the female faculty who taught at those institutions during most of her era.

My most recent study is a comparative exploration of the education and early careers of three women physicists. All three demonstrated great talent in physics, at least at the beginning of their scholarly lives, but all had some difficulties forging careers in the Canadian academy. Of the three, only Elizabeth Allin succeeded in remaining both in physics and in Canada. Elizabeth Laird, whose career unfolded in the late nineteenth and early twentieth century, was forced to seek both her doctorate and university level teaching in the United States, obtaining the first from Bryn Mawr and finding the second at Mount Holyoke, where she quickly became head of a small but vital department. A generation later, Allie Vibert Douglas shifted from physics to astrophysics when studying for her doctorate in the early 1920s; by the late 1930s, she had left her home physics department and McGill University to take on the deanship of women at Queen's.

The study of these three women is intended to be part of a collection of essays in which, with the help of three collaborating editors, I have finally delved more deeply into the prickly question of women's relationship to the professions.[37] In this projected volume, school and university teaching are explored in tandem with other kinds of professional work that women have engaged in. The collection as a whole examines the ways in which individual women and groups of women have fared in particular professions, how women have interpreted 'professionalism' in their everyday lives, and the encouragement as well as the barriers they have encountered. Not surprisingly, over and over again, the professions studied are shown to be gendered in complex ways; for many women, indeed, attempts to enter or to work in these professions have been productive of stress, while professionalism for many of our subjects – as, indeed, for many of the essays' authors – remains a problematic concept. Parental and 'professional' responsibilities clash; many of the women whose careers are explored in our volume remained single or chose to be childless. There are also strong hints that place is significant, along with gender. Becoming a professor of physics in the small university community of central Canada was difficult enough; becoming a composer and professor of music in British Columbia meant bucking both US and central Canadian musical establishments. At the same time, it is apparent that the professions, perhaps especially those that women have created or been able to make their own, have provided vital, and sometimes extraordinary, opportunities for many women.

Here, it seems useful to return to the story of Ontario's teachers in the fall of 1993. As workers, they were ready to go on strike. But they also saw themselves as professionals, who ought to return to the classroom in recognition of their students' and society's claim to their services. Indeed, we must acknowledge these teachers' multiple identities, for many of them are undoubtedly parents as well as workers, professionals and protesters.[38] All are also members of complex communities, where the need for their services is great.

My wish to acknowledge ambiguity and multiple identities may explain the turn to biography. In this, once again, I appear to have been part of a larger trend. Perhaps only in the lives of single individuals is it possible to glimpse the complexity of motivation and experience that make up human history. Biography may also be a more accessible form of historical writing, an important attraction, as I have always wanted to reach out beyond the academy to general audiences. This is a goal that has seemed frustratingly difficult to accomplish in a Canadian setting, although hope springs eternal.[39]

I will probably continue to work with individual stories. Oral histories of women working in universities are on the agenda, as is the publication of a memoir of her early life that Allie Vibert Douglas penned in her retirement and entitled 'Pilgrims were we all'.[40] I want to bring the insights of the Australian historian, Alison Mackinnon, and of the Swedish social scientist, Inga Elgqvist-Saltzman, to bear on women's quest for commitment, autonomy and meaning in working lives that are complicated – and enriched – by the multiple responsibilities of job, family and community.[41] Like feminist historians everywhere, feminist educational historians no longer wish to make heroes or heroines of the 'great' in history; perhaps it is still acceptable, however, to find a measure of heroism in the lives of ordinary travellers. Women's teaching work, professional and personal lives and roles remain contradictory, ambiguous, challenging. Allie Vibert Douglas put it well. Pilgrims were we all. I can only add that pilgrims we remain.

Acknowledgements

I wish to thank the many students and friends who helped with the research reported in this chapter, most recently and especially, Cathy James and Alyson King. For funding it, thanks are also due to the Ontario Institute for Studies in Education/University of Toronto and the Social Sciences and Humanities Research Council of Canada.

Notes

1 I am grateful to Sandra Acker, of the Ontario Institute for Studies in Education/University of Toronto, for keeping me posted.
2 The five Ontario teachers' associations are the Ontario Federation of Secondary

School Teachers, Federation of Women Teachers' Associations of Ontario, Ontario Public School Teachers Federation, Ontario English-Catholic Teachers Federation and Association des enseignantes et des enseignants franco-Ontariens.

3 As the strike wound down, the president of the Ontario Federation of Secondary School Teachers, Earl Manners, emphasized this very point. 'No one is ever going to be able to take away from the history books what has been accomplished in the past two weeks'. *The Globe and Mail* 8 November 1997.

4 The schools and colleges were Forest Hill and Bishop Strachan in Toronto, and Smith College in Massachusetts. I spent a third undergraduate year at the University of Geneva and did my MA at the University of Toronto.

5 See A. Prentice (1978) The public instructor: Ryerson and the role of the public school administrator, in N. Macdonald and A. Chaiton (eds) *Egerton Ryerson and his Times*. Toronto: Macmillan.

6 S.E. Houston and A. Prentice (1988) *Schooling and Scholars in Nineteenth-Century Ontario*. Toronto: University of Toronto Press, ch.6.

7 A. Prentice (1977) *The School Promoters: Education and Social Class in Mid-Nineteenth Century Upper Canada*. Toronto: McClelland and Stewart. The other missing chapter had already been published elsewhere. See A. Prentice (1972) Education and the metaphor of the family: the Upper Canadian example. *History of Education Quarterly* 12(3): 281–303. Reprinted in M.B. Katz and P.H. Mattingly (eds) (1975) *Education and Social Change: Themes from Ontario's Past*. New York: New York University Press.

8 Wendy Bryans was completing (1974) ' "Virtuous women at half the price": the feminization of the teaching force and early women teacher organizations in Ontario'. MA thesis. University of Toronto.

9 For me, the highlight of the conference was meeting Barbara Roberts, a lifelong friend, whose enthusiasm for women's history and women scholars helped to kindle my own.

10 A. Prentice (1975) *Social History/histoire sociale* 8(May): 5–20; reprinted in S.M. Trofimenkoff and A. Prentice (eds) (1977) *The Neglected Majority: Essays in Canadian Women's History*. Toronto: McClelland and Stewart; and in J.M. Bumsted (ed.) (1986) *Interpreting Canada's Past: Volume I. Before Confederation*. Toronto: Oxford University Press.

11 The thesis was published posthumously. M. Danylewycz (1987) *Taking the Veil: An Alternative to Marriage, Motherhood and Spinsterhood in Quebec, 1840–1920*. Toronto: McClelland and Stewart. G. Boulad (trans.) (1988) *Profession: religieuse. Un choix pour les Québécoises, 1840–1920*. Montreal: Boréal.

12 M. Danylewycz, B. Light and A. Prentice (1983) The evolution of the sexual division of labour in teaching: a nineteenth century Ontario and Quebec case study. *Social History/histoire sociale* 31 (May): 81–109; reprinted in J. Gaskell and A. Mclaren (eds) (1987 and 1990) *Women and Education: A Canadian Perspective*. Calgary: Detselig. Our paper noted, especially, that the findings of M. Strober and A. Lanford (later published in *Signs*) did not seem to apply, in the Canadian counties we studied. See M. Strober and A. Lanford (1986) The feminization of public school teaching: a cross-sectional analysis, 1850–1880. *Signs* 11(2): 212–35.

13 See S. Laskin, B. Light and A. Prentice (1982) Studying the history of an occupation: quantitative sources on Canadian teachers in the nineteenth century. *Archivaria* 14 (summer): 75–92. Unfortunately this article was marred by printing errors, including the omission of the code for understanding a table illustrating statistics available for the different provinces, over time.

14 See A. Prentice and S.L. Laskin (1993) The quest for universal schooling, 1851–1891, Plate 55 in R.L. Gentilcore (ed.) *Historical Atlas of Canada. Volume II: The Land Transformed, 1800–1891.* Toronto: University of Toronto Press.

15 A. Prentice *et al.* (1993) Education: variety and separateness, 1851–1891, Plate 54 in ibid.

16 M. Danylewycz and A. Prentice (1984) Teachers, gender and bureaucratizing school systems in nineteenth century Montreal and Toronto. *History of Education Quarterly* (spring): 75–100; (1986) Revising the history of teachers: a Canadian perspective. *Interchange* 17(2): 135–46. See also Danylewycz (1983) Sexes et classes sociales dans l'enseignement: le cas Montréal à la fin du 19è siècle, in N. Fahmy-Eid and M. Dumont (eds) *Maîtresses de maison, maîtresses d'école: femmes, famille et éducation dans l'histoire du Québec.* Montreal: Boréal.

17 Like her thesis, this too was published after Marta's death. M Danylewycz and A. Prentice (1986) Teachers' work: changing patterns and perceptions in the emerging school systems of 19th and early 20th century central Canada. *Labour/le travail* (spring): 59–80; reprinted in J. Ozga (ed.) (1988) *Schoolwork: Approaches to the Labour Process of Teaching.* Milton Keynes: Open University Press; in A. Prentice and M. Theobald (eds) (1991) *Women Who Taught: Perspectives on the History of Women and Teaching.* Toronto: University of Toronto Press; and in J.M. Bumsted (ed.) (1993) *Interpreting Canada's Past: Volume II, Post-Confederation,* 2nd edition. Toronto: Oxford University Press.

18 Her brother also took the lives of Marta's parents and uncle, as well as his own. He evidently believed that his family was carrying genes that had produced mental instability in both himself and his mother. Jealousy of his sister may also have been involved in his own illness, which became apparent at about the same time she was offered her first tenure-stream position. The problems of Marta's family may be attributed, in part, to their bitter experiences in the Ukraine and in Germany, prior to, during and following the Second World War; but our own culture of violence in North America – and the ease with which guns may be purchased and carried across the American–Canadian border – are also implicated. A brief account of Marta's life and death may be found in the preface to Danylewycz, *Taking the Veil,* or in the French version of her monograph, *Profession: religieuse.*

19 A. Prentice (1985) Themes in the history of the Women Teachers' Association of Toronto, in P. Bourne (ed.) *Women's Paid and Unpaid Work.* Toronto: New Hogtown Press. See also A. Prentice (1984) From household to school house: the emergence of the teacher as servant of the state. *Material History Bulletin* 20(Autumn): 19–29.

20 A. Prentice (1990) 'Friendly atoms in chemistry': women and men at the Toronto Normal School', in D. Keane and C. Read (eds) *Old Ontario: Essays in Honour of J.M.S. Careless.* Toronto: Dundurn Press.

21 R. Heap and A. Prentice (1993) 'The outlook for old age is not hopeful': the

struggle of female teachers over pensions in Quebec, 1880–1914. *Histoire sociale/Social History* (May): 67–94.

22 J.R. Abbott and A. Prentice (1986) Policy, gender and conflict: teachers and the state in Ontario and Quebec, 1850–1920. Paper delivered to the biennial meeting of the Canadian History of Education Association, Halifax, Nova Scotia.

23 P. Staton and A. Prentice (1987) Teachers and the quest for health. Paper presented to the Canadian Research Institute for the Advancement of Women Annual Meeting, Winnipeg, Manitoba.

24 A. Prentice (1981) Patriarch or public servant? Teachers and professionalism in mid-nineteenth-century Ontario. Paper presented to the Workshop on Professionalization in Modern Societies, University of Western Ontario, London, Ontario. This paper nevertheless proved useful to R.D. Gidney and W.J.P. Millar in the writing of their section on teachers in Gidney and Millar (1994) *Professional Gentlemen: The Professions in Nineteenth-Century Ontario*. Toronto: University of Toronto Press.

25 S.E. Houston and A. Prentice (1988) *Schooling and Scholars*; A. Prentice, P. Bourne, G.C. Brandt, B. Light, W. Mitchinson and N. Black (1988) *Canadian Women: A History*. Toronto: Harcourt Brace Jovanovich; 2nd edition (1996) Harcourt Brace Canada.

26 M.R. Theobald and A. Prentice (1991) *Women Who Taught: Perspectives on the History of Women and Teaching*. Toronto: University of Toronto Press.

27 See, especially, M. Theobald (1984) 'Mere accomplishments'? Melbourne's early ladies' schools reconsidered. *History of Education Review* 13(2): 15–28, and A. Zainu'ddin (1984) 'The poor widow, the ignoramus and the humbug': an examination of rhetoric and reality in Victoria's 1905 Act for the Registration of Teachers and Schools. *History of Education Review* 13(2): 29–42. Both essays are reprinted in Prentice and Theobald, *Women Who Taught*.

28 I think particularly of David F. Allmendinger, Jr, Ann Firor Scott and Kathryn Kish Sklar. See Allmendinger (1979) Mount Holyoke Students encounter the need for life-planning, 1837–1850. *History of Education Quarterly* 19(1): 27–46; Scott (1979) The ever widening circle: the diffusion of feminist values from the Troy Female Seminary, 1822–1872. *History of Education Quarterly* 19(1): 3–25; and Sklar (1973) *Catharine Beecher: A Study in American Domesticity*. New Haven, CT: Yale University Press.

29 J.M. Selles (1996) *Methodists and Women's Education in Ontario, 1836–1925*. Montreal and Kingston: McGill-Queen's University Press; E.J. Errington (1995) *Wives and Mothers, School Mistresses and Scullery Maids: Working Women in Upper Canada, 1791–1840*. Montreal and Kingston: McGill-Queen's University Press.

30 S. Gelman (1994) 'The history of women teachers in Ontario's public secondary schools: 1871–1930'. PhD thesis. University of Toronto; S. Smyth (1989) 'The lessons of religion and science: the congregation of the Sisters of St. Joseph and St. Joseph's Academy, Toronto, 1854–1911'. Ed.D. University of Toronto; A. Lathrop (1997) 'Elegance and expression, sweat and strength: body training, physical culture and female embodiment in women's education at the Margaret Eaton Schools. Ed.D. University of Toronto. Articles include S. Gelman (1990) 'The "feminization" of the high schools'? Women secondary teachers in Toronto, 1871–1930. *Historical Studies in Education/Revue d'histoire de l'éducation* 2(1):

119–48; E. Smyth (1994) 'Much exertion of the voice and great application of the mind': teacher education within the congregation of the Sisters of St. Joseph of Toronto, 1851–1920. *Historical Studies in Education/Revue d'histoire de l'éducation* 6(3): 97–113; E. Smyth (1997) 'Writing teaches us our mysteries': women religious recording and writing history, in B. Boutilier and A. Prentice (eds) *Creating Historical Memory: English-Canadian Women and the Work of History*. Vancouver: UBC Press.

31 A. Prentice (1989) Scholarly passion: two women who caught it. *Historical Studies in Education/Revue d'histoire de l'éducation* 1(1): 7–25; reprinted in Prentice and Theobald (eds) *Women Who Taught*.

32 A. Prentice (1991) Bluestockings, feminists, or women workers? A preliminary look at women's early employment at the University of Toronto. *Journal of the Canadian Historical Association* NS2: 231–61.

33 B. Boutilier and A. Prentice (1997) Locating women in the work of history, in Boutilier and Prentice (eds) *Creating Historical Memory*. My essay in the collection is entitled 'Laying siege to the professoriate'.

34 A. Prentice (1996) The early history of women in physics: a Toronto case study. *Physics in Canada* 52(2): 94–100.

35 A. Prentice (1997) Elizabeth Allin: physicist, in E. Cameron and J. Dickin (eds) *Great Dames*. Toronto: University of Toronto Press. Parts of Ormsby's story appear in Prentice (1991) Bluestockings, feminists or women workers?; Prentice (1997) Laying siege to the professoriate. See also Prentice (1996) The early history of women in physics.

36 D.M. Hallman (1992) 'A thing of the past': teaching in one-room schools in rural Nova Scotia, 1936–1941. *Historical Studies in Education/Revue d'histoire de l'éducation* 4(1): 113–32; reprinted (1994) in P. Bourne *et al.* (eds) *Feminism and Education: A Canadian Perspective*. Toronto: Centre for Women's Studies in Education, Ontario Institute for Studies in Education.

37 E. Smyth, S. Acker, P. Bourne and A. Prentice (eds) *Challenging Professions: Historical and Contemporary Perspectives on Women's Professional Work*, manuscript submitted to University of Toronto Press, Toronto. My essay in the collection is entitled 'Three women in physics'. Two path-breaking Canadian books in this field are M. Kinnear (1995) *In Subordination: Professional Women 1870–1970*. Montreal and Kingston: McGill-Queen's University Press; and N. Fahmy-Eid *et al.* (1997) *Femmes, santé et professions: histoire des diététistes et des physiothérapeutes au Québec et en Ontario, 1930–1980. L'affirmation d'un statut professionel*. Montreal: Fides.

38 For an earlier discussion of some aspects of this theme, see A. Prentice (1990) Multiple realities: the history of women teachers in Canada, in F. Forman *et al.* (eds) *Feminism and Education: A Canadian Perspective*. Toronto: Centre for Women's Studies in Education, Ontario Institute for Education.

39 It is frustrated, in part, by the many problems of publishing in Canada. The market has always been small; our geography makes distribution difficult and expensive; gaps between scholarly and trade publishing seem almost unbridgable; many of our presses and bookstores are British or, increasingly, American branch plants or chains; book reviews, despite the valiant efforts of a few, frequently neglect Canadian publications and, especially, much women's history.

40 Typescript, A. Vibert Douglas Papers, Queen's University Archives. The memoir, accompanied by a scholarly introduction, is intended for the University of Toronto Press Echo Series, edited by Elspeth Cameron and Janice Dickin.

41 A. Mackinnon (1997) *Love and Freedom: Professional Women and the Reshaping of Personal Life*. Cambridge and Melbourne: Cambridge University Press; I. Elgqvist-Saltzman (1992) Gravel in the machinery or the hub of the wheel?, in M.L. Eduards *et al.* (eds) *Rethinking Change: Current Swedish Feminist Research*. Uppsala: HFSR. See also A. Mackinnon, A. Prentice and I. Elgqvist-Saltzman (eds) *Education into the Twentieth-Century: Dangerous Terrain for Women?* London: Falmer Press.

4 Reflections on writing a history of women teachers

Kathleen Weiler

For almost a decade, beginning in the late 1980s, I conducted research on rural women teachers in one area of the North American West – Tulare and Kings Counties in California in the period 1850–1950.[1] As is true for many other feminist scholars, my choice to write this particular history emerged from my own history and desires. In writing this history, in a sense I explored my own past, since I was born and raised in a small town in California, the daughter and niece of women teachers in country schools. When I undertook this history, I held the unexamined belief that I could come to understand the lives of these women and that in writing their history I would provide witness to their valuable and unrecognized worth. But when I began formal research into this world through interviewing retired teachers and reading local school records and state documents, these guiding assumptions became less sure. I came to see more clearly that the social and cultural world of my mother and other teachers was built on assumptions of white and Protestant hegemony. And what I saw as autonomy and pride in their work coexisted uneasily with evidence of increasing state control and community surveillance. The more I explored this history, the more complex it became. In this chapter, I consider some of the underlying epistemological concerns that guided my attempt to write this history of women teachers – issues that are common both to the enterprise of writing history and the project of feminism. I then discuss some examples from my own ongoing research, not to provide definitive answers or guidelines, but to illustrate theoretical debates and to raise questions.

Feminist theory and women's history

Both feminist theory and women's history have produced rich and original work. In the second wave of the women's movement in the late 1960s, feminists began to explore the lives of women who had been 'hidden from history'. The focus of these histories was on the oppressions of patriarchy.

But feminist historians soon shifted their focus to include studies of women's resistance to the dominant order. These two approaches of either documenting patriarchal oppression or celebrating women's resistance continue to shape feminist history and the history of women teachers, even as historians have moved to more complex levels of analysis of women teachers' work in relation to the state and economy or of the discursive constructions within which women teachers imagined themselves or were imagined. Perhaps inevitably, as feminist historians have produced an extensive and impressive corpus of work, conflicts over interpretation and approach have emerged.[2] These conflicts reflect debates among feminist scholars and within history as a discipline, as poststructuralism and deconstruction have challenged the traditionally empirical approach of historians.[3]

Like theorists such as Dominick LaCapra and Hayden White, feminist poststructuralist historians, most notably Denise Riley and Joan Scott, have argued that history is an imaginative construction resting on certain rhetorical effects, but unlike these male theorists, they have emphasized as well that it has been deeply gendered.[4] As is true of many other feminists who are attempting to write about women in the past, I have been influenced both by the ongoing political commitment of feminist historians and by recent poststructuralist theory and historiography. Here I want to articulate some of my own developing theoretical concerns, particularly my understanding of three key concepts that have come to shape my own reading and approach. These are the interrelated concepts of knowledge, language and subjectivity. By knowledge I refer to the debate about universal versus particular truth claims and the nature of historical evidence, the question of what exactly are our sources of understanding the past; by language, the question of discourse and its relationship to experience as the source of our knowledge of the past; and by subjectivity, the question of essence and identity.

First, there is the question of historical knowledge, the nature of the evidence about the past and the kinds of truth claims that can be made about it. As is true of many other feminists, I write from a situated and conditional perspective, emphasizing my own reading and partial perspective in presenting what I read as important and true. It is typical of feminist theorists to view knowledge as both contextual and historical. This is particularly true of socialist or materialist feminists, who have incorporated a materialist analysis of oppression and a dialectical method deeply influenced by Marxism into their feminist analysis of gender. Feminist materialist theorists like Rosemary Hennessy and Anna Yeatman have built upon the earlier work of such theorists as Nancy Hartsock, Sandra Harding and Dorothy Smith to emphasize the material and practical life experiences and activities of women as the source for their knowledge of the world.[5] Just as Hegel argued for the privileged perspective of the slave, or Marx for the privileged perspective of the worker, these feminist theorists have argued that women have a particular epistemological standpoint because of their oppression. In a similar vein, Patricia Hill Collins has argued for the importance of seeing knowledge as emerging from practical life experiences defined by race as well as gender and class.[6] Such theorists argue that women's differing experiences of oppression, like the experiences of Hegel's slave or Marx's worker, provide a knowledge or standpoint that is in some sense 'truer' in that it reveals more of power relationships than does the hegemonic knowledge of those who control and exploit them and who seek to obscure that control. While I continue to believe that this approach has much to teach us, it also seems important to consider not only women's 'life activities', as Hartsock suggests, but also the ways in which different women are positioned as subordinate or 'other' in discourse, and to consider that everyone, including the 'oppressed', understands experience through language.

As is true for other epistemologies of difference, feminist standpoint epistemology rests upon the recovery of outlawed or denigrated knowledges. But recovering and celebrating hidden knowledge, what Foucault has called 'dangerous memories'[7] can lead to an acceptance of memory and experience as sources of a 'true past'. Poststructural feminist historians such as Catherine Hall, Joan Scott and Denise Riley have argued that the category of 'experience' itself is one that needs to be carefully examined. For Scott the object of historical inquiry shifts from an empirical documenting of the facts of the past to the analysis of the way meaning is created through language. As Scott says, 'To do this a change of object seems to be required, one which takes the emergence of concepts and identities as historical events in need of explanation'.[8] This kind of historical epistemology takes as the object of study, as knowledge, the processes by which people make sense of their lives. Scott and Riley argue that rather than documenting the narratives of experience of historical actors, historians should analyse the 'historical processes that, through discourse, position subjects and produce their experiences'.[9] This is similar to Kimberle Crenshaw's comment that 'one important way social power is mediated in American society is through the contestation between the many narrative structures through which reality might be perceived and talked about'.[10] Theorists such as Scott, Riley and Crenshaw are concerned with language as a way of ordering and evaluating what becomes 'experience' and of understanding the past as constantly contested and constructed through competing discourses.

The argument about language is in many ways an argument about texts, about what texts can tell us. The most extreme 'linguistic' perspective seems to imply that we can understand the past only through the workings of language, that the past is available only through texts and that thus the focus of historical analysis must be textual. Although this position has made a valuable intervention in making historians more cautious about their claims of knowing the 'true past', it has also raised dangers of its own – of slighting other kinds of evidence and failing to raise questions other than those of the workings of language. Linda Gordon, for example, argues that while the analysis of representations can help us understand the ways that language works to justify power, this analysis of language does not mean that the material past did not exist and should not be explored.[11] Thus to become sensitive to the linguistic turn makes the historian less innocent, but does not, I think, necessarily erase a concern with understanding the material past.

It is the sensitivity to the constructed quality of memory and experience that has led feminist theorists in a number of disciplines to suggest the use of the term 'subjectivity'. Subjectivity has been employed to try to capture this quality of the social construction of the self; it implies the struggle and contest over identity, the ways in which selves are unstable, shifting, constructed through both dominant conceptions and resistance to those conceptions, and suggests the incomplete and sometimes contradictory quality of our lives both in the present and as we construct our pasts through memory. Emphasizing the constructed quality of subjectivity also implies the constructed nature of gender. The belief in the social construction of gender is central to feminist thought. By insisting on the artificial nature of historically defined aspects of gender, feminist theorists point to the instability and contradictions in gender systems and the possibilities for individual manipulation and resistance to them. People are not simply defined by ideological constructs of what they should be, but negotiate expectations, both external and internalized in their own consciousness, in the context of material need and desire through competing discourses. In this sense they engage in the construction of their own gendered subjectivities, in Teresa deLauretis's terms, 'within the context of existing practices, discourses, and institutions'.[12]

Along with considerations of the nature of experience and the evidence of texts, feminist historians have taken up the debate about the meaning of the concept 'woman'. Judith Butler points out, 'In a sense, what women signify has been taken for granted for too long, and what has been fixed as the "referent" of the term has been "fixed", normalized, immobilized, paralyzed in positions of subordination'.[13] This line of analysis, deeply influenced by the critiques of Black, Asian and Latina women, has pointed to the complexity of socially given identities. African-American women's historians have called on feminist historians to take into account what Elizabeth Higginbotham calls the 'metalanguage of race' in their study of women's history.[14] Like postcolonial theorists, Higginbotham points out that the coherent identity 'woman' obscures the meaning of race in a racist society, class power or oppression, age, or other kinds of differences or deviations from a mythical norm. These theoretical developments have led to a questioning of the concept of a coherent subject moving through history with a single identity and instead suggest the constant creation and negotiation of selves emerging from competing and contradictory discourses within structures of material constraint. The construction of gendered subjectivities through discourse, the contradictions of our various ways of categorizing and understanding what happens in our lives and who we are, naming ourselves, becomes the point of entry for historical analysis.

Women teachers' narratives

Women teachers' narratives and the descriptions of their lives by contemporary observers both draw upon existing representations of what it means to be a teacher and what it means to be a woman. The descriptions of outside observers tend to draw upon dominant representations to give meaning and shape to the lives they describe, while in their own accounts women teachers represent themselves both through the dominant discourses and through counter memories. These oppositional meanings recall Carolyn Steedman's comment that 'personal interpretations of past time – the stories that people tell themselves in order to explain how they got to the place they currently inhabit – are often in deep and ambiguous conflict with the official interpretative devices of a culture'.[15] A theoretical reading of the narratives of women teachers raises questions about the complexity of the construction of meaning and identity through discourse. But a feminist approach addresses not only the contradictions of competing discourses, but also the context in which narratives are produced and the relationships of power through which various accounts are given.[16] This approach raises a number of questions for researchers: what kinds of knowledge do narrative texts provide? How can we read them? How are we as researchers implicated in the creation of social knowledge? A recognition of the situated quality of narratives demands not only that historians be conscious both of their own assumptions as they gather 'evidence', but also that they consider the context in which such evidence (as texts or narratives) is produced.

To illustrate the ways in which these theoretical concerns shape a feminist history, I turn now to some examples of narratives – published texts and oral testimony – from my recent study of women teachers in California. In my analysis, I have been influenced by the theoretical approaches outlined above that suggest ways of reading these narratives of teacher's lives critically as discursive constructions produced in specific historical contexts. Although I made use of other documentary evidence such as the US manuscript census and county and state school records, my major sources for trying to understand the meaning of teaching for women was through first person accounts and life history narratives. I used a variety of sources – among them privately printed autobiographies, newspaper accounts of teachers and schools, narratives written by retired teachers for retired teachers' newsletters and journals, accounts of school visits by state officials, as well as twenty-five oral histories I collected between 1988 and 1993. But as has become increasingly clear to me, these sources do not provide a transparent picture of past lives; each kind of evidence needs to be read for the context and conditions of its production and with a consciousness that my own location as a feminist seeking to 'recover' the lost lives of women has led me to select certain texts as significant and to highlight certain themes within them. As a contemporary reader of historical texts and an oral historian eliciting life history narratives, I have attempted to draw out these contradictions and highlight the workings of power in their production. In the following discussion, I explore the different kinds of evidence provided by different kinds of texts.

As a white feminist scholar writing in the late 1990s, I am concerned with race as well as class and gender. And that concern with race implies not only a focus on the lives of women of colour, but also an acknowledgement of whiteness as a racial construct shaping white women's lives. California education was profoundly defined by racial categories from its founding. For Black women teachers, race shaped their lives much more overtly than did gender. White women teachers were constrained by their gender, but their race privilege was accepted as natural and was not even mentioned in the white teachers' narratives I have collected. By 1900, segregated schooling for African-Americans had taken on its familiar form as a *de facto* but no longer *de jure* practice. But teachers in the formally integrated schools, even when the majority of students were children of colour, continued to be almost exclusively white. In 1900, the US census listed only two teachers in the category 'Indian, Negro or Mongolian' for the entire state of California.[17] In 1910, sixteen 'Negro' and twenty 'Indian, Chinese or Japanese' teachers are listed.[18] African-American teachers had taught in the segregated coloured schools in the nineteenth century, but when the separate coloured schools were closed, the possibilities of employment for Black teachers disappeared. The evidence of the lives of these early African-American teachers is scanty and often is found in descriptions by contemporary white observers. In seeking to know the lives of Black women teachers, we frequently know more about the ways white observers constructed them within racist and patriarchal discourse than we do their own consciousness or life experience.

In my research on the women teachers of Tulare and Kings Counties in California, I have found some evidence of the lives of a handful of African-American women teachers. But this evidence itself needs to be interrogated. For example, consider the example of two African-American women teachers – Mary Dickson and Margaret Prince. The kind of historical understanding that we have of the lives of these two women is constrained by the nature of the sources available to us. Darlene Clark Hine has pointed out that even when we have the autobiographies or letters of nineteenth or early twentieth century African-American women, we need to read them with an understanding of the conditions of their production.[19] Hine argues that given the realities of racism and of sexual violence, African-American women tended to conceal their inner selves from a hostile world. But as she points out, while hiding or misrepresenting the inner self may have been an understandable strategy for survival, it presents the historian with serious difficulties in trying to understand the lives of Black women. In the case of Mary Dickson and Margaret Prince, the historian is dependent on quite different sources: one is the observation of a white observer in the 1880s; the second is the words of a Black woman solicited in an oral history interview with a Black scholar in the 1970s. The context in which these two texts were produced has shaped the evidence in very different ways; these texts reveal as much about the workings of culture and ideology as they do of specific material conditions.

According to Tulare County school records, Mary Dickson taught in the Visalia Colored School between 1881 and 1884. In this period, teachers who did not have a Normal School certificate were required to take and pass the county teachers' examination. In December 1881, fourteen prospective teachers took the Tulare County teachers' examination in Visalia. Six passed, but only one received a first grade certificate. This was Mary Dickson, an African-American woman 'about twenty three' who had come to Visalia from the Colored School in Vallejo. Besides the presence of her name on the county list, the only other evidence I have found of Mary Dickson is in an article from the *Visalia Delta* describing the teachers' examination of 1881.[20] This article, entitled 'Successful Candidates', in fact is what the unnamed (and I assume male) journalist calls 'a pen portrait' of Mary Dickson. The teachers' examination included both written and oral components; the oral section of the 1881 examination was open to the public and the *Delta* journalist was present. Mary Dickson received the highest mark on the examination, but the journalist does not speculate on where she might be sent to teach or indicate that she would be sent to the Visalia Colored School, by other reports a shabby, one room school on the outskirts of town, rather than to the town's new graded grammar school. Writing in 1881, he takes for granted that Mary Dickson would teach in a segregated school, no matter what her performance on the examination. Instead, he provides his 'pen portrait', a detailed description of Mary Dickson's body and manner. He is fascinated with her beauty and accomplishments, precisely because, as he says, 'she belongs to the race properly termed "colored".' Although the journalist mentions her intellectual accomplishments, his main concern is her body:

She belongs to the race properly termed 'colored' and this fact adds interest to the subject in view of her remarkable success. She has the medium height of women; her form is full, straight, rounded and symmetrical, and as near perfect as the form of a handsome woman can well be; her hands and feet are narrow, and her fingers denote artistic taste, her hair is remarkably abundant, is straight with occasional graceful waves, and of course is black as night.

In this description, Mary Dickson is presented as the object of the journalist's desire, using terms such as 'full, straight, rounded', 'perfect', 'handsome', 'artistic', 'abundant' to describe her, and then emphasizing the contradictions between these 'Caucasian' qualities and her identity as a member of the 'race properly termed "colored"' and his description of her hair: 'of course . . . black as night'. He goes on to describe her

> large, black, intelligent eyes, and more expressive than which there are none. Negatively, the cheek-bones have not the prominence noticeable in the black race, and the chin, though prominent, betrays no evidence of African blood. Her mouth is almost faultless, the lips inclining to fullness, but only agreeably. The tout ensemble of the face is a slight rounding of the cheeks and the elongation that belongs to the Caucasian race; and perhaps handsomer features, altogether, are not to be found in California.

She is for him the exotic 'other', subject to what literary critics have called the gaze of the dominant observer, in this case not just the male gaze, but the white gaze as well.[21] It is almost as though she represents to him a white woman trapped inside a Black body.

It is important historically to know of the Visalia Colored School, of Mary Dickson, and of her intellectual accomplishments. Her life expands our knowledge of the work and achievements of nineteenth century African-American women teachers. And the article in the *Visalia Delta* describing her reveals a great deal about the intersection of exoticism, sexuality, and racism marking white discourse. But it tells us nothing about Mary Dickson's inner life. Darlene Clark Hine has discussed the ways in which African-American women protected themselves by failing to reveal their inner thoughts in their written work in this period. In the case of Mary Dickson, we do not even have her own words. She exists for us through the imagination of the *Visalia Delta* journalist, as exotic, fascinating, desirable, and other. We know nothing of her thoughts or feelings, or the condition of her work or life. After 1884, she left the Visalia Colored School. I have found no further evidence of her. What kind of claim of knowing her can we make?

We have a different source of knowing about the life of another African-American woman teacher, Margaret Prince, who taught at the all-Black school at Allensworth in Tulare County between 1914 and 1919. In this case, we have Margaret Prince's own account of her life, solicited by a Black scholar, Eleanor Ramsay, who conducted an interview with Margaret Prince while Ramsay was a student in anthropology at Berkeley for her 1977 PhD dissertation on Allensworth.[22] The interview seems to have taken place in the early or mid-1970s. In her narrative, Margaret Prince frames her life as a struggle to obtain an education and decent work in a racist society. Margaret Prince grew up in Pasadena in what she describes as a loving and supportive family. She was the only Black graduate of Pasadena High School in

1911 and went on to be one of two Black students at the California State Normal School in Los Angeles, which later became UCLA. And once she graduated, she faced the racist realities of California education, in which only white teachers would be hired except in segregated Black schools:

> Here is where I had my first real setback, for I rudely discovered that my ability to control and direct my professional career virtually ended with the completion of my formal training . . . At the time, the only Los Angeles school hiring Black teachers, Home Street School, had only two staff positions. The school served Furlong Tract, the Black section located just outside Los Angeles City Limits. Home Street School certainly did not offer serious employment opportunities for the many Black teachers resident in the Los Angeles area.[23]

But in the summer of 1914, William Payne, the principal of the Black school at Allensworth and a friend of Margaret Prince's family, offered her the position as primary school teacher at Allensworth. Allensworth was a colony of African-American settlers that had been established in the arid southern San Joaquin Valley a few years earlier. Although the Allensworth School was a public school and was not formally segregated, in practice all the children were African-American.

Allensworth was marked by idealism and hopes for a better future.[24] For the African-Americans who settled there, the school was in many ways the key to these hopes. But for Margaret Prince, it was also a choice that was no choice at all. As she told her story to Eleanor Ramsay in the 1970s, she remembered her move to Allensworth in the context of her family's history of forced choices and limited opportunities. She recalled the life of her grandmother, who had been forced to work as a maid, travelling with rich white families and separated from her own children and family.

> My parents too well knew that the only employment locally available to our people was in the service industry. Thus, they quietly accepted the fact I would be separated from the family nest. As I now remember my parents' beaming faces at my graduation – twenty strong in the fourth row in the Pasadena High School auditorium – they must have known then about my destiny. For their own reasons, my parents chose not to tell me then, that to break the occupational pattern of the Prince family, I would have to leave home, just as my grandmother had done twenty-six years before. Continuously though, they reminded me, 'To have an education is to be somebody.'[25]

Remembering her life in the 1970s, Margaret Prince frames her identity as an African-American teacher through a consciousness of the long African-American struggle for education in the United States. She documents racist practices and presents the attitude of her family as one of quiet determination ('they must have known about my destiny'). In reading her testimony it is also important to consider the circumstances and historical moment that framed Margaret Prince's narrative. She was interviewed by an African-American woman scholar at a time in which Black students were first admitted to white dominated institutions like the anthropology department at Berkeley. A major focus of the research of these students was documenting the rich history of the African-American freedom struggle. While Mary Dickson was constructed as a mute exotic other by the white journalist in 1881, Margaret Prince speaks as a powerful and committed woman in her interchange with a Black researcher.

As another example of the impact of audience and historical moment, consider the evidence of the autobiography of Grace Canan Pogue, published in the early 1950s, a deeply conservative time in the United States in which the language of feminism had essentially been lost in everyday discourse. Grace Canon Pogue was a white Protestant teacher in the country schools of Tulare County; her narrative is framed in the conventional theme of sacrifice and caring for others.[26] This representation, recalling the nurturing 'true woman' of the common school movement, constructs and gives meaning to lives in memory, but it also often reveals a pattern of caring and responsibility that frequently marks women teachers' narratives. Grace Canon Pogue's narrative also calls forth the convention of moral guardianship, speaking out for the good of the community from a position of ethical guide. Her narrative also reveals the hidden workings of class.[27] Teachers, particularly women teachers, are difficult to place within conventional conceptions of class. In rural California, teachers were seen as 'respectable' and although they did not control wealth or exercise political power, they often, like Grace Canon Pogue, represented themselves as the defenders of the moral order, as middle class. None the less, as was also true for Grace Canon Pogue, teaching was in fact a necessary source of livelihood for many women teachers, and their wages were equivalent to those of semi-skilled male labourers. Grace Canon Pogue's autobiography is written through a discourse of the nurturing and morally upright woman teacher, but it also reveals the material needs of a struggling family dependent on her teacher's salary.

Grace Canon was an outstanding student in high school, winning an essay contest on 'The California Fruit Ranch' and graduating as valedictorian. But once she graduated, Grace was faced with the realities of her class and gender:

> A period of mental adjustment followed High School graduation. For four years, dreams of Stanford University had taken shape. A girl needed more units to enter Stanford than were required of a boy. I had the units. Also my recommendation said, 'Rank in class, distinguished.' But . . . the idea of working my way through college didn't appeal to my family.[28]

In this passage, Grace describes barriers of both gender and class; however, in her presentation, she does not denounce these barriers as unjust, but accepts them as natural. For example, she uses the phrase 'mental adjustment' to describe her emotions, which surely must have included deep disappointment if not anger at not being able to attend college. She accepts Stanford's different entrance requirements for boys and girls without comment. Although she met the higher requirements for girls and was accepted at Stanford, she accepts her family's decision that as a girl she should not work her way through school. Instead, once she graduated from high school, she went to work in a cannery, a common practice among girls from farming families in rural California at this time.

But Grace Canon did not remain a cannery worker. At the age of 19, she passed the county teacher's examination and was immediately offered a position in the mountains at the one room school at Yokohl. In her description of this first job, Grace does not mention her need to earn money, but presents this position as the fulfilment of her life's ambition:

> It was decided that Sister and Mother and Dad and I would live at Yokohl and Sister would be one of my pupils. My ambition to teach was about to be realized. When I was a little girl, I had declared my intention to be a matron of an orphans' home; then came a dream of being a missionary. But my love for children and my yearning for an opportunity to guide them in the right paths could be realized in the teaching profession. And so, by the time I reached my teens, I was determined that a teaching career was what I wanted.[29]

Here Grace ignores her earlier ambition to attend Stanford and instead presents as her deepest desire (from the time she was a little girl) the opportunity to serve others as a moral guide (matron of an orphans' home, missionary, teacher). This presentation of herself as moral guide (like the missionary or the matron of the orphans' home) simply ignores the material conditions and limitations she describes. Her family could not afford to send her to Stanford; because she was a girl they would not allow her to work her way through college. In taking a job in a mountain one room school, she supported her parents and her sister. Later in her narrative she marries, and in hard economic times supports her husband and son with her teacher's salary. Throughout she presents these material realities without comment; when she reflects on her inner life or the meaning of her choices, she employs the representation of a Christian moral woman.

Her narrative also ignores the themes of adventure or coming of age, themes that appear in many other teachers' narratives, particularly in their depictions of 'the first school', a mark of the transition from childhood to adulthood. The first teaching job was often the first time away from home for these young women and offered them their first opportunity to earn real wages. Accounts of the first year of teaching in one room country or mountain schools are often filled with descriptions of physical dangers overcome. In the narratives of California teachers, for example, rattlesnakes often appear, and the teacher most commonly dispatches the snake as a mark of her competence and courage. Accounts of the responsibilities and dangers of the first school are presented without reference to authoritative images of nurturing or self-sacrificing womanhood. Instead they recall the discourse of the 'new woman', or of the 'flapper', or of earlier nineteenth century narratives of women travellers as brave adventuresses. All of these images counter Grace Pogue's vision of the maternal and self-sacrificing 'true woman'.

In reading autobiographical accounts, particularly those of 'ordinary' women like Grace Pogue, whose lives would otherwise be unknown, it is a temptation to accept their self-presentation as both transparent and representative. But as Marjorie Theobald has argued (Chapter 2 in this volume), the representation of women teachers as morally upright, self-sacrificing, and heroic needs to be read as precisely that: as a representation of social reality, not necessarily the truth for all women, or even for any single woman. And, of course, it is also important to remember the conditions of the production of Grace Pogue's text. Her autobiography was privately published, and would have been circulated among members of the community in which she still lived and of which she was a respected member. She wrote in the early 1950s, in the revival of 'true woman' ideology and repressive politics in the United States. This was not a moment in which expressions of a woman's anger or her criticism of patriarchal practices would be welcomed. Grace Pogue's narrative thus not only reflects conventional representations of the woman teacher, but also in another sense reproduces them and keeps them alive in the virulently sexist 1950s, when her book was published.

As a final example of the ways that women teachers' lives are represented and may be read, consider the following examples from a series of oral history interviews I conducted in Tulare and Kings Counties between 1988 and 1992. In oral history, women's narratives are elicited by the historian; this raises further questions about the ways subjectivities are presented and become historical evidence. The question of responsibility and the nature of the interaction between feminist researcher and woman narrator has been addressed by a number of feminist scholars.[30] In a study of women teachers, Kathleen Casey argues that a feminist researcher must respect her 'subject' as a subject, that is, a human being with the right to define the meaning of her own life.[31] She enjoins us as feminists to avoid a moralistic judgement of the narratives we have requested and have been generously given, and to try to demystify the production of these narratives by acknowledging the relationship between researcher and researched. My own experience exemplifies the ways that oral accounts are shaped by the setting and relationship between researcher and narrator. As the interviewer, I asked for the gift of these country women's stories and established the context in which these stories were produced. In my case, I was uneasily positioned as an urban university professor, a distant and possibly judgemental figure; women told me their stories with a wary consciousness of who I might be and how I might receive these stories.

The following excerpts are taken from a series of interviews in which I was exploring the nature of the married women teachers' bar during the depression. The stricture that women teachers could not be married was never officially made law in California, as it was, for example, in Pennsylvania, but the bar was widely enforced in California. In Tulare and Kings Counties, the bar against married teachers varied from place to place. In the 1920s, the practice was still enforced in many towns, but smaller districts would hire married women or allow women teachers who were already employed and who were well known in the district to continue teaching after marriage. The retired teachers I interviewed all mentioned the existence of the marriage bar. When I asked Ellen A. why she thought school boards refused to hire married women, she said, 'They just wanted to be dictatorial. Husbands were supposed to provide for you.' Miriam J. mentioned that she quit teaching when she married. When I asked why, she said:

> It was the thing to do in those days. When you got married you weren't supposed to have a career, you were supposed to stay home and keep house. I guess you know that. I suppose you can become interested in keeping house. It's just a little boring. I persuaded my husband to let me go back and teach.

In these comments, Ellen A. and Miriam J. described common practices of discrimination against married women teachers and ways that individuals resisted them. But they also framed their comments in ways that showed their disapproval of these practices: Ellen A. says school boards wanted to be 'dictatorial', and Miriam J. ironically describes housework as 'just a little boring'. In both cases, they may well have been influenced by their perception of who I was, an outsider, a woman professor who had a career, who probably was critical of the marriage bar.

In another example, however, Ruth G. provided a more contradictory account. Ruth G. also left teaching during the depression when she married. In the interview, the following interchange took place:

> *Ruth G.:* I got married and they weren't hiring married teachers. But I didn't want to teach then anyways.
>
> K.W.: That's interesting too. Once you got married at Thermal they wouldn't have kept you on?
>
> *Ruth G.:* No, they wouldn't have over at Oakland Colony either, that's the school out by Tulare. The principal was married, but she had been there quite a while. A woman. Well, she

taught it as a one teacher school. But they wouldn't hire married teachers after that. There weren't enough jobs really.

K.W.: Did they give reasons?

Ruth G.: No, except there were, there was a surplus of teachers, and that was one way of not hiring. Married teachers, their husbands could support them. Other than that I don't know.

K.W.: Wasn't that kind of hard on you, to give up your job in the depression?

Ruth G.: Well, he was working. He made enough. Ninety-eight dollars a month, and it was ample compared to now. I subbed some, quite a bit. No, that amount seemed to go as far as, a great deal more than now-a-days. I can remember, on our honeymoon, in September, and we'd drive by these schools with people in them and I'd sit there and cry and he'd say, this is a heck of a honeymoon.

K.W.: You were crying because . . .

Ruth G.: I wanted to teach.

Ruth G.'s account contains striking contradictions and breaks. At the beginning of this interchange, she says she didn't want to teach after she was married; the story of crying when she passed a school on her honeymoon seems almost to escape from her narrative. While discussing living on 'ninety-eight dollars a month' ('that amount seemed to go as far as, a great deal more than now-a-days') she then begins a seemingly unrelated story: 'I can remember, on our honeymoon'. Consider as well the circumstances under which this story was told. I conducted this interview in the summer of 1990. I was a professor from 'back East'. Even though I was born in the valley and had grown up there, by leaving and particularly by going as far as Massachusetts (not to a more familiar place like Texas or Kansas, which are also known as 'back East') I was identified as an easterner, probably a liberal, and possibly, since I was a woman professor, a feminist. Ruth G. had married into a well known conservative family of early settlers to the valley. When I looked at her, I saw a Republican! My relationship with Ruth G. was polite on both sides, but wary. Throughout her narrative, Ruth G. presented to me a past in which things turned out all right, in which the authorities acted wisely, and traditional values were upheld. Like all of us in recalling our pasts, she was constructing a story for the circumstances of the telling.

Conclusion

Accounts of women teachers' lives, their own memories, the ways they frame the choices they made, the way they are viewed by observers, all need to be examined as constructs produced at specific historical moments, under particular circumstances, with different audiences in mind. It is important to consider the conditions under which testimony is given, in terms of not only the dominant issues of the day – the way that womanliness or teaching is presented in the authoritative discourse, for example – but also the relationship between speaker and audience. Think of the differences between a written text like Grace Pogue's (privately published, and thus almost certainly to be circulated among members of the community in which she lived), an account of an observer like the Visalia journalist fascinated with Mary Dickson as the exotic 'other', the interchange between researcher and subject in an oral history interview when both are positioned 'on the same side', or see one another as potentially hostile, on opposite sides.

A feminist history that begins with a concern with the constructed quality of evidence moves uneasily between historical narrative and a self-conscious analysis of texts. There is the seductive attraction of narrative, to write the past as a coherent story or plot, framed by implicit or explicit judgements and perceived as a moral lesson. On the other hand, there is the analysis of representations, a critical suspicion of the evidence of written texts or the oral accounts produced through questioning, and a concern with the contemporary biases of the historian/critic/narrator.

Giovanni Levi has argued for a history in which 'the historian is not simply concerned with the interpretation of meanings but rather with defining the ambiguities of the symbolic world, the plurality of possible interpretations of it and the struggle which takes place over symbolic as much as over material resources'.[32] This is similar to Roland Barthes's comment that history would be less 'mythological' if it were presented in modes that 'overtly called attention to their own process of production and indicated the "constituted" rather than "found" nature of their referents'.[33] In writing the history of these women teachers' lives, I was trying to consider the ways in which they constructed their pasts through the discursive categories available to them, while acknowledging that my own questions and categories 'constitute' a story, in Barthes's term. Carolyn Steedman wrote:

> Visions change, once any story is told; ways of seeing are altered. The point of a story is to present itself momentarily as complete, so that it can be said, it does for now, it will do; it is an account that will last for a while. Its point is briefly to make an audience connive in the telling, so that they might say: yes, that's how it was; or, that's how it might have been.[34]

As is true of any historian, I can only analyse and understand the evidence of lives through discursive categories while recognizing and acknowledging my complicity in the narratives I call forth and the narrative I construct. In my history, I hope to present both a story and a meditation on what it means to be a teacher and a woman and to try to capture what, in Steedman's words, 'might have been'.

Notes

1 K. Weiler (1998) *Country Schoolwomen: Teaching in Rural California 1850–1950*. Stanford, CA: Stanford University Press.

2 See, for example, the exchange between L. Gordon and J. Scott (1990) *Signs* 15(4): 848–59; also the earlier discussion over women's culture and resistance among E. DuBois, M.J. Buhle, T. Kaplan, G. Lerner and C. Smith-Rosenberg (1980) Politics and culture in women's history. *Feminist Studies* 6: 28–36.

3 J. Newton (1989) History as usual? Feminism and the new historicism, in H.A. Veeser (ed.) *The New Historicism*. London: Routledge, p.152.

4 H. White (1987) *The Content of Form: Narrative Discourses and Historical Representation*. Baltimore, MD: Johns Hopkins Press; D. LaCapra (1985) *History and Criticism*. Ithaca, NY: Cornell University Press. See also A.-L. Shapiro (1992) Introduction: history and feminist theory, or talking back to the beadle. *History and Feminist Theory*. Middletown, CT: Wesleyan University Press.

5 N. Hartsock (1983) The feminist standpoint: developing the ground for a specifically feminist historical materialism, in S. Harding and M.B. Hintikka (eds) *Discovering Reality: Feminist Perspectives on Epistemology, Metaphysics, Methodology and Philosophy of Science*. Boston, MA: D. Reidel; S. Harding (1986) *The Science Question in Feminism*. Ithaca, NY: Cornell University Press; R. Hennessy (1993) *Materialist Feminist and the Politics of Discourse*. New York: Routledge; D. Smith (1987) *The Everyday World as Problematic*. Boston, MA: Northeastern University Press; A. Yeatman (1994) *Postmodern Revisionings of the Political*. New York: Routledge.

6 P.H. Collins (1992) *Black Feminist Thought*. Boston, MA: Unwin, Hyman.

7 M. Foucault (1980) *Power/Knowledge: Selected Interviews and Other Writings 1972–1977*. New York: Pantheon Books.

8 J. Scott (1992) Experience, in J. Butler and J. Scott (eds) *Feminists Theorize the Political*. New York: Routledge, p.33; D. Riley (1988) *Am I That Name?* Minneapolis: University of Minnesota Press; C. Hall (1992) *White, Male and Middleclass*. New York: Routledge.

9 J. Scott, Experience, p.25.

10 K. Crenshaw (1992) Whose story is it anyway?, in T. Morrison (ed.) *Race-ing Justice, Engendering Power*. New York: Pantheon.

11 See L. Gordon (1990) Response to Scott. *Signs* 15(4): 852–3.

12 T. deLauretis (1984) *Alice Doesn't*. Bloomington, IN: Indiana University Press.

13 J. Butler (1992) Contingent foundations: feminism and the question of postmodernism, in J. Butler and J. Scott (eds) *Feminists Theorize the Political*. New York and London: Routledge, p.16.

14 E. Higginbotham (1996) African-American women's history and the metalanguage of race, in J. Scott (ed.) *Feminist and History*. Oxford: Oxford University Press.

15 C. Steedman (1987) *Landscape for a Good Woman: A Story of Two Lives*. New Brunswick, NJ: Rutgers University Press, p.6.

16 I have discussed some of these questions in K. Weiler (1992) Remembering and representing life choices: retired teachers' oral history narratives. *International Journal of Qualitative Research in Education* 5(1): 39–42. See also M. Nelson (1992) Using oral histories to reconstruct the experiences of women teachers in

Vermont, in I. Goodson (ed.) *Studying Teachers' Lives*. New York: Teachers College Press; L. Passerini (1987) *Fascism in Popular Memory: The Cultural Experience of the Turin Working Class*. Cambridge: Cambridge University Press; Popular Memory Group (1982) Popular memory: theory, politics, method, in R. Johnson, G. McLennon, B. Swartz and D. Sutton (eds) *Making Histories*. Minnesota, MN: University of Minnesota Press; R. Samuel (1988) Myth and history: a first reading. *Oral History* 16(1): 10–17.

17 US Bureau of the Census (1907) *Statistics of Women and Work*. Washington, DC: Government Printing Office, p.111.

18 Bureau of the Census (1914) *Thirteenth Census of the United States 1910 Vol. IV Population, Occupation Statistics*. Washington, DC: Government Printing Office, p.440.

19 D.C. Hine (1994) Rape and the inner lives of black women in the Middle West, in V. Ruiz and E. DuBois (eds) *Unequal Sisters*. New York: Routledge.

20 Successful candidates. *Weekly Delta*, December 30, 1881: 1.

21 This description recalls the 'orientalizing' described by Said in his discussion of the representation of the exotic Other. E. Said (1979) *Orientalism*. New York: Vintage Books.

22 E.M. Ramsay (1977) 'Allensworth: a study in social change', PhD dissertation. University of California at Berkeley.

23 Margaret Prince Hubert as cited in Ramsay, Allensworth, p.148.

24 For a more extensive discussion of the role of education in the Allensworth colony, see K. Weiler (1990) The school at Allensworth. *Journal of Education* 173(3): 9–38.

25 Margaret Prince Hubert as cited in Ramsay, Allensworth, p.146.

26 See for example J.R. Martin (1992) *Homeschool*. Cambridge, MA: Harvard University Press; M. Grumet (1988) *Bitter Milk*. Albany, NY: SUNY Press; C. Gilligan (1982) *In a Different Voice*. Cambridge, MA: Harvard University Press; G. Pogue (1957) *The Swift Seasons*. Hollywood, CA: Cloister Press.

27 For an interesting discussion of the question of teachers' class location see M. Danylewycz and A. Prentice (1991) Teachers' work, in A. Prentice and M. Theobald, *Women Who Taught*. Toronto: University of Toronto Press.

28 Pogue, *The Swift Seasons*, p.29.

29 Pogue, *The Swift Seasons*, p.32.

30 See in particular S.B. Gluck and D. Patai (1991) *Women's Words*. New York: Routledge; G. Etter-Lewis and M. Foster (1996) *Unrelated Kin*. New York: Routledge.

31 K. Casey (1993) *I Answer with my Life*. New York: Routledge.

32 G. Levi (1992) On microhistory, in P Burke (ed.) *New Perspectives on Historical Writing*. University Park, PA: Pennsylvania State University Press, p.95.

33 As quoted by H. White (1987) *The Content of Form*. Baltimore, MD: Johns Hopkins Press, p.35; R. Barthes (1973) *Mythologies*. London: Palladin.

34 Steedman, *Landscape for a Good Woman*, p.22.

5 Connecting pieces: finding the indigenous presence in the history of women's education

Linda Tuhiwai Smith

I am surrounded, quite literally, by the work of indigenous Maori women who have engaged in some aspects of the history of Maori women's education. Some of this work I have supervised or examined as theses and the bound copies share shelf space with other books and reports. Other reports, videos, audiotapes and boxes of archival material are stacked precariously on other shelves or are stuffed underneath my desk in a desperate pretence at tidiness. These are the gatherings of my own research – some completed; other projects are still in progress and still others await a moment of inspiration. Graduate students, including those who have completed their work, come into my office to discuss their ideas and bring their latest draft. Most of the students are older Maori women; several have had many years of teaching and community service. The younger ones make up in sharp insight and enthusiasm what they may lack in life experience. Their combined projects span the topics of health, family histories, life histories, youth issues, sexuality, truancy and domestic violence.

In this chapter I reflect through three pieces of work on a series of issues related to narrative inquiries into the lives of indigenous women in Aotearoa New Zealand. The issues are informed by my own research efforts, by those of colleagues and students with whom I work, and by my discussions with students who have participated in a graduate class. The class is called 'Tikanga Rangahau; The Issues of Research by Maori, with Maori and for Maori'. Most of the students are mature Maori with many years of experience in education. Many of them are women. In Maori terms many of the students are like my aunts and uncles, to others I am like their aunt or older sister. They bring with them to their studies years of experiences and a depth of cultural knowledge. Most of the older students are fluent in Maori language. They are, year after year, a rich resource of cultural knowledge and insight. Over the years my interest in the history of women's education has been rather ambivalent. Like many of my students I have shared a resistance to the historical accounts of Maori as written by white historians. I consider it important that indigenous people write our own histories. I am however deeply interested in the way that stories are made and narrative lines are traced and developed. I am also interested in the way indigenous peoples interact with, challenge, resist and make history. The following pieces of work are reflections both on the nature of historical inquiry for Maori and on a pedagogical approach to working with indigenous students.

I have focused primarily on the ways we as indigenous women often have to find the indigenous presence inside histories already told. Our inquiries often begin with the oral testimonies of women and elders or the collaborative recollections of groups of women 'around the kitchen table'.[1] The agenda for historical inquiry is frequently determined by the priorities of our own community contexts investigating land claims and health concerns alongside educational research. The three 'pieces' recounted here are used along with many other examples to provide the basis for class discussions about research. They are stories of Maori women whose lives in some way were involved with education. They are also stories about my colleagues and me and our everyday work as Maori women academics in a research and teaching environment.

The woman in the photograph

She was hidden in the back row, standing on the side. At first, it seemed that the woman in the faded school photograph was not one of the pupils' mothers. Then there was a sense that the woman was not just a teaching assistant, she appeared to be much older than most teaching assistants.

She was hidden in the National Archives, enclosed within official records relating to New Zealand's Native Schools system. The file from the National Archives mentioned a woman of 'good blood' who not only was the head-teacher but also had founded a residential school for Maori girls and funded it privately in 1875.

> Mr Hislop: [Mary] is a half-caste, of good blood by both parents, I believe. She was educated at Three Kings Institution. She speaks English perfectly. You can judge her ability as a writer of English in her letters in the attached file. She is altogether ladylike and attractive in person, bearing and manners. . . .
> Mary: I send you my last appeal for the assistance so long promised and withheld from me, in confidence, that you will, before it is out of your power to do so, see that I have some return made to me for the heavy losses I have sustained in carrying out my school . . . this is all from Mary.[2]

The woman, the photograph, the community, the files, the school, the past, had been all so neatly stored, disconnected by time and place, fragmented in various collections and then quietly ignored. Mary it appears not only was the first Maori woman headteacher but also was probably the first woman headteacher in New Zealand.[3] To have pieced together the connecting threads of this woman's presence in educational history seemed almost serendipitous. It happened as part of a much larger research project that is conducting oral histories of people who were either students or teachers in New Zealand's Native Schools system (1867–1969).[4] Two features of this research project were very different from any other research into the Native Schools system. The first was a focus on collecting the oral histories of the people who experienced such schooling and the second was the involvement of Maori researchers in the project.[5]

At the time we put the story of Mary together, several of us had been writing our contributions to a book on this research. We were exchanging ideas and photocopied archival material and oral history transcripts as we worked out the sequence and themes of photographs and ideas. A history was there, stored in photographs and the files of the National Archives, everything from letters, to receipts, to the minutes of school committees, official policies and school attendance registers. It was an ordered history of a hundred years of government schooling of Maori. The policies of assimilation, the denigration of language and culture, the disdain for communities, the accounts of epidemics and disasters, the Native Land Court,[6] the attitudes of teachers and government departments were all there neatly protected as an official account of Native Schools. A history was there too in the oral histories gathered from past students and teachers who had attended schools from across the country. Within the oral histories were people's names and personalities, children's stories and community perspectives. There were family genealogies and stories of family decision making as some children stayed home to care for their younger siblings or went to work to support their families while other siblings went to school unaware until later in their lives how much their older sisters or brothers had sacrificed. There were also private collections and photographs kept lovingly by families who understood that the old papers and photographs were somehow significant.

In discussions of the story of the woman in the photograph in the research class, my students' initial reactions were as mixed as my own. No comment was made on Mary's significance to the history of women's education. They were resigned to the fact that her story had been ignored by historians of education. Students reacted to the paternalistic tone of the officials who wrote about her 'good blood' and ability with English language. They were able to draw out the racial assumptions behind the classification of terms such as 'half caste' and comment on the way these terms were used in Native policy. They were upset that considerable attention was paid in the reports to the character of the woman's husband. He was referred to as a 'pure

blood' Maori of good quality. They were angry that her story had been forgotten. Mostly, however they were sad. It was sad that her image had been
locked away in the archives. It was sad that her letters, so beautifully written, had been hidden alongside the letters of thousands of other anonymous
people. 'What about her family?' one student asked, 'they probably don't
know that all this material exists'. 'If she were my ancestor,' another student
added, 'I would go and get her back, tell those archive people to hand it all
over, they don't know how to care for her, they don't deserve her'. The class
debated various issues related to the repatriation of indigenous materials,
the respect for ancestors, the role of archives, the role of Maori women in
education. Most students interpreted the lack of knowledge about Mary and
her place in educational history as just one further example of the margin-
alization of Maori in New Zealand history. They were able to cite several
similar examples and could talk confidently about the invisibility of Maori
women, the lack of voice, the subordination of alternative views of history,
the representation of Maori and indigenous women generally in western
texts. The discussion ranged freely both in terms of topics covered and
theoretical perspectives brought to bear on the discussion. By the time we
stopped for a coffee break energy levels were high. I was worried.

Later, I added two points for students to consider. The first point was like
a riddle that went something like this: there are many stories in our archives.
Some are stored, recorded in writings and photographs. Some are in the collective memories of people. Some are in our genealogies. Even though we
may be looking at one story, we would not necessarily see it, or, if we did,
we might mistake it for another story. How can that be? The second point
was that perhaps the woman's story was not really in the archives at all. Her
story was partially in the fragmented pieces of historical material that were
in different files of the archives. But perhaps her story was also partially in
the approach taken to the research, and partially in the way we as a generation of Maori regard our past. The story could not have been put together
without an approach that added in the oral histories of the people whose
lives were deeply affected by the Native Schools established in their communities. It was also unlikely that the story would have been considered significant in a time when indigenous priorities were not concerned with
reclaiming our past. Perhaps, I suggested, we are part of the story, without
us it would not exist.

The women in the books

Increasingly the stories of indigenous women are being told both through
the writing of indigenous women themselves and in 'as told to' biographies.
I refer to some of these as indigenous granny stories. Although I have written my own such story I have gradually come to the conclusion that I do not

really like most indigenous granny stories.[7] Many seem far too romanticized to be real. I probably suffer from some kind of granny envy as most granny stories are of strong, powerful but loving, and culturally correct grannies who have overcome extreme hardship to become significant community icons and repositories of knowledge. My own grandmother was often downright horrible, highly opinionated, completely one eyed on some matters and definitely politically incorrect, in need of a major decolonization programme! My grandmother often infuriated people. She was contradictory, exasperating and feisty. She was a demanding, knowledgeable, sharp, commanding and interesting woman. I remember asking her once why she wasn't a nice old lady like grandmothers were supposed to be.

I am probably therefore not the most sympathetic person to send a book to about a wonderful Maori woman who had been given away as a young woman to serve the Church and her people for most of her life. However I was sent the book in the hope that I would write a review. The book, *Heeni: A Tainui Elder Remembers*, is authored by Heeni Wharemaru with Mary Katherine Duffy.[8] It had the feel of a doctoral thesis even when I opened the pages, an 'as told to' account with far too many explanatory statements in the text to be the woman's own story. It had indeed been a doctoral thesis written by an American anthropologist who gave a brief account of her methodology in the introduction. The book then told the story of this woman's life from her beginnings as a young girl, her family circumstances, her growing up as a young woman and then the rest of her life as it unfolded in historical sequence. Duffy adds in the editorial note that the story was not told in this sequence 'as in any natural dialogue' but was catalogued in line with a chronological plan made by Heeni herself. Duffy also comments on her own editorial 'intrusions', the second of which was 'to make substitutions to compensate for language inadequacies; for example where Heeni had struggled for an English word or phrase to express a Maori idea or concept'.[9]

While reading this biography I was also reading Julie Cruickshank's *Life Lived Like a Story*, a three star granny story of First Nations women in British Columbia.[10] In Cruickshank's work the approach taken is a more integral part of the stories of the women she interviewed while simultaneously being separated into various sections of the book. She addresses directly the different narrative styles used by the women she interviewed and the various ways in which their narrative styles quietly but persistently challenged her own views of how both research and narrative should proceed. According to Cruickshank, 'Oral testimonies are very different from archival documents and are never easily accessible to outsiders'.[11] Cruickshank's discussion of the oral testimonies and the way they develop as narratives made a great deal of sense and connected with my own understandings of the ways in which older Maori women also talk about their lives.

The two books were written for very different audiences. The biography of Heeni was clearly written for a Maori audience that is hungry for stories of positive role models and the wisdom of elders. It also fulfils a commitment probably made by the writer to 'give something back' to the people with whom she lived and whose hospitality she shared. A book of this kind affirms a cultural view that wisdom resides in elders and provides many examples of cultural practices often referred to as part of our oral history but rarely written about and published. The book is also given formal support by the Tainui tribe and is described in the foreword as a treasure.[12] While I admired the woman whose story was being told, I did not like the book. I wanted to read the thesis. I wanted to find out why the woman's life was told the way it was told when it was clear that this was not the sequence used in the interviews. If the chronology was Heeni's herself I wanted to ask why that was so, what was that about? I also wanted to find out how the story had been theorized. Cruickshank's book was written for an academic audience. The women's stories, their own words, formed only part of the book. While I can imagine the book being passed around indigenous communities and given as gifts to visitors I do not see it being read so avidly from cover to cover as the story of Heeni. There is value in the book written with Duffy for a Maori audience because it is both accessible and educational. Both books however raise the same questions, questions asked by other indigenous women. Why are we being written about by non-indigenous women? Why are our lives told by others? What does it mean for us as indigenous women to have our lives told by others? Does it really matter?

These questions stimulated a lively debate. Students who come from the same tribal group as the woman in the first book find the discussion difficult as they know of, and respect, the woman whose story is being told. They are ambivalent about the official sanctions given to the book by the tribal leadership and are horrified that the story was told to an 'American woman!' Other women in the class talk about wanting their stories to be told by their own daughters or granddaughters. Some are curious about the extent to which the story has been 'sanitized' for public consumption. Other students commented on some of the details of the book affirming various cultural practices. A lengthy discussion was held about the cultural reasons behind young children being 'given away' for adoption and the significance then of being given to the Church. Others commented on the concept of service to 'the people' and the cost of such lifelong service to women and their choices and opportunities. The class also speculated on the reasons why a Maori woman might prefer to tell her life history to a white woman. Perhaps 'she came straight out and asked,' it is suggested, or 'it was the right time, wrong woman, but right time'. Perhaps the American had learned the process and understood how to enter the network, her introductions came from people who knew the cultural protocols. 'I would not be that cheeky,' claimed a younger student; 'Yes you would,' laughed someone else, 'but you would have been told to get in line, you're too junior.' It is agreed that somehow our own insider relationships can sometimes be disadvantageous and that our own positions within the family or community can determine certain forms of access to the knowledge of elders. The women in the class also make the point that Maori women are able to make those decisions themselves even if their own families object. In principle the students wanted their own stories to be told by indigenous writers, preferably someone from their own area or community.

The women in the video

Hukarere is a residential Maori girls' school first opened in 1875 by the daughters of Anglican missionaries. The school has had an enormous impact on the education of Maori girls, many of whom became significant community and national leaders. Although, as in many missionary schools, the curriculum was based on domestication and training young girls to become the wives of Maori farmers, the school was held in high regard by Maori families. Several generations of women from the same families and communities had attended Hukarere. In 1993 a colleague, Kuni Jenkins, who had also attended Hukarere as a student, decided to focus her research on the politics of Maori girls' schooling using the history of Maori girls' education at Hukarere leading through to the school's closure in 1992 as a focus of her study.[13] Her action based research model rapidly turned into a study of the reopening of the school and Kuni was soon appointed as the new principal. The Hukarere project became a much wider social project involving several colleagues in my university's Department of Education in fundraising and developing strategies to re-establish the school.

One strategy, decided upon by a small group of Maori staff, was to make a video that could be used to help tell the story of Hukarere through the words of past students who were attending a school reunion over a weekend. Sufficient funds were raised to make a video and a professional film crew was hired to film the events of the reunion and conduct some interviews. A Maori woman doctoral student with a background in acting was employed to carry out the interviews. We worked out some themes around which the interviews would be structured and discussed general ideas about the way we wanted the interviews to be conducted. Consent forms were developed for the women who agreed to be interviewed for the project. One colleague, Leonie Pihama, had experience as a film producer and we relied on her knowledge to manage the logistics. The rest of us combined did not have the technical knowledge to operate the departmental video recorder. We did however have views about the representation of Maori women and discussed these over many informal sessions.

The reunion was held with women attending from all over the country.

The oldest woman was in her nineties and had been sent to Hukarere at the age of 6. Other women had been sent to Hukarere from the remote Chatham Islands. They ranged in age from their nineties through each decade down to the current students who were 13 and 14 years old. We decided to try and interview women in small groups rather than carrying out individual interviews. One pairing was the woman in her nineties with her daughter then in her seventies. A group of three consisted of two sisters from the Chatham Islands and a friend. Another grouping was of friends who had all been at school together. Some interviews were of women by themselves. Interviews were conducted in English or Maori language depending on the women's preference. The loosely structured thematic approach to the interviews worked well because it gave the interviewer some prompts without imposing either topics or pace on the women. The 90-year-old, Eve McGee, first attended Hukarere in 1914. The video images capture her delightfully wicked sense of humour and bright eyes while her daughter sits respectfully laughing at stories she has probably heard many times before. The group of three turn in towards each other and continue a story from an older sister to a younger sister. The interactions between the women being interviewed, their tears and their laughter, their shared story making, occur with little interruption from the interviewer. As we began the task of editing the many hours of film we found it painful to decide which parts of the interviews to cut. We ended up with a very long video that needed an intermission when we held our world premiere for our families and friends.

For indigenous peoples residential schooling was a common feature of attempts to destroy language and culture by removing children from the influences of their families and communities. This occurred in Canada, Australia, New Zealand, the Pacific Islands and other parts of the colonized world. The legacy of those schools is still being felt and has been the basis of claims made by indigenous peoples against the social policies of various governments. The story of Hukarere is also a story of women who hated the place and were adamant that they would never ever return. That story is one that students expect, it confirms their view of colonial history. But the joyful, loyal and proud memories that the women in the video hold about their own experiences challenges the all encompassing and very bleak view that colonial schooling was so destructive that the students who attended must have known and should have resisted. The idea that Maori women could hold such positive views of their education and yet still be Maori also challenges the belief that education was only about assimilation of language and culture. The story of Hukarere forces students to look more deeply and to theorize the role that schooling played for Maori girls and women. Hukarere had a highly academic curriculum that would have given Maori women access to university and professional careers. That curriculum had been put in place by Pakeha women, missionary daughters, who held quite different beliefs about the purposes of schooling for Maori girls. The curriculum was changed to a technical and much more domesticating curriculum after intervention by the state.[14] The possibilities for Maori girls that were available within schooling and the alternative educational philosophies of individual teachers challenge students' understanding of the role of agency exercised by indigenous women that is often missing in the broad sweep of colonial history and the way it is told.

Connecting the pieces

There are connecting themes to the three pieces discussed in this chapter that relate to some approaches to narrative inquiry currently underway in a range of indigenous women's projects. There is a historical context to inquiries about the educational lives of indigenous women and men that frames most indigenous approaches to research. For Maori women inquiries into the educational past are often journeys into a terrain deeply shadowed by histories of colonization. A dominant theme in the educational history of indigenous peoples has been one of pain, oppression, cultural assimilation and failure. Official government inquiries, for example, into the 'stolen children' of Australia have affirmed the stories told by indigenous peoples of educational and social policies and practices that have wreaked havoc and disruption on the lives, languages, values, social relations and cultural practices of generations of indigenous children and indigenous communities.[15] The accounts of the past in relation to indigenous peoples are depressingly familiar across the world. Yet the task of reclaiming our own pasts, retelling our own stories of struggle and resistance, renaming and representing our experiences, and celebrating our survival as indigenous peoples has become a major project for indigenous women. There is for example a burgeoning indigenous women's literature that addresses the difficult issues that have confronted women's lives and the achievements of women that are worth sharing and celebrating.[16] There are also highly active academic networks of indigenous women that promote the participation of indigenous women in a wide range of research related activities.

It is frequently this broader project that motivates many Maori women to journey into the memories and archives of our educational past. It is important for ourselves to find the traces left by previous generations of indigenous women, locate them and then in the words of my student seek ways to 'bring them home' if not in a material sense then in the way we acknowledge and write about the stories they helped shape. It is also important for the history of education and the history of women's education in New Zealand that the presence of indigenous women is seen, acknowledged and understood. The stereotypical view of indigenous women as passive recipients of Native schooling policies denies the very active role Maori women often had as community leaders who saw possibilities in education for their families, their communities and themselves.

One approach that is evident in the way many Maori women students carry out a historical study is to find connections to the past through the living. This partly reflects Maori genealogical ways of thinking that shape all relations between people and between people and the environment. It is through genealogies that the past is traced. Embedded in genealogies are many histories. Some genealogical lines connect all members of an *iwi* (tribe) while others connect one part of an *iwi* with another part. Many of my older Maori students have this system embedded like a template in the way they think about the past. Their inquiries begin with the living and then step back into the past. Connecting to the living also partially reflects a cultural understanding that history is happening now and is not something that happened a century ago. The history of women's education for many Maori students is as much about the women who are involved in education now as it is about women who lived and died fifty or a hundred years ago.

From indigenous perspectives there is also a determination that research of any kind into indigenous people's lives cannot continue unproblematically as it has in the past. Research is expected to make a positive difference, to be reciprocal and collaborative, to be transformative.[17] In this new context historical educational research often suffers a problem of relevancy. Unlike the activity around treaty claims – research that has huge economic and political implications for various Maori tribal groups – educational research is not always regarded by Maori organizations as relevant or exciting.[18] In the education field there is also little support as schools cope with the contemporary and therefore more pressing issues facing Maori. However, individuals and families are often very supportive of projects that involve the recollections and oral histories of elders. The Native Schools project has received enormous support from both Maori and Pakeha (non-Maori) who have contributed their own collections and photographs. There is an awareness that the history of the schools does indeed reside in the memories of people and deserves to be told. It has been our experience that some families cling tenaciously to the memories and papers of their grandparents and that women play key roles as keepers of family memories.

In our communities there is often a demand to tell stories that are positive and that challenge a history of negative representations of Maori women. The indigenous granny story often serves this purpose as it provides an example of a revered woman whose life can enlighten and educate younger people who have 'lost' their culture. There is a tendency to situate these stories as moral lessons and to use their lives to teach the next generation. The stories often set up unrealistic expectations of Maori identity that define cultural authenticity around a social context framed either by the depression years of the 1930s or the post-1945 period of New Zealand rural life. Related to such stories are others that are designed to celebrate the lives of indigenous or Maori women. These stories promote positive role models and provide examples of women who have achieved in various fields of life.[19] The fact that such stories need to be told says something about the ways that Maori women have been represented in the media, in educational texts and political discourse. These stories fulfil a social purpose that I do not dispute. However they do not in my view tell a story that gives even adequate attention to the subtleties, contradictions, richness of women's lives. Some stories become too laden with a responsibility to demonstrate qualities of achievement or leadership. Often the focus is given to women whose impact on the national scene has been defined as significant.[20] The more acceptable their work is to the dominant Pakeha society the more often their lives are seen to have been successful and worthwhile.

While I have focused mainly on the finding of an indigenous presence in the history of women's education, the telling of Maori women's lives raises a number of issues related to the ways in which their stories are told or represented. The emphasis here is not necessarily on the story but on the storyteller or narrator of a life and the skill of 'telling' that she possesses. It is in this area that my students struggle. I decided at one point that students expected historical writing to be entirely descriptive, lacking any form of analysis, hugely dull and always conforming to a strict chronological sequence, from birth to death. Furthermore they expected to expunge all traces of their own voices and to rely either on the voice of the woman they have interviewed, another more 'expert' voice or on an 'archival' voice to develop their story.[21] While as a generalization many Maori students are also superb storytellers in an oral setting, telling a story through the written text requires very different skills. In telling the stories of the women whose lives they have researched it is important to me that as writers they tell a story that meets not just the criteria of a historical account but also the demands of a strong piece of writing. It is in their writing that they have a voice and through which they can honour the lives of the women they have researched. It is also through their writing that they can reflect critically on the ways in which they have shaped the narrative, selected the stories, framed the background, filled in the details and arranged the presentation of women's lives.

The need that students have to tell a woman's life in chronological order intrigues me because students acknowledge the fact that their mothers and grandmothers do not talk about their lives in that order. But in the retelling the students have learned that real life stories must begin at the beginning. As readers they expect the same narrative. It is as if women's lives have to follow a pattern of 'growing up'. As Julie Cruickshank had discovered it is not the way that some indigenous women tell their lives or make sense of their lives. Maori women quite often begin with a complicated genealogical chart that sets out their relationships to others or possibly an account of their tribal or community history within which they are positioned. Sometimes they will begin with a talk about a mountain. It is not until some

Maori women are much older, often very old, that they begin to see themselves having an individual existence. Perhaps that is when their lives begin. In historical inquiries it is often the case that large chunks of a life are missing, that what we find are fragments of a woman's life, small moments and glimpses that in themselves are fascinating. The finding of a woman in an archive or photograph becomes part of her story. Her presence is significant even though we may never be able to reconstruct anything further about her. We may know enough to connect her with her descendants and that also becomes part of telling her story, the journey home.

Notes

1 More particularly our discussions occur around food, but the kitchen table discussion is shared by other groups of women.
2 National Archives Native Schools, Taumarere School 1879–81, File BAAA 101 561f.
3 Her first name is Mary but, as the research is still in progress, we are still completing our contacting of families and individuals.
4 The Native Schools System Oral Histories research is funded by the Marsden Fund and administered by the Royal Society of New Zealand. The project leader is Dr Judith Simon. The research covers all the Native Schools known to have existed and interviews have been conducted all over New Zealand.
5 The research methodology is based on two streams of investigation, and two teams of researchers, Maori and Pakeha (white). The Maori researchers carry out the interviews and archival research of the Maori participants who were either students or teachers in the Native Schools.
6 The Native Land Court was established in 1865 to alienate Maori land. The court sat all over New Zealand and school logbooks record attendance at the Native Land Court as a major factor in the disruption of communities as parents were often away at the court for days and weeks.
7 L.T. Smith (1990) The view from my grandmother's veranda, in L.T. Smith and R. Whaitiri (eds) *Te Pua 1: A Journal of Maori Women's Writing*. Research Unit for Maori Education, University of Auckland.
8 H. Whakamaru with M.K. Duffy (1997) *Heeni: A Tainui Elder Remembers*. Auckland: HarperCollins.
9 Ibid., p.11.
10 J. Cruickshank (1990) *Life Lived Like a Story*. Vancouver: University of British Columbia Press.
11 Ibid., p.3.
12 This was written by Dame Te Atairangikahu, the highest ranking chief of the Tainui people, who is referred to generally as the Maori Queen.
13 As part of this research Kuni has also collaborated on a book, K. Jenkins and K. Morris Matthews (1995) *Hukarere and the Politics of Maori Girls' Schooling*. Hukarere Board of Trustees and Palmerston North: Dunmore Press.
14 Ibid., pp.23–42.
15 See the report *Bringing Them Home: National Inquiry into the Separation of*

Aboriginal and Torres Strait Islander Children from their Families (1997). Human Rights and Equality of Opportunity Commission, Commonwealth of Australia, Canberra.

16 See for two examples, *Te Pua: A Journal of Maori Women's Writing*. Research Unit for Maori Education, University of Auckland; J. Harjo and G. Bird (1997) *Reinventing the Enemy's Language Contemporary Women's Writings of North America*. New York: W.W. Norton.

17 G.H. Smith, (ed.) (1994) *Maori and the Issue of Research*. Research Unit for Maori Education, Monograph 9, School of Education, University of Auckland.

18 The Waitangi Tribunal was established by legislation to deal with Maori claims against the Crown that breached the Treaty of Waitangi which was signed between Maori and the British in 1840. The Tribunal can deal with claims that go back to 1840 but 'tribes' have to carry out the research that establishes the breach. There are currently several hundred claims at various stages of development involving massive areas of land.

19 There are a range of both books and magazine articles that are snapshot biographies of selected Maori women often accompanied by beautiful photographs. Some books are photographic essays, almost calendars, that represent Maori women as stunningly beautiful and successful role models. Often the same women appear in several different books as personalities not just positive role models.

20 The term *'whaea o te motu'* or 'mother of the nation' has become a fashionable term for designating women who have made an impact on the national scene and has been used to describe the significance of women who have died. Unfortunately the term is often applied by the media and gives the very strong message to Maori that the only good Maori woman has to be acceptable to non-Maori society and also be dead.

21 A favourite expert for Maori women and Maori men is bell hooks. By an archival voice I refer to a style that reads like the person was dead when they wrote the piece.

Part II

NARRATIVE INQUIRIES

6 Disciplining the teaching body 1968–78: progressive education and feminism in New Zealand

Sue Middleton and Helen May

In April 1997, we were checking the page proofs of our new book, *Teachers Talk Teaching 1915–1995: Early Childhood, Schools and Teachers' Colleges*. Searching for ideas for the cover, we consulted our photograph albums. The illustration shows the image that we suggested and our publishers produced.[1]

A computer generated collage, our cover picture is what media theorists term a simulacrum (a copy without an original).[2] The two teachers in the centre of the picture are Sue (left) and Helen (right). Yet in 1972, when the original photographs were taken, we had never met. We were then 25 years old and, 25 years later, we were fascinated by the educational and wider social theories, or discourses, that 'wrote' or 'inscribed' the bodies in the photo – our own bodies as mini-skirted teachers, Sue's high school students in their uniformed rows and Helen's primary school pupils in their 'civilian' clothes. What were the educational ideas-in-action (or discourses) that gave form to these rows, demeanours and postures – so characteristic of New Zealand schools in the early 1970s?

In exploring this question, this chapter introduces a tiny portion of the life history interview data gathered for our broader project, the aim of which was to map the tides and currents of educational thought in New Zealand in the twentieth century. Relying primarily on policy documents, many previous histories of educational ideas had viewed the educational terrain 'from the top'. Instead, we sought to construct a view 'from the bottom up' – as lived and described by 150 New Zealand teachers and former teachers from as far back as living memory would allow.[3] The resulting book is a textual counterpoint of interwoven themes. In this chapter we take up one of these and explore 'progressive education' in action in the years from around 1968 to the late 1970s. Rather than make the feminisms of the time our central object of study (as each of us has done elsewhere),[4] we chart the broader spectrum of progressive ideas that shaped, and were produced in, the educational settings of the time and that created a context of constraints and possibilities for second-wave feminist activism in education.

Feminist educationists have seen numerous links between feminism and progressive education. Discussions of these have focused on political, psychological, historical and empirical connections. From a political standpoint, many 1970s and 1980s feminists – liberal, radical, socialist, etc. – saw progressivism's emphasis on students' experience as a basis for learning as compatible with feminist practices of consciousness raising. Psychological rationales gained ascendancy in the 1980s as radical feminists of the object relations and other psychoanalytic persuasions saw student centred teaching styles as exemplary of (biologically determined or socially constructed) 'women's ways of knowing'.[5]

It is historical/ empirical relationships between feminism and progressivism that concern us in this chapter. For, although many of the major progressive theorists have been men, historians have recorded how the everyday practices of progressive, or child centred, teaching took root first, and most firmly, in early childhood centres and in the junior years of primary schools[6] – domains dominated by women teachers – rather than in the senior years in primary (elementary), or in intermediate (middle) and secondary (high) schools. Yet these sectors have usually been researched and theorized separately and the often unpaid work of women in early childhood education has been rendered invisible in general educational philosophy, history and sociology texts. Seeking to bridge these divides by studying the ebbs, flows and cross-currents of lived theories and debates within, across and between these sectors, Helen interviewed 75 early childhood and primary school educators, and Sue spoke with 75 intermediate and secondary school teachers. Because the resulting interview transcripts amounted to 3,000 pages,[7] this brief chapter can give only broad impressions, rather than details, of the lived educational theories – progressive, feminist and otherwise – that washed through, around and between New Zealand's educational sectors in the 1970s.

We begin with a brief definition of progressive education and explain how we have used Foucault's conceptualizations of the body, discourse and capillary power to help us contextualize the teachers' narratives politically, historically, geographically and culturally.[8]

Freedom, discipline and Foucault

The international movement, theories and practices known popularly as progressive education became influential on many New Zealand educators' thinking and practices – particularly in infant education – during the 1920s and 1930s.[9] Critical of the regimented drills of traditional schooling, progressive ideas were centred around the Enlightenment values of liberty and rational autonomy. The more 'sociologically' oriented (e.g. Deweyan) versions focused on the collective, or social, benefits of education – the teaching and practice of democracy in schools would create citizens who would preserve democratic values in adult life.[10] The more individualistic (psychoanalytic or psychological) models were based on the idea that there were (natural) 'stages' of human development and that the role of the teacher was to observe, facilitate and monitor the progress of the developing child.[11] By the mid-1950s, this constellation of ideas and approaches to learning and teaching (derogatively labelled by their critics as 'playway') had become dominant in many of New Zealand's preschools and in the infant classes of primary schools.[12] While post-Second World War secondary school curriculum and other policy documents were centred around social objectives like 'education for democracy' (social engineering), teaching and disciplinary practices in most high schools remained highly regimented and it was not until the early 1970s that the more student centred pedagogies were widely encouraged or practised at secondary school level.[13]

While advocates of progressivism might describe it as centred on freedom of student choice, and therefore as antithetical to the compulsion characteristic of traditional school disciplinary practices, a Foucauldian analysis conceptualizes it differently. Foucault saw pedagogies as key objects for historical investigation in his broader research agenda on the sites and mechanisms of 'capillary' power. Since the eighteenth century, he argued, 'technologies' for the rationalized, bureaucratized and professionalized surveillance and administration of populations had, in western societies, gradually replaced the preindustrial feudal systems that had relied on the personality, divine right and bodily presence of the sovereign and his/her delegated agents. Like blood in the capillaries of the human body, the disciplinary knowledges of professionals – articulated to the powers of government – flowed through the intersecting conduits of professional networks, social institutions and information systems.

Viewing freedom and subjection as flip-sides of the same coin – as complementary rather than contradictory – he argued that 'The Enlightenment, which discovered the liberties, also invented the disciplines'.[14] The democratic forms of government characteristic of western capitalist states rested on the ideal (or fantasy) of individual rational autonomy – the core Enlightenment value. Yet the social order required citizens who were not only autonomous and free, but who were, at the same time, both economically productive and subjected (rendered governable). As products of the Enlightenment, institutions of public schooling straddle this contradiction. Children in school learn to be both autonomous and governable – free and subjected.

Within schools – as in other apparatuses of regulation – the bodies of individuals are subjected to the 'panoptic' (all-seeing) gaze of authorities: 'a relation of surveillance, defined and regulated, is inscribed at the heart of the practice of teaching, not as an additional or an adjacent part of it, but as a mechanism that is inherent in it and which increases its efficiency'.[15] This 'relation of surveillance' – so central in teachers' everyday work – includes monitoring the spatial locations of students (where they may be and with whom they may mix); the postures students may assume within their allocated spaces inside and outside the classroom (static or moving; sitting in rows or in groups, in desks or on the floor); and the surveillance and standardization of their dress and demeanour.

As Walkerdine has argued, student centred pedagogies do not 'liberate' children from the regulatory surveillance of adults.[16] Rather, the processes of discipline, regulation and normalization become more covert: 'the child supposedly freed by this process to develop according to its nature was the most classified, catalogued, watched and monitored in history. Freed from coercion, the child was much more subtly regulated into normality.'[17] Within progressivist environments, she observed, 'Discipline became not overt disciplining, but covert watching [as] the classroom became the facilitating space for each individual under the watchful and total gaze of the teacher.'[18] Writing about child centred learning in primary schools, Walkerdine noted that the freedom of children meant less space for the teacher, who became 'the servant of the omnipotent child, whose needs she must meet at all times.'[19]

A Foucauldian approach to the study of discipline includes the 'disciplines' in the sense of the professional and administrative bodies of knowledge (including progressivism, critical or radical pedagogies, and feminism)[20] by which students and teachers are categorized, classified or otherwise 'known' by those in authority. Also included are the (psychological, etc.) criteria that teachers use to measure students' 'success', 'growth', 'maturity', 'conduct' and any written or electronic records of these. In addition, it encompasses the standards by which schools and teachers are assessed by inspectors and auditors and the overarching policies, theoretical rationales (or discourses) that inform their evaluations.

What, then, were the progressive and other educational discourses that were lived by New Zealand teachers and students in early childhood centres and schools in the 1970s? Where did they come from? How were they encountered, taken up, and/or resisted by teachers and students? How did these discourses 'write' their bodies? Finally, what questions does this exploration of the broader discursive context raise with respect to the emergence of second wave feminisms in education?

Protest movements and neo-progressivism

During the 1960s many of the post-Second World War baby boom generation – students whose parents may not have had access to higher, or even secondary, education – were moving to the cities and studying in colleges and universities. The sense of marginality that many of us who were such students felt in academic environments – as female and/or Maori and/or working class – together with the sense of possibilities afforded us by the economic prosperity of the time, fuelled radical critiques of education and wider social protests. In the late 1960s, the hippy movement, the student revolts, anti-Vietnam War protests, anti-Apartheid demonstrations and American Black Civil Rights all had their repercussions on some New Zealand students and teachers.

As the postwar baby boom cohorts entered teaching in the early 1970s, ideas from these movements blended with previous progressive educational ideas and influenced mainstream educational policies and teaching practice. Earlier forms of progressivism had been strongly shaped by academic disciplines: philosophy (John Dewey), psychoanalysis (Susan Isaacs and A.S. Neill) and the various developmental psychologies (Jean Piaget, Erik Erikson and, later, Carl Rogers and J.S. Bruner). In contrast, rooted as they were in the protest movements, the newer versions (we shall term these 'neo-progressivism') had a more popular base. All, however, had in common an emphasis on personal growth, on individual autonomy, rights and choices and on creating classroom environments, curricula and decision making processes that fostered democratic practices and values. The availability and intertwining of both 'generations' of progressivism created an atmosphere in which more experienced teachers and administrators shared with their younger colleagues a desire for more liberal classrooms. With two successive liberal/progressive Ministers of Education – the Labour Government's P. Amos (1972–5) and the National Government's L. Gandar (1975–8) – the wider political climate in New Zealand was supportive of such innovation.

Many of our interviewees encountered progressive, and more radical ideas, for the first time as students at universities or teachers' colleges. One Maori man commented on the politicizing effects of his studies at Auckland University in 1968:

> with papers like anthropology we looked at culture and all that sort of thing – injustices. New Zealand history cemented my view that I had to do something about it . . . We were getting very political then, the Maori – the Black Panther movement, Bastion Point [a land-rights protest] . . . Certainly university made me more aware politically of what was happening in this country.

These insights were compatible with international critiques of the part played by schooling in colonial oppression. Revolutionary Third World writers such as Frantz Fanon were read in some more radical circles in New Zealand universities.[21] Jack Shallcrass (b.1922),[22] a leading teacher educator and civil libertarian, recalled that:

> [Paulo] Freire came to stay with me when he was in New Zealand in 1975. He was really the genesis of my teaching in my last ten years at the university. How do you empower people? That was a constant doubting question. How do you actually make people a significant part of the process?

The discourses of the liberation movements were appropriated and adapted to urban settings in western countries. Deschoolers and advocates for free or alternative schools outside the mainstream system conceptualized children as oppressed by adults.[23] Andy Begg (b.1940) explained that although there were philosophical and organizational differences between New Zealand's two publicly funded alternative high schools, both had decision making processes that gave the opinions of parents, teachers and students equal weight:

> The most important organizational aspect was the school meeting and it was made very clear by me within the original terms of reference on which the school was set up that the school meeting should have all the powers of the Principal and my job as the Director (or Principal) was to put their decisions into action. So as far as possible everything that came to me as Principal should go to school meeting . . . everything, every appointment of staff and so on was done by the school meetings or by subcommittees of it. The school meeting with students, staff and sometimes parents was very important.

These, and less radical, progressive ideas were popularized by a boom in the commercial publishing of affordable paperback books – usually American – written for teachers by teachers who described their innovative educational programmes in difficult urban settings. Among these were Postman and Weingartner's *Teaching as a Subversive Activity*, Herbert Kohl's *The Open Classroom*, John Holt's *How Children Fail* and Jonathan Kozol's *Death at an Early Age*.[24] Although the theoretical and political allegiances of these authors varied, all shared the broad ideas that the problems faced by teachers in urban schools resulted from social injustices in the cities and society more generally (such as poverty and/or racism); that the authoritarian structures and programmes characteristic of most (American) schools were inappropriate to the urban conditions of the time; and that, if children and teenagers were to become effective and socially aware citizens of a democracy, democratic practices such as student choice must be central in their school experiences. Commercial booksellers were important in disseminating these ideas and models in New Zealand:

I went into Roy Parsons [a Wellington book store], and the elder Parsons was onto Penguin Education Specials. And I used to go in and ask if there were any new Penguin Specials, and he'd hand them out to me and sometimes discuss them. So it isn't teachers that taught me.

Andy Begg remembered his first staff meeting at Auckland's new Green Bay High School in 1973 under the principalship of Des Mann:

It was just wonderful. The first letter we got after we had been appointed told us that we'd have a staff meeting in the last week of January and how before that we were to read *Teaching as a Subversive Activity*. This was from the Principal and this just seemed mind blowing.

Graham Robinson (b.1926) explained how the neo-progressive ideas were disseminated in his professional networks in Christchurch:

Ideas came from America. We did a lot of reading . . . I got to know these books through the people I was working with . . . English Association people talked about them, passed them around, and discussed them. The whole atmosphere was a ferment of activity, excitement, and discussion . . . It was a time of great excitement in education – the world seemed at your feet. And we were pretty free to go ahead.

Disciplining the student body

'In thinking of the mechanisms of power', said Foucault, researchers should 'think of its capillary form of existence, the point where power reaches into the very grain of individuals, touches their bodies and inserts itself into their actions and attitudes, their discourses, learning processes and everyday lives.'[25] In this and the following sections, we illustrate how progressive ideas circulated through and between early childhood centres and schools, inscribed the bodies of students and teachers, and repartitioned time and spaces in educational settings.

Progressive teaching methods encouraged more movement in classrooms by students and teachers. Seeking bodily comfort, freedom of movement and informality, some of us who were teaching struggled to liberalize our schools' requirements with respect to the way we dressed. Some of our male colleagues caused outrage when they refused to wear ties, grew their hair and sideburns and wore jeans. Our mini-skirts made free movement in the classroom difficult: 'When you lifted your hand up to write on the blackboard, it wasn't a particularly good thing to be doing!' Not surprisingly, trousers became acceptable work clothes for women. The influx of young and trendy teachers exacerbated classroom management dilemmas for some of their older colleagues, as 'Audrey Hall' (b.1928) commented:

> I found boys very lazy as students. A lot of them never settled down and did a decent period of work, or their homework. I was older by then. A younger teacher can get a rapport with students, almost a hero worship. They see you as a role model and notice what you're wearing, and comment on it, too – quite a different sort of relationship. But coming in as a middle-aged woman to boys' classes you really had to be very bossy and authoritarian. A feeling of 'We're all in this together, let's get to work' didn't seem to work. I like a relaxed way of teaching, but I found that at that school I had to be very authoritarian.

With younger teachers sharing their students' tastes in popular music and clothes, the youth culture became more evident in schools. Kindergarten teacher 'Angela David' (b.1942) recalled how 'the music had changed, there was Peter, Paul and Mary being sung in the kindergartens. The kindergarten used to get into a mess . . . there was lots of creativity.' A young teacher (b.1947) remembered Naenae College:

> In my English classes we chose our own themes. We did something on war and something on rock music. Bob Dylan, Simon and Garfunkel and Joan Baez – I used the words of their songs as poems. Some of that stuff was on the hit parade at the time. And I was doing some folk singing in the Chez Paree [a Wellington coffee bar] in the evenings. So I had my guitar; I wore mini skirts, long hair and boots and I related well with the kids.

The acceptance and visibility (or audibility) of the youth culture in the more liberal secondary schools irritated some older teachers:

> Onslow College was one of the first high schools in New Zealand where there was no school uniform. There were no prizes, no prize-giving, no

formal three-hour examinations. Much more relaxed. They always had, for example, school students playing rock music over the loud speaker, which just about drove me mad. Every interval and lunch time you'd have this blaring. They took turns to run the radio station, and they went on protest marches.

The publication in New Zealand of the Danish *Little Red Schoolbook* introduced high school students to the rhetoric of protest movements and applied it to their situation.[26] In a climate in which students' rights were seen as important, some challenged the contradiction between the 'freedom of expression' that they were offered by liberal/progressive discourses and their positioning as passive recipients of teachers' normalizing practices:

> The former Principal had had the school absolutely screwed down tight, and the new Principal was faced with mutiny from the boys – sit ins on the school field over caps. He abolished caps, and the Board of Governors thought that that was the end of the world. The sit-ins were about wearing caps, and long hair and all that stuff. It was the time of the *Little Red School Book,* a time of great ferment. Student power.

The refusal of many high schools to relax uniform requirements trivialized their educational function for some of their more questioning students. 'Nell Wilson' (b.1955) resisted her school's attempt to standardize her appearance:

> The uniform was a grey skirt and a white blouse. So I made a tie-dye grey skirt which didn't go down well at all. I was constantly called into the Senior Mistress's office and given lectures . . . I had quite long hair, and used to wear it in all different kinds of ways. We had a 'gals' assembly and Mrs Owens walked up and down the aisles and picked out girls who had to go on stage for having inappropriate hairstyles. That included me who on this particular day had these pigtails just above my ears – like Pippi Longstocking pan handles . . . As a result of things like that, I was so sick of the place that I didn't do a senior year.

A few high schools abolished uniform. While for some this signalled an increase in personal freedom, for those whose families were unable to provide them with good clothing it was a source of discomfort. 'Rangi Davidson' (b.1956), who had himself attended a private Maori boys' boarding school, had regarded his own school's uniform as important in helping him to develop a sense of self-worth:

> I'm basically a traditionalist and a disciplinarian . . . I like to wear a tie for school. I believe in the importance of a uniform for self-esteem and all that sort of thing. The uniform gives you a sense of belonging to something and if it's a nice uniform it makes you feel good. If you don't dress well, you don't feel so good.

Rangi's concerns with the well-being of his urban Maori students illustrates the impact of the increasing diversity of school student populations. In response to the urbanization of Maori and the immigration of Pacific Islanders, teachers debated how best to cope with increasingly multicultural classrooms, as a Wellington high school principal explained:

> By 1970 it was a different school. You could stand on the stage and you could look at the school. The hair colour was different. Whereas it had been sort of light brown, the occasional blonde, and the occasional red head, it was a much darker mix with the Chinese and the Indian and the Greek, and the Pacific Islanders coming in. And at the same time as we were realizing that our school was changing we were looking at major changes in educational direction, and I'm really always heartened that it was teachers that took the plunge – *Education in Change* was a keynote document.

Education in Change was published in 1969 by the secondary school teachers' union.[27] Grounded in humanistic psychology, its recommendations – like those in several other key reports in the early to mid-1970s – were in tune with progressive thinking: 'education forms a major part in the process of individual and social growth and should be self-motivating because its rewards are inherent. This report is directed towards the development of a concept of self-motivated learning.'[28]

In the more liberal/progressive secondary schools, such ideas generated major upheavals in the ways they were structured and brought about changes in teaching practice. Traditional streaming [tracking] – based on what from the 1920s to the 1960s were seen as 'objective' tests – had disproportionately relegated Maori and working class Pakeha (white New Zealanders) to the non-academic streams. This stratification became increasingly obvious as urbanization brought about an influx of brown students into predominantly white urban schools and centres. Reconceptualizing cultural difference as valuable diversity rather than as deviance or inferiority, the discourses of cultural pluralism (or multiculturalism) provoked many high schools to destream during the 1970s.[29] Destreaming tore down the 'fences' that had segregated students who took different courses (academic, home craft, commercial, agricultural or industrial) and reclassified the student population into coeducational groupings of mixed ability and mixed race. Teaching in non-streamed classes made whole class instruction difficult and forced secondary teachers to develop the kinds of individualized and small group teaching methods which up till this time had been characteristic only of primary schools. Some found these changes difficult:

> I think non-streaming requires a particularly gifted teacher. Streaming requires a major effort on the part of teachers to preserve, particularly the slower kids' self-esteem, but non-streaming required really hard

working, gifted teachers, and group teaching – which secondary teachers have never been very good at.

Concerns with the diverse backgrounds of students as formative of their learning and behaviour were reflected not only in teaching methods, but also in disciplinary practices outside the classroom. Corporal punishment fell out of favour and was replaced by behaviourist techniques of positive reinforcement, which were being taught in teachers' colleges and universities. 'Eric Cotton' (b.1939) described the new 'social work' orthodoxy with respect to the monitoring of students' whereabouts and behaviour:

> I was a Dean and that was a huge job. I would spend day after day looking for girls around the town – I saw the rougher side of life that I didn't even think existed . . . I would be in my classroom, and there'd be a knock on the door and there'd be one of the girls saying, 'We need to see you for a moment.' So I'd leave some work for the class and say, 'What's your problem?' Mainly Samoan girls, who were getting a really hard time at home. They'd say, 'We've got this problem.' 'Where abouts are you? How many of you?' They'd usually have gone into the girls' toilet.

Consistent with the shift towards progressivism in high schools, by the early to mid-1970s, the Department of Education was introducing new syllabuses in which the postwar version of equality of opportunity ('equal means the same')[30] gave way to one of education for diversity – cultural pluralism and student choice. Patricia Harrison (b.1931) was on the committee that wrote a new secondary school English syllabus:

> We looked at the whole of pop culture – where kids were at – the way they developed language, how they learned best. We looked at the fact that students needed more than just reading and writing basic skills, but that they needed a greater facility with language and a confidence in using it . . . it began because of the exposure of young people to television [introduced to New Zealand in 1960] and the media and it was looking at language in a much wider context . . . It was looking at the needs of young people and the different pressures. I mean the pressure of advertising, the pressure of television, the pressures from the Maori moving in from the rural to the urban area and just being without any kind of focus or roots. All those things impacted and came together. I think there were people who were truly educationalists and we just sparked each other off.

Repartitioning time and space

'Discipline', wrote Foucault, 'proceeds from the distribution of bodies in space'.[31] In bureaucratic organizations, including schools, disciplinary power breaks down complex multiplicities into simple units ... carefully repartitioned in a basically cellular space: for each individual a place and for each emplacement an individual. It breaks down activities and actions into simple, momentary movements, thus allowing their control and ordering through routines and timetables.[32]

In many schools and centres, the shift away from authoritarian, and towards progressive, pedagogies necessitated substantial repartitioning and reclassification of time and space. James Doyle (b.1966) was a primary school pupil and recalled that his teacher had sat at a child's desk:

> It was right in the middle of the room facing the front. He was just part of the group ... He dressed very casually. His pottery was very artistic. He had a wheel in the back of the classroom and he had a kiln there ... I remember him getting into trouble because he wasn't covering all the curriculum ... we spent a lot of time doing pottery. I remember him discussing it with us saying, 'We're meant to do this and we had better get it done.'

There was widespread enthusiasm in primary schools for open plan classrooms: walls came down, age groups were mixed, and – in the more progressive ones – children moved freely between activities and teachers. Barbara Harold (b.1952) worked with 5–8 year olds:

> We were able to put into practice the things we thought about developing the kids' independence and allowing kids to make their own choices and to move freely around. Centres of interest, children's independence and individual contracts were very much to the fore in the mid-1970s.

Such changes also characterized many preschools – both kindergartens (state supported with professional teachers) and playcentres (run by parent volunteers). So called free play was now being conceived in more political terms to do with the rights and autonomy of children. The earlier Freudian and psychological underpinnings of progressivism were not lost, but were overlaid with more immediate ends, as Joan Brockett (b.1927) recalled: 'If you asked teachers their aims, the children's happiness would come right to the surface. It was very important.' Some teachers tested the limits of necessary order, questioning old assumptions, often over things that were quite small, such as the limited colours of paint allowed, and sizes of brushes and paper. But cumulatively this dissatisfaction became an explosion as teachers began to dismantle the unwritten rules of the kindergarten curriculum as 'Angela David' (b.1942) explained:

> We set up the shelves in the storeroom where kids could actually move in and out and decide what sort of junk they wanted. I guess I was empowering kids at that time and allowing kids to make choices. We used to make up just the mixture of cornflour and we gave the children

the dyes and they could decide all the colours, so kids were learning. That's when I first introduced being called by my Christian name and that was quite radical in those days.

Georgina Kerr (b.1947) sought to transform the whole approach to learning:

We had this brain wave where somebody says, 'Let's look at the physical layout of the place maybe that will help us initiate some change.' We wanted the whole curriculum area to just transform and to be a place where kids can learn. Not where kids learn to behave but where kids can learn in a way that they want to learn. So we looked at furniture and that was the revolution. We looked at the layout, we looked at where things were, and it just went from there and then the theories started to come out.

Tony Holmes (b.1946) described the playcentre he supervised in the 1970s as 'socially anarchic':

[We would have] the naive view that structure isn't really required at all. The idea is that the material and the environment is provided and the kids just go for it as long as they don't actually interfere or destroy each other in the process. We just let them go for it . . . The role of the adult was to provide for the child's free exploration as a Piagetian 'little scientist'. You create the environment for children to learn but it was very much hands off. The only time that there was real intervention was when there were disputes . . . As long as the session flowed and children enjoyed themselves and enjoyed exploring the environment then they weren't to be touched unless they came to you.

In some kindergartens there was an explosion in creative art work. Many kindergartens lost their traditional neat and tidy look; the junk piled higher, the weavings hung lower, and every surface became a possibility for paint: 'I remember sitting on the floor doing weaving, creating this amazing weaving with children and all these natural environment resources that we'd collected and had this great array of children around me', recalled Jane Barron (b.1956). There was, however, concern that empowering children led to chaos, as one preschool adviser explained:

The idea was fine, but nobody had worked with the teachers on the practice. It had to be kept in some kind of order so that the kids could work properly. They became laissez-faire. And you had these awful situations arising where children had no limits. Yet the idea was great. It was sad, because there were wonderful people wanting to do their best, and not quite knowing when to intervene and when not to . . . I think they felt that if they interfered too much, or stopped children or said no to them, they would stop their curiosity from coming to the fore and they would stop their learning in some way or interfere with the process that was going on.

Teachers often used other ways to impose 'order', as Margaret Carr (b.1941) recalled:

> I've got wonderful memories of boys being hauled in at half past ten to do a painting – you'd drag these reluctant children in to do a painting and maybe a puzzle. The indoor activities, table top activities, were planned and initiated by adults . . . The children all had things sussed. They'd whiz around, and I can remember one of the children saying, 'What is it today – Oh making a bear, OK!'; then making a bear in three minutes flat and then he was allowed to go off and do what he wanted to do. So they subverted the system as much as they could. Fortunately children are very good at subversion!

But as Cushla Scrivens (b.1939) found, the 'content' whims of teachers could seem bizarre to children:

> I can remember going to one kindergarten and the student had decided that the theme for the week would be green. This was Thursday and I heard some child at the paints with these six pots of mixed greens say 'Not bloody green paint again' – I felt for him. But usually things were a bit more imaginative.

Feminism and progressive education

We conclude by following the blending of second wave feminist ideas with progressive education and trace how these both supported and contradicted it. While progressivism had been simmering in many female dominated educational institutions since the 1920s, feminism – as a mass movement – had been quiescent since New Zealand women had been the first in the world to win the franchise in 1893. As elsewhere in the western world, a second wave of feminism gathered momentum in the late 1960s. By the mid-1970s, education had become pivotal in the resurgence of both the liberal and more radical (women's liberationist) strands of feminism.

Young 'women's libbers' adopted shock tactics – street theatre; demonstrations; writing and displaying provocative tracts, posters and magazines. Often highly educated and articulate, they gained high media profiles. Catherine Lang (b.1957), a student at Hamilton Girls' High School, recalled the public outrage at visiting feminist Germaine Greer's flaunting of convention in a public address: 'Germaine Greer came and said "bullshit". So we read her book.[33] It was just amazing. I was this stroppy feminist thereafter.'

Greer and other women's liberationists (later termed radical feminists) focused on embodied sexuality as a political issue. With their exhortations to engage in sexual – including lesbian – experimentation, their gritty rhetoric spoke to many younger women (such as university and teachers' college students). Living away from parental surveillance, and increasingly gaining access to cheap and reliable contraceptive technology, many revelled in the permissive freedoms of the 'sexual revolution'. Coinciding historically, and interacting theoretically and politically, with the sexual revolution were the liberalization of sexuality education in schools, the formation of gay liberation and lesbian feminist groups, and the introduction of welfare benefits to enable single mothers to keep and raise their babies rather than be forced to give them up for adoption.[34]

While radical feminist politics focused on the body and women's essential differences from (and oppression by) men, liberal feminists minimized gender differences and sought equality in public life. We who were the daughters of the post-Second World War baby boom were the first generation of women to have universal access to secondary schools and widespread opportunities to enter higher education. However, while the liberal/progressivist discourses that informed public policies had promised us equality of opportunity in education and in the workforce, the reality we experienced was often one of inequality. As young feminist students and beginning teachers, our concerns were fuelled and supported by the few older women who had attained key positions, such as Phoebe Meikle and Geraldine McDonald, who – alone and in tiny networks – had laid the groundwork for the later more popular campaigns for 'women's rights'. Although their political antecedents and rhetoric were different, feminist educators of liberal and radical persuasions combined forces to lobby for the removal of 'sex role stereotyping' in education.

Taught in the top stream of a girls' school by feminist teachers, Catherine Lang (b.1951) commented on the link between (liberal) feminism and academic/ professional success – girls in the less academic streams (destined for working class occupations) encountered more conservative expectations:

> I didn't get the 'work until marriage' in the A stream but the C's [commercial] and G's [general] were being prepared for domesticity. You were still supposed to make choices based on the models around of women who didn't have children, or older women who had come back into teaching and didn't have to juggle young children and a career [but] we also had younger women teachers who were pregnant and taught right up until their babies were born.

We have argued in this chapter that the wider political climate was supportive of critiques of, and progressive innovations in, formal education. In 1975 (International Women's Year), the New Zealand Department of Education sponsored a conference on *Education and the Equality of the Sexes*. Noeline Alcorn (b.1939) described this as:

a key event. The principal of [Auckland Teachers' College] thought he ought to send someone and, since I was about the most senior woman he said would I like to go? I can still remember Geraldine McDonald's session on 'Let us Now Praise Famous Men' (which became a classic).

On recommendations from that conference, the Department of Education set up structures and policies, and commissioned research with the aim of removing of sex role stereotyping from the curriculum, encouraging girls into non-traditional subjects and helping more women teachers move into senior positions.[35]

Looking back in hindsight, these issues raise questions about the 'fit' between feminist and progressive educational agendas. As others have pointed out,[36] there can be conflicts and contradictions between feminist and progressive teaching strategies, since progressivism's emphasis on student choice may allow sexist and racist attitudes and practices free expression. In contrast, many feminist educational initiatives have been necessarily directly interventionist, for example insisting on 'choices' of non-sexist games, texts and activities; or on those that were 'non-traditional' for a child's sex. In the 1970s – as in the late 1990s – feminist educational interventions have been opposed from libertarian (as well as conservative) standpoints.

Amidst the activism of the 1970s women's movement, the issue of child-care came to the forefront. Indeed, it was as graduate students and mothers of 1-year-old daughters attending the Victoria University crèche that we, the authors, first met. While kindergartens and playcentres had been officially designated as 'preschool education', childcare had – since the nineteenth century – been classed as a welfare service. Feminist demands for the right to affordable quality childcare, were radical challenges to the normalizing administration and regulation of family life. In Foucauldian terms, they challenged the partitions within and between domestic and public spaces. In an interview with Helen in 1986, Cathy Lythe talked about the barriers:

> You suddenly realize that you are up against something that is bigger than just childcare. Childcare was just a manifestation of it. As long as you did nothing for childcare you could keep women in their place . . .
> *Was it feminist action . . . ?*
> There were no structural links with the women's movement. They were not the doers . . . The theoretical jargon was fine but the people who were really going to sell it were people already doing it . . . Children in childcare deserve the same treatment, the same housing, the same conditions, as any other children.

This interview was published in a journal which contained a photograph of an activist, Pam Croxford, portrayed with her children in a protest march during the early 1970s. The placard around her toddler's neck captured the strident mood, 'FREE MUM, FREE DAD, FREE ME, FREE CHILD-CARE'.[37] Another activist was Duilia Rendall who, as a single mother before the Domestic Purposes Benefit, needed childcare. She spent many years working in Wellington to ensure that childcare was available without stigma to single parents. 'Year after year preparing those bloody submissions and justifying it always – always justifying'. In an interview with Helen in 1987 she recalled a not atypical meeting with a National Government minister:

> It must have been at least my fifth deputation . . . That was the meeting where Bert Walker expounded his great philosophy of childcare . . . Bert said to us, 'Now ladies, my wife stayed home with our children, why can't all you wives stay at home with your children?'

Helen Orr (b.1947) returned to nursing in 1968 and placed her young infant in childcare: 'The reaction of everyone was shock and horror that I had chosen to pass my child onto someone else. I justified it in that she was a trained nurse and was of equal calibre to myself. I struck gold.' In 1975 the Dunedin Community Childcare Centre was established with an explicit connection with the women's movement, as a project funded from a grant for International Women's Year. Anne Smith (b.1942) was involved in the venture and, as a new academic at Otago University and a childcare user, she became active in the political campaign:

> We wanted it to be for everyone, but it was more of a feminist thing for women who wanted to work or had to work. But we also had quality principles that we wanted too. We had some ideals about it being for children too . . . We talked about parent involvement. We would use what there was in psychology or whatever to plan an environment that we thought was good for kids.

Pat Hubbard (b.1931) worked at this centre. Like Anne Smith she wanted a quality programme but acknowledged the strong element of feminism:

> I think the non-sexist thing was very important from the beginning because of International Women's Year and feminism. I had long talks with Marie Bell who was on a committee for producing non-sexist books. Marie was one of the earliest official visitors.

Anne Smith used her academic position to support the positives of childcare through research, training and advocacy, and she made contact with a group of women interested in broadening early childhood to be inclusive of childcare. 'Val Burns, Ros Noonan, Wendy Lee, Anne Meade . . . I guess it was a link between feminism and early childhood that came together at that time'. Seeing progressivism and feminism as compatible rather than contradictory, Anne Smith was concerned to ensure that 'The feminist arguments had to be accompanied by some which were child centred.' A series of women's conferences and conventions throughout the 1970s became platforms for launching childcare onto the political stage, moving it away from its associations with welfare and charity, and towards the education sphere.

In 1976 the Muldoon National Government was elected amidst the trauma of a sharp economic recession. Abrasive in personality, confrontational with liberal/left protesters, and conservative with respect to the role of women, Muldoon appointed a conservative Minister of Education (M. Wellington), who proceeded to undo what critics saw as excessive permissiveness in the curriculum and – supported by fundamentalist Christians – to stem the tide of feminist activism in educational settings. Unlike in the USA, the reign of social conservatism was to be shortlived. The election of the fourth Labour Government in 1984 – grounded as it was in a strong feminist and Maori base – promised quite radical feminist and other social reforms. Labour's first Minister of Education, R. Marshall, worked to extend liberal/ progressive programmes and provisions. But this was not to last. The Prime Minister (David Lange) replaced Marshall as minister after the 1987 election and it was his Labour Government that wholeheartedly adopted neo-liberal economics and set about restructuring the state – including education – in radical ways. The story of 'new right' reforms in New Zealand has been told elsewhere. These adopted a contradictory blend of devolution and centralized control of curriculum content, standards and assessment. Since the election of the National Government in 1990, feminist structures in state bureaucracies have been steadily removed, the educational climate has shifted to an emphasis on 'success' and competitiveness between individuals and institutions. However, the presence of strong libertarian feminists in National has ensured that official recognition of at least a minimalist feminist libertarianism remains.[38]

Epilogue

We leave you – as we began – with a formal photograph of ourselves in our educational environment (Helen on the left, Sue on the right). This was taken in June 1997, when we launched *Teachers Talk Teaching* with a party. Our colleagues and many of those whom we had interviewed for the book were there. Here we stand – again posed for the camera – no longer clad in mini-skirts, but wearing the casualized formality of the senior feminist academic. Such a scenario would have been unimaginable in 1972, when the previous photographs were taken.

Since the early 1970s and the resurgence of second wave feminism, there has been an unprecedented boom in feminist theorizing, research, publishing and university teaching – in the separate domain of women's studies and within mainstream disciplines such as education studies. In the 1990s, there has been evidence of a 'pure/applied' split.[39] The pure, or high, forms of feminism are evident in the emphasis on abstract theory in some women's studies departments and the traditionally more elite humanities subjects. Applied feminist scholarship is more characteristic of professional courses such as education, management, and law.

Feminist narrative histories, such as those in this book, view the social world not 'from the top', but from the bottom up. And in this, Foucault's toolkit remains useful. Those of us who work to understand, support and initiate progressive and feminist education can learn much from Foucault's warning that – as scholars, writers and activists – we should not be pre-occupied with abstract theorizing of

> the regulated and legitimate forms of power in their central locations; with the general mechanisms with which they operate, and the contin-ual effects of these. On the contrary . . . [we should be] concerned with power at its extremities, in its ultimate destinations, with those points where it becomes capillary, that is in its more regional and local forms of institutions.[40]

Notes

1 Used by permission of Dunmore Press, Palmerston North, New Zealand; S. Middleton and H. May (1997) *Teachers Talk Teaching 1915–1995: Early Childhood, Schools and Teachers' Colleges*. Palmerston North: Dunmore Press.

2 M. Poster (1995) *The Second Media Age*. New York and Cambridge: Polity Press and Basil Blackwell.

3 We included those who saw themselves as 'ordinary' as well as the more well known; Maori and Pakeha; and sought to represent experiences from all parts of New Zealand (which has only 3 million people in a land the size of the UK); all sectors; all types of school pupil 'mixes'; rural, urban and small towns; differing school and personal philosophies. For methodological details see S. Middleton (1996) Doing qualitative educational research in the 1990s: issues and practicalities. *Waikato Journal of Education* 2: 1–23.

4 H. May Cook (1985) *Mind That Child: Childcare as a Political and Social Issue in New Zealand*. Wellington: BlackBerry Press; H. May (1992) *Minding Children, Managing Men*. Wellington: Bridget Williams Books; S. Middleton (1993) *Educating Feminists: Life-Histories and Pedagogy*. New York: Teachers College Press.

5 These arguments are developed more fully in Middleton, *Educating Feminists*, pp.112–16.

6 H. May (1992) Learning through play: women, progressivism and early childhood education, 1920s–1950s, in S. Middleton and A. Jones (eds) *Women and Education in Aotearoa 2*. Wellington: Bridget Williams Books.

7 We used the NUD-IST software package (see note 3).

8 The use of Foucault's work in theorizing life history interviews is developed more fully in S. Middleton (1998) *Disciplining Sexuality: Foucault, Life-Histories and Education*. New York: Teachers College Press.

9 H. May (1997) *The Discovery of Early Childhood*. Auckland: Auckland University Press, Bridget Williams Books and NZCER.

10 M. Greene (1988) *Dialectic of Freedom*. New York: Teachers College Press.

11 V. Walkerdine (1984) Developmental psychology and the child-centred pedagogy: the insertion of Piaget into early childhood education, in J. Henriques, W. Holloway, C. Urwin, C. Venn and V. Walkerdine *Changing the Subject*. London: Methuen.

12 May, Learning through play; May, *The Discovery of Early Childhood*.

13 S. Middleton (1996) Towards an oral history of educational ideas in New Zealand as a resource for teacher education. *Teaching and Teacher Education* 12(1): 543–56.

14 M. Foucault (1977) *Discipline and Punish*. Harmondsworth: Penguin, p.222.

15 Ibid., p.141.

16 Walkerdine, Developmental psychology.

17 V. Walkerdine (1992) Progressive pedagogy and political struggle, in C. Luke and J. Gore (eds) *Feminisms and Critical Pedagogy*. New York and London: Routledge, p.18.

18 Ibid., p.19.

19 Ibid., p.21.

20 C. Luke and J. Gore (eds) (1992) *Feminisms and Critical Pedagogy*. New York

and London: Routledge; E. McWilliam (1995) *In Broken Images: Feminist Tales for a Different Teacher Education.* New York: Teachers College Press.

21　D. Awatere (1984) *Maori Sovereignty.* Auckland: Broadsheet Books.

22　Names in quotation marks are pseudonyms; names without quotation marks are real names. The insertion of birthdates indicates whether the excerpt refers to the interviewee's childhood, adolescent or adult experiences in education.

23　I. Illich (1971) *Deschooling Society.* Harmondsworth: Penguin.

24　N. Postman and C. Weingartner (1971) *Teaching as a Subversive Activity.* Harmondsworth: Penguin; H. Kohl (1969) *The Open Classroom.* New York: New York Review; J. Holt (1974) *How Children Fail.* Harmondsworth: Penguin; J. Kozol (1968) *Death at an Early Age.* Harmondsworth: Penguin.

25　M. Foucault (C. Gordon, ed.) (1980) *Power/Knowledge: Selected Interviews and Other Writings 1972–1977.* New York: Pantheon, p.39.

26　S. Hansen and J. Jensen (1972) *The Little Red Schoolbook.* Wellington: Alister Taylor.

27　New Zealand Post-Primary Teachers' Association (1969) *Education in Change.* Auckland: Longman Paul.

28　Ibid., p.xiv.

29　S. Middleton (1992) Equity, equality and biculturalism in the restructuring of New Zealand schools. *Harvard Educational Review* 62(3): 301–22.

30　S. Middleton (1992) Gender equity and school charters: theoretical and political questions for the 1990s, in Middleton and Jones (eds) *Women and Education in Aotearoa 2.*

31　Foucault, *Discipline and Punish,* p.141.

32　P. Patton (1979) Of power and prisons, in M. Morris and P. Patton (eds) *Michel Foucault: Power, Truth, Strategy.* Sydney: Feral Publications, p.121.

33　G. Greer (1971) *The Female Eunuch.* London: McGibbon and Gee. While she was in New Zealand, Greer was arrested and tried for obscenity on the grounds of a protest over her use of the word 'bullshit' in a public address.

34　S. Middleton, *Disciplining Sexuality.*

35　H. Leahy (1996) 'Focusing on a fault line: gender and education policy development in Aotearoa, New Zealand', unpublished MEd thesis. Victoria University of Wellington; S. Middleton (ed.) (1988) *Women and Education in Aotearoa 1.* Wellington: Port Nicholson Press.

36　K. Clarricoates (1978) Dinosaurs in the classroom: a re-examination of some aspects of the 'hidden curriculum' in primary schools. *Women's Studies International Quarterly* 1: 353–64; V. Walkerdine (1987) Sex, power and pedagogy, in M. Arnot and G. Weiner (eds) *Gender and the Politics of Schooling.* London: Hutchinson, pp.166–74.

37　*Childcare Quarterly* 7(1) 1986: 11.

38　Leahy, 'Focusing on a fault line'; Middleton, *Educating Feminists*; S. Middleton and H. May (1997).

39　K. Morris Matthews (1993) 'For and about women: a history of women's studies in New Zealand universities, 1975–1990,' unpublished DPhil thesis. University of Waikato.

40　Foucault, *Power/Knowledge,* p.96.

7 'To cook dinners with love in them'? Sexuality, marital status and women teachers in England and Wales, 1920–39

Alison Oram

Attitudes and ideas about women's sexuality changed significantly over the first half of the twentieth century. From being supposedly asexual in the nineteenth century, by the time of the Second World War middle class femininity could encompass sexual desires and sexual pleasure, at least within marriage. Changing discourses of gender and sexuality affected various sections of British society differently, but women teachers constitute a particularly interesting group. Specific tensions were created in their personal experience as a result of clashes between the gender-specific occupational structures they inhabited and dominant forms of femininity. As a result, women teachers were obliged to consciously engage with and analyse their sexual and marital status.

Changing discourses of femininity and sexuality

The women teachers discussed in this chapter worked in state elementary and secondary schools and can be seen as both ordinary and atypical women. They were ordinary in the sense that they were a large body of women workers whose family origins lay variously in the respectable working class, lower middle class and less affluent professional middle class. They lived their daily lives in the context of the same norms of femininity and family structures as other women.

Throughout the twentieth century the dominant expectation for women has been that they should marry. Represented as women's natural destiny, marriage was the only permitted place for the expression of female sexuality and provided the context for other fundamental feminine roles – motherhood and homemaking. Marriage brought women firmly into relationship with men; into heterosexuality, financial dependence and a caring role. To be unmarried was therefore to lack the basic ingredients of femininity and to have failed as a woman. The wider context of the falling birthrate, eugenic fears and the increasing popularization of 'new psychology' meant that the importance of motherhood and sexual fulfilment for feminine identity became strengthened during this period, and increased both the pressure to marry and the aberrant connotations of spinsterhood.

The expectation that women should marry did not change over the first half of the twentieth century, but it did gain a new edge in relation to ideas about female sexuality. Particularly influential in this was the work of the British sexologist Havelock Ellis. First published before the First World War, Ellis put forward the radical argument that it was normal for women to experience sexual desire and pleasure. More conservatively, however, he also recommended that this sexual instinct needed to be exercised, in marriage and motherhood.[1] These ideas found a wider constituency in the 1920s, especially through marriage manuals such as Marie Stopes's *Married Love*, first published in 1918.[2] British 'new psychology' similarly stressed biologistic 'instincts' and the importance of the 'normal family' for the healthy development of adults and children, and also contributed to the valorization of marriage.[3]

Both sexology and the new psychology presented marital heterosexuality as desirable and indeed necessary for women's health and happiness. Conversely, the repression of sexual and parental instincts might lead to anxiety and even mental illness. Single women thus faced the dangers of sexual repression and frustration which resulted in complexes and neuroses. Those who had deliberately avoided or rejected marriage could be further pathologized as frigid. As the idea of marriage as a psychological as well as a social necessity for women gained ground in the interwar years, single and celibate women who lacked an outlet for their sexual and parental instincts were increasingly vulnerable to being seen as warped and unfulfilled.[4] Existing negative stereotypes of spinsters as failures in femininity were augmented by this new pathologizing of spinsters' sexuality, while, at the same time, eugenic concern about the quality and quantity of the nation's children reinforced the idea that spinsters were failures because they were not mothers.

Women who married, on the other hand, were represented as contributing to national well-being, as well as being more fulfilled as individuals. The coupling of femininity with motherhood was given new prominence by the losses of the First World War. The middle class birthrate had dropped rapidly before the First World War, but in the 1930s eugenic concern with class differentials in fertility was overtaken by alarm that the birthrate had fallen to below replacement levels. Teachers – the 'cream of British womanhood' – continued to be seen as one of a number of key groups in the less affluent middle class among whom marriage should be encouraged.[5]

Professional identities and the marriage bar

Yet teachers' professional position set them apart. While teaching was a respectable, feminine and relatively easy to enter occupation in this period, it was also gendered as a masculine profession, offering a rewarding lifelong career after higher education and training. It was work with children, but it was also intellectual work, public service, and it offered some approximation to professional material rewards. All these elements were very important to many women teachers who forged a strong professional identity and attachment to, and pride in, their work. For example, women teachers did not necessarily wish to give up their work on marriage – for professional as well as for financial reasons. Teaching was the only occupation to offer reasonably high pay to large numbers of women. This financial security, which included a future pension, allowed women teachers to more easily recognize and avoid the dependency of marriage. Unlike most women, they were not obliged to marry in order to achieve a reasonable standard of living.

In the early 1920s a marriage bar was more widely enforced in teaching and, as a result, it became increasingly difficult for women teachers to combine their profession with marriage. Until this time it was sometimes possible for women teachers to continue after marriage if they desired. In a few areas there had been quite a strong tradition established of married women teaching in elementary schools – for example in London and some rural districts – and during the First World War married women had been encouraged to return to teaching. In 1921 as many as 18.9 per cent of women teachers were married.[6] But by 1926 about three-quarters of all local authorities operated some sort of marriage bar, and in the 1930s, the proportion of women elementary teachers who were married had dropped to about 10 per cent, although this figure conceals great local variations.[7] In the mid and late 1930s the situation eased slightly when the London County Council and a few other local authorities reviewed and raised their marriage bars, though in 1939 between 80 and 90 per cent still operated a bar.[8] Women secondary school teachers were similarly subject to marriage bars in the period, and had, in any case, little tradition of employment after marriage.

Marriage was an important signifier of successful adult femininity, but one which most teachers were unable to attain at the same time as practising their profession, especially in the interwar years, because of the marriage bar. Marital status was not a static condition, however. The increased interwar emphasis on the psychological problems of the 'unfulfilled spinster' added to the already difficult choices about marriage and created particular pressures for those women teachers who remained single. How could these discourses be negotiated? The varying ways that women teachers understood their lives – their subjectivity – shows how elements of personal identity are constructed.

The idea of subjectivity suggests a continuous and historically produced process, not a fixed state of being. Self-definitions and identities may shift as women move through the life cycle and take up different positions in relation to family, marriage and employment. It also acknowledges instability and conflict within people's identities.[9] In order to make sense of their lives, women teachers were obliged to negotiate differing and often contradictory requirements across workplace rules such as the marriage bar, family life, romantic and sexual desires, and the dominant social meanings of woman-hood. Because women teachers' professional lives did not easily fit conventional models of femininity, there were tensions in their subjectivity and life choices around sexuality and marriage in particular. A consequence of these pressures was that women teachers were likely to become conscious of these conflicts and constraints.[10]

Recent debates about memory and representation in oral and autobiographical evidence suggest how this method can provide a means of examining the different ways that knowledge and meaning are produced in people's lives.[11] To examine teachers' understandings of their life choices I carried out 12 interviews with retired women teachers, half of whom had worked in secondary schools and half in elementary schools. Half of this group married. Other life histories were selected from the University of Essex Oral History Archives, 'Family life and work before 1918' and from accounts by teachers in the Mass-Observation Archive at the University of Sussex.[12]

Choices around marriage

To achieve 'true femininity' – sexual fulfilment, a 'home of one's own' and motherhood – women teachers had to marry. However, in most local education authorities (LEAs), especially after the First World War, marriage involved giving up a secure post. Economic independence, sexual expression and motherhood could not be achieved together, either within marriage or outside it, without forfeiting respectability or femininity. The experiences of individual women teachers show how they became aware of these conflicts at an individual level and how they dealt with them. Teachers prized their economic and professional independence, and so were confronted in different ways with impossible choices concerning marriage and professionalism and work. But feminine marriageability, spinsterhood and sexuality were such personal issues that they could not be lightly ignored or easily negotiated.

One major pressure towards marriage was the stigma of remaining single. The general social attitude was that unmarried women were failed women, as the story told by one teacher illustrates:

Married women had more status. I went to teach in South Wales, where single women were more denigrated than they were in London. I was very struck by that. It was hard to put your finger on it, but one of the staff said to me, one day, that one of the miners' wives had said to her – this is a miner's wife speaking to a teacher – 'You know, you must enjoy life mustn't you, when you've got over the shame of being single.' And the teacher was amused at this, not having thought of herself like that. But it was a very general attitude.[13]

The view expressed by the miner's wife can also be read as a complex recognition that remaining single brought benefits as well as social disapprobation. The teacher had not equated femininity with marriage, for herself, and so could afford to be amused by the misunderstanding in the remark. Nevertheless the powerful social stigma of spinsterhood is also clear here.

For some teachers – or indeed for many teachers some of the time – even a strong professional identity and love of their work was not enough to set against the whole weight of negativity attached to spinsterhood and the slur of unfemininity. One secondary schoolmistress felt this pressure very keenly and described how 'later on I very nearly got married because of the status. Because, really, you got the stereotype of being almost inhuman if you were not married.'[14]

This may have been mitigated slightly by class differences in attitudes to single women. A social niche for the professional middle class spinster was fairly well established from the late nineteenth century, acceptable because the types of profession available, teaching and nursing, were seen as using traditional feminine qualities. It meant that all women teachers could associate themselves with a specific identity and a 'permission' to be single, albeit one which was becoming increasingly undermined by the discourses discussed above.[15] This could counter the 'shame' and unwomanliness of the failure to marry, though often to a very limited extent.

For those teachers who sought marriage however, even courtship posed problems. A major difficulty for women teachers was that of meeting suitable potential husbands in the first place. As an adolescent, the future teacher was to some extent segregated from her peers, whatever her social class, by the necessity of studying. One survey of secondary school teachers published in the mid-1930s commented:

As a girl, the teacher has often had fewer opportunities of contact with members of the opposite sex than those, for example, who leave school at fourteen, and who are probably walking out with their boy friends whilst she is sitting at home preparing her lessons. If, after her school days are ended, she goes to a women's college, she is normally hedged in by rules governing her association and conduct with men.[16]

Even the minority of teachers who went to mixed colleges and universities may have had little time or inclination for courtship. One respondent, Miss

Wainwright, described socializing with men students on her postgraduate teaching course at Cambridge, but on terms of friendship rather than romance. It was seen as unusual to be keen on having boyfriends.[17]

Even in social circumstances where they might meet men, teachers were hindered by the negative image of women teachers as unattractive, unmarriageable spinsters. This was partly because they were seen as clever and therefore unfeminine. One teacher reflected:

> Actually, once you were a teacher, you didn't think you would get married . . . Teachers used to go to great lengths to say they were anything but teachers – if they went on holiday or anything like that, they'd never admit to being teachers, because that would put off every man in sight. So young teachers . . . said they were secretaries or something like that . . . I think people were afraid of teachers then . . . there were more people who were afraid of the bluestocking . . . There was definitely a feeling in society generally that you wouldn't want to be too clever if you were going to be married.[18]

This seems to have particularly affected secondary school teachers. I have found no evidence of elementary school teachers disguising their occupation. Teachers who denied their profession in this way recognized that marriageable femininity in this period was symbolically constructed as inferior in status to masculinity; women had to be younger, shorter and less intellectually competent than their husbands.

An important, though unquantifiable group of women teachers were not especially committed to their profession, and were content to give up teaching for marriage and conventional femininity. One single teacher, who was planning to marry soon, answered a Mass-Observation question on marriage by expressing a degree of complacency and satisfaction at having fitted into the norm so successfully:

> Even though I know now whom I am going to marry, eventually, I can clearly remember that before meeting my future husband, it was my considered opinion (as well as a conviction based on instinct) that for me a career, however successful, would be unsatisfactory, compared with happy marriage and family life, with children.[19]

This teacher represented her experience in terms of dominant ideas about natural instincts and the normal woman's route to happiness.

But a variety of personal, professional and financial pressures, including a strong sense of independence and self-worth militated against marriage being an easy choice for many women teachers. To marry in her twenties after only a few years of teaching was a difficult choice for the woman teacher quite apart from the marriage bar, since it would entail wasting the investment made in her education and training. Teachers who had accepted public money in grants for training – the majority – were obliged to sign 'The Pledge' whereby they promised to teach for five years after training.[20]

While this acted as a direct disincentive to early marriage, indirectly it also signalled that the teacher had a wider value as a woman than that conventionally measured by the ability to find a husband. State and familial investment in their education both enabled and required women teachers to think carefully about marriage as a personal goal. As a result of her qualifications and professional position, the young teacher may have regarded herself as set apart from the ordinary run of young women whose route led them from a dead-end job straight into marriage. Women civil service clerks, for example, did not develop a professional identity as did teachers, and positively chose marriage as a way of consolidating and improving their status.[21]

Financial obligations for family members meant that some women teachers could not seriously consider marriage. Miss Drysdale described the structural constraints of 'The Pledge' and the marriage bar, but it was clear that these formal constraints were less important than the need to support her elderly mother: 'I always felt that I couldn't get married because I must hang on to the job. The job was more important because it was a case of bringing money into the home.'[22] As the central breadwinner, this teacher did not have a real choice; she believed that her duty lay with her family and was comfortable with this role. The financial sacrifice made by many families to support their daughters through teacher training may have enhanced the woman teacher's sense of responsibility towards parents and siblings and caused them to renounce or defer marriage.

Some women teachers valued their personal independence and directly contrasted this with what marriage could offer. One teacher wrote to Mass-Observation at the point of having to make a decision about whether to marry:

> It seems more pleasing to me to be facing a day where I shall be away from home earning my own living than if circumstances were such that I should have to be attending to the breakfasts of a husband and family. No, I do not want my mother's life, or the life of any one of the women in our avenue, to cook dinners with love in them.[23]

Being a teacher enabled this woman to weigh up her true inclinations and reject a life of domesticity. Even secondary school teachers, who had no tradition of continuing after marriage, felt the stress between marriage and their profession. One married secondary school teacher said in 1939: 'I did wish to teach and I do wish to teach and I think it exceedingly hard lines on anybody at all who wishes at the same time to marry.'[24]

The desire for marriage and the recognition of its costs in professional terms were in constant tension for many women teachers – particularly the younger women. One young woman teacher who fell in love with a young master in the boys' department of her school found that his salary was not sufficient to keep them both and provide for a family. 'I shall be miserable if I have to give up my work or my man,' she said.[25] If a marriage bar was in force, the only means of enjoying a heterosexual relationship while keeping a teaching post was either to marry secretly or cohabit secretly with a male partner. Either option carried many risks in this period. 'Living together' was morally unacceptable and would bring instant dismissal if revealed, as would concealment of marriage. While it is unlikely that there were more than a few cases of cohabitation among teachers in the interwar years, it is not difficult to find evidence of both solutions. One teacher married secretly and moved from Liverpool to Oldham to hide the fact, wearing her wedding ring round her neck. Her 'fiancé' visited her every weekend with the connivance of her landlady.[26] There were also dismissals and legal cases involving teachers who had secretly married.[27]

These solutions were possible only in large towns and cities and even then were risky and anxiety provoking. Some teachers did consider having sexual relationships outside marriage in the interwar years.[28] These young women teachers valued their work, but also wanted to form relationships with men and eventually marry. We might speculate that the increased attention drawn to women's sexual needs in the interwar period gave them greater strength to negotiate socially unacceptable solutions to their dilemma. One London teacher described the circumstances which enabled her to live with her partner for several years before they were able to marry, and the tensions which accompanied such a transgression of social mores:

> I was living with David, and that had to be kept very quiet. It was only the fact that [my headmistress] was such a good friend and let me use the school for addresses and all that and helped me out in every way . . . It would have been really serious if they had found out. The phrase 'living in sin', it really meant that, and as you were sinful you weren't the right sort to have anything to do with children, so you both would have lost [your teaching] Certificates, so we had to be awfully careful. We lived in a state of constant terror because if you were ill staff might call on you . . . I remember one was coming one day, I remember saying to David, 'come along, remove all traces of male habitation', so he pulled his dressing gown down from the bedroom door, but it was a tension.[29]

She stressed that such women teachers were not making political points about Bloomsbury-style free love; they would certainly have married if they could: 'as soon as the bar was lifted a whole lot got married'.[30]

Negotiating spinsterhood

Sexology and psychology had also categorized lesbian sexuality for the first time, and created an ambiguous overlap with spinsterhood. Now that the sexual instinct was identified in every woman, the deviant categories of spinster and lesbian could easily be confused, and female friendship increasingly came into question. Media attention to lesbianism in the 1920s also raised public awareness.[31] Single women teachers were often targeted in these new representations – by the popular press, doctors, educationalists and anti-feminist men teachers – as unfulfilled celibates, as predatory lesbians, as man-hating feminists, and hence as undesirable role models.[32] Furthermore, in making a case against the marriage bar, women teachers' organizations sometimes used the argument that the experience of marriage and mother-hood made women especially fitted for teaching, an argument that became increasingly powerful. But the other side of this argument was that single women teachers, who had not 'lived the full and complete woman's life', could be seen as narrow, less psychologically well balanced and a potentially bad influence in the schools.[33] Their professional status could be under-mined as well as their femininity.

As perceptions of spinsterhood became increasingly negative, it is likely that it became more difficult for individual women teachers to reconcile or explain their failure to marry. Since discourses of spinsterhood predomi-nantly involved notions of personal cost and denial, it was hard for teachers to understand their marital status other than as an individual failing of femininity. This was particularly the case for single women teachers in their thirties onwards, who had quite evidently not found their feminine destiny within marriage and were now 'confirmed spinsters'. How could they describe their lives to themselves and to others in terms of dominant ideas of femininity?

The influence of changing ideas about spinsterhood on women teachers themselves is difficult to assess, though they were likely to be circulating among educated and middle class women, and perhaps especially among teachers who studied human psychology in a professional capacity. But though influential, these ideas were not hegemonic, even in the 1930s after the new psychology had been quite widely popularized, and single women teachers as individuals took them on in varying ways. Some teachers did internalize the view that they had stunted lives.[34] Teachers who wrote to Mass-Observation regarded their colleagues (and by extension themselves) as being 'as shallow as teaspoons' and as leading 'very narrow lives'.[35] One exhibited considerable self-hatred and frustration in declaring, 'I loathe and detest living in a school, and think that women who teach are the most awful things that ever happened.'[36]

Many teachers felt obliged to negotiate at least some aspects of the spin-ster image, while ignoring other elements. There was certainly a concern among many single women teachers to affirm their albeit unfulfilled hetero-sexual normality. Mary Clarke (a successful headmistress) was keen to stress that she was attracted to men, though she never married: 'although I had been from childhood susceptible to the charms of the other sex, I was not prepared to accept marriage on these terms.'[37] Other teachers suggested that a boyfriend or fiancé had been killed in the First World War (in many cases genuinely of course), or in more general terms that they belonged to the postwar generation for whom there were insufficient men. A wide cohort of women used this tactic to deflect doubts about their normality.[38]

The views of those teachers who wrote to Mass-Observation about themselves are interesting, since they show attitudes in the late 1930s (or in some cases during the Second World War), when it might be supposed that new ideas about women's instincts and sexuality had become widely disseminated. However, as a self-conscious, self-selecting sample they may not have been typical. One teacher who replied to Mass-Observation had taken on the new ideas, but they were in competition with her professional identity and her opinion that the marriage bar was unfair: 'In the past I would have preferred marriage and children, but would have felt resentful about giving up my work. I believe marriage is essential to a woman for her complete development and realization'.[39] Some teachers were prepared to acknowledge certain feminine instincts, but to fulfil them in less conventional ways. One single woman teacher wrote: 'I have a very strong maternal instinct (which was, I suppose, what compelled me to seek out a child to adopt, which I did in 1921 at the age of 36)'.[40]

When women teachers expressed positive feelings about their spinsterhood, they may have moulded their subjective experiences to fit into acceptable conventions. The testimony to Mass-Observation of one 62-year-old spinster provides a good example of this point:

> I cannot remember ever having thought about marrying. I'm sure that I did not deliberately decide against it. I think I was too busy thinking about my profession and other things to bother about it. I liked the company of men, but never met one whom I had the slightest inclination to marry, and never had a love affair. While I think that a happy married life is probably preferable to a happy single life, when I see other people's husbands my usual feeling is one of thankfulness that I haven't one of my own.[41]

The writer is careful not to reject marriage and men in principle, or the idea that happy marriage is the best way to live. In this way she accedes to dominant ideas about marriage and normal femininity. But everything in her own experience mentioned here contradicts this norm, including prioritizing her work over marriage and judging her friends and acquaintances' husbands as unattractive. Women teachers felt obliged to show familiarity with current ideas, but did not necessarily accept them wholesale.

Some women in this period took on the new psychology and reworked it into a more positive version for single women, by utilizing and developing the idea of 'sublimation'. This was the term given to 'the process by which instinctive emotions are diverted from their original ends and redirected to purposes satisfying to the individual and of value to the community.'[42] This theory suggested that spinsters could avoid repressing their sexual and parental instincts, which might have harmful consequences such as 'nerves' and neuroses. Instead, through self-knowledge and awareness, single women could more healthily sublimate these drives and direct them to happier ends, via female friendship, and by working with children, for example. The psychiatrist Esther Harding saw female friendships as the place where single women's emotional life and sexual drives could be expressed, rather than being repressed.[43] The notion of sublimation was a particularly effective retort for women teachers who could argue that, far from being dangerously repressed, their parental instincts and sexual drives were beneficially sublimated in their work – to the good of themselves, their pupils and society as a whole.

The idea of sublimation was indeed disseminated in discussions about women teachers. In her 1935 survey of secondary schoolmistresses, Mary Birkinshaw observed: 'for the majority of teachers the society of men is restricted and the marriage bar is applied. Some among them do not mind. Their sexual impulses are sublimated satisfactorily in teaching.'[44] Individual teachers showed some awareness of these ideas and used them. A respondent to Mass-Observation wrote: 'I have always felt that if marriage did not present itself, one could only become mature by throwing oneself into other activities – certainly not by hankering after marriage.'[45]

Women teachers' associations also used the sublimation model on behalf of teachers. The 1933 president of the Association of Assistant Mistresses suggested that most women desired marriage, but that:

> If we do not [marry], let us see that we do not waste our lives in vague repinings, becoming abnormal and irritable, difficult to live with and impossible to work with. It is quite possible to survive our disappointment, to be abundantly happy, and to use those qualities which would have made us good wives and mothers in making our work a more vivid and beautiful thing.[46]

The feminist teachers' union, the National Union of Women Teachers (NUWT), also used these ideas to counter attacks made on its members as frustrated spinster teachers. In 1935 a Dr Williams alleged that women teachers were 'embittered, sexless or homosexual hoydens who try to mould the girls into their own pattern'. This accusation was angrily repudiated by the NUWT: 'he should know that in the vast majority of cases a woman teacher's work is a complete outlet for her maternal instincts. Her womanly impulses are sublimated and diverted, but splendidly employed.'[47] Interestingly, the NUWT was reverting here to the older idea that women's instincts were primarily maternal rather than sexual.

Women teachers could also emphasize other, more traditional, elements of personal identity or self-hood as a counterweight to their failure to achieve marriage, though this was not always a completely satisfying answer. One way of resolving femininity with spinsterhood was to draw on feminine roles based on the family. One teacher in her thirties wrote of her alternative role as aunt: 'I still want to get married, and I still want a family of my own. I think they are two of the best things in life. But I have stopped expecting either and will just have to become a gracious spinster and a devoted aunt.'[48]

A more powerful familial identity was that of daughter, especially if this involved close integration into the family, caring for elderly parents or contributing financial support, as many teachers did. Contemporary statistics and surveys show that many women teachers – probably at least one-third – had dependants, most commonly elderly or ailing parents.[49] There was a strong social expectation that it was a daughter's role to care for her elderly parents; it was seen as morally laudable and to some extent was publicly recognized. In this way, some women teachers, like Miss Drysdale cited above, could counterpose their failure to marry by pointing to dependants they had to support and care for, an honourable and womanly duty, though one less archetypally feminine than marriage and motherhood.

Women teachers who not only had disdained marriage but also had formed emotional and perhaps sexual bonds with other women had further issues to contend with. It might be assumed that women teachers who lived with a friend had to negotiate the increasing doubt about 'obsessive' female friendships, possible aspersions on their femininity, and the growing social awareness of lesbianism by the 1930s. One advice book to spinsters, published in 1935, observed that 'within recent years the subject of sexual inversion or homosexuality has become a topic of frequent discussion in certain sections of society' and that as a result, 'friendly couples of the same sex are now much more readily suspected of homosexual tendencies than would have been the case, say, twenty years ago'.[50] However, despite this awareness, women teacher couples may still have been regarded benignly. Their education, respectability and middle class status may have protected them from suspicion, particularly if they were older and seen to have left the years of youth and sexual attractiveness behind them. Coupling up with a friend may well have been construed as sensible for those women unfortunate enough to have been left without a man.

Women teachers themselves varied widely in their awareness of these issues. One 29-year-old secondary schoolmistress reported in 1939: 'Though I loved teaching I found the life unbearable, chiefly through petty instructions, a high moral atmosphere, homo-sexuality, and the empire-building tone of the school.'[51] However, an elementary teacher of the same generation suggested that consciousness of lesbianism was not very widely shared:

> I would say right up to the second world war, homosexuality, lesbianism were almost terms which you didn't use and didn't recognise. Lesbianism – I just didn't know what it was all about. No one ever said two women living together were lesbians.[52]

Thus spinster teachers were not necessarily going to be subject to 'a readiness to suspect an "unnatural relationship" whenever two women live together.'[53] Even in the 1930s, after the new psychology had been widely popularized and after the high profile trial in 1928 of Radclyffe Hall's lesbian novel *The Well of Loneliness* for obscenity, the effects of the sexualization of spinsters were partial and fragmented.

Women teachers' professional associations, especially the small feminist NUWT, also provided social networks within which friendships could be established and sustained without social disapprobation. These friendships would have carried a range of emotional significance, from casual friendships maintained to share social activities, to lifelong partnerships. These latter relationships were reminiscent of those forged in prewar suffrage days when female friendship had been seen as a positive virtue. One brief example stands for many. The prominent NUWT activist and feminist Miss Emily Phipps (b. 1865), moved to Swansea in 1895 where she later became headmistress of the Swansea Municipal Secondary Girls' School. 'Her closest associate was another Swansea headmistress, Miss Clare Neal, who had come with her to Swansea.'[54] Clare Neal died in 1937 and her obituary in *The Woman Teacher* was clear about the depth and meaning of her friendship with Emily Phipps. It described the period at the turn of the century when they had both taught in the same Swansea school:

> it was then that the friendship which already existed between Miss Phipps and Miss Neal was further deepened and strengthened so that it became a life-long unbroken association. To her chosen friend, Miss Phipps, she was the light that never failed.

This account of her life also described a number of ways in which the partnership was publicly accepted by colleagues and friends.[55]

Conclusion

Women teachers faced new challenges between the wars as public discourses contributed to the increased sexualization of women in marriage, and concurrent criticism of spinsters. It was suggested that the professional abilities of single women teachers were undermined by their marital status as spinsters, and they were subject to increasing aspersions on their sexuality and femininity. At the same time, teachers' choices around marriage and sexual expression were tightening up as marriage bars were more widely imposed. In this context how could teachers both pursue their professional commitment and live within social expectations of femininity?

The evidence suggests that women teachers negotiated this in a whole variety of ways. They were in a unique position to identify and critique the gendered structures of the profession and society which created impossible choices for them and which they sometimes addressed politically. This awareness did not always make it easier to construct a comfortable individual personal life, however. In taking on dominant ideas and reworking them, women teachers occasionally made radical challenges to contemporary moral codes around marriage and sexuality – by cohabiting with male partners, for example. More frequently they used traditional and well established forms of femininity, such as that of the dutiful daughter, to counter negative stereotyping. Despite the emerging stigma of lesbianism, they also continued important feminist traditions of community by engaging in female friendships and partnerships.

Acknowledgements

I would like to thank Annmarie Turnbull and Anna Clark for their helpful comments on the draft of this chapter.

Notes

1 For detailed discussion of Ellis's work see M. Jackson (1994) *The Real Facts of Life: Feminism and the Politics of Sexuality c.1850–1940*. London: Taylor and Francis, ch.5. J. Weeks (1981) *Sex, Politics and Society: The Regulation of Sexuality since 1800*. Harlow: Longman, pp.146–52. R. Porter and L. Hall (1995) *The Facts of Life: The Creation of Sexual Knowledge in Britain, 1650–1950*. London: Yale University Press, chs 7–9.

2 M.C. Stopes (1995) *Married Love: A New Contribution to the Solution of Sex Difficulties*, 29th edn. London: Gollancz.

3 L. Hearnshaw (1964) *A Short History of British Psychology 1840–1940*. London: Methuen, pp.166–7, 238–9. Weeks, *Sex, Politics and Society*, p.155. For an example see J.A. Hadfield (1924) *Psychology and Morals: An Analysis of Character*. London: Methuen, pp.162–4.

4 L. Bland (1983) Purity, motherhood, pleasure or threat? Definitions of female sexuality 1900–1970s, in S. Cartledge and J. Ryan (eds) *Sex and Love: New Thoughts on Old Contradictions*. London: Women's Press, pp.17, 21. S. Jeffreys (1985) *The Spinster and her Enemies: Feminism and Sexuality 1880–1930*. London: Pandora, chs 5–10.

5 *Times Educational Supplement* (*TES*), 19 December 1931, p.473.

6 *TES*, 29 December 1927, p.569.

7 Public Record Office. Ed 24/1744. Returns for 1926. *TES*, 16 November 1929, p.504; 24 February 1934, p.59.

8 *TES*, 20 July 1935, pp.257–8; 7 December 1935, p.59. National Union of Women Teachers (NUWT) Records, Institute of Education Archive, London. Box 176, Report, 31 May 1938. For further details about the marriage bar, see A. Oram (1996) *Women Teachers and Feminist Politics 1900–39*. Manchester: Manchester University Press, especially pp.57–72.

9 This use of the concept of subjectivity springs from recent debates in feminist history about the importance of meaning and language as well as material causes in

understanding women's position and gender relations in the past. C. Hall (1992) *White, Male and Middle-Class: Explorations in Feminism and History*. Cambridge: Polity Press, pp.21–4. D. Riley (1988) *'Am I That Name?': Feminism and the Category of 'Women' in History*. London: Macmillan. J. Scott (1986) Gender: a useful category of historical analysis. *American Historical Review* 91: 1053–75. M. Maynard (1995) Beyond the 'Big Three': the development of feminist theory into the 1990s. *Women's History Review* 4(3): 259–81.

10 A major argument of my book is that tensions between professionalism and femininity contributed to the widespread politicization of women teachers as feminists. Oram, *Women Teachers and Feminist Politics*, chs 1–3.

11 A. Portelli (1981) The peculiarities of oral history. *History Workshop Journal* 12: 96–107. J. Scott (1991) The evidence of experience. *Critical Inquiry* 17: 773–97.

12 These latter were Monthly Diaries 1937–39 and Directive Replies 1939–45: Attitudes to Marriage. The Mass-Observation material is copyright of the Trustees of the Mass-Observation Archive at the University of Sussex, and reproduced by permission of the Curtis Brown Group Ltd, London.

13 Interview with Miss Vera Reid (b. 1910), 6 September 1989 (all names of interviewees are pseudonyms, except for Mrs Nan McMillan).

14 Ibid.

15 C. Dyhouse (1981) *Girls Growing Up in Late Victorian and Edwardian England*. London: Routledge and Kegan Paul, pp.78, 174; M. Vicinus (1985) *Independent Women: Work and Community for Single Women 1850–1920*. London: Virago, chs 1 and 8.

16 M. Birkinshaw (1935) *The Successful Teacher*. London: Hogarth Press, p.77. And see P. Summerfield (1987) Cultural reproduction in the education of girls: a study of girls' secondary schooling in two Lancashire towns, 1900–50, in F. Hunt (ed.) *Lessons for Life: The Schooling of Girls and Women 1850–1950*. Oxford: Basil Blackwell, pp.164–6.

17 Interview with Miss Sarah Wainwright (b. 1914), 26 May 1989. Also see A. Barlow (1969) *Seventh Child*. London: Duckworth, p.46.

18 Interview with Miss Sarah Wainwright, 26 May 1989.

19 Mass-Observation Archive, University of Sussex. Miss Howard (pseudonym). Respondent no. 3541. Aged 25, physical education teacher. Directive Replies: Attitudes to Marriage, March 1944.

20 It was quite common for teachers to have to postpone marriage in order to pay back these LEA loans. Interview with Miss Vera Reid (b. 1910), 6 September 1989.

21 K. Sanderson (1988) 'Social mobility in the life cycle of some women clerical workers', unpublished PhD thesis. University of Essex, pp.49–50, 141, 201, 211, 227, 278–9.

22 Interview with Miss Ruth Drysdale (b. 1904), 8 September 1989.

23 Mass-Observation Archive. Miss A. Hibberd (pseudonym). Respondent no. 0078. Aged 37, infant teacher, Prestwich, Manchester. Monthly diaries, April 1937.

24 Association of Assistant Mistresses (AAM) (January 1939) Annual Report, p.43.

25 *The Star*, 24 May 1935.

26 J. Greaves (1982) A woman in education fifty years ago. *Spare Rib* 124 (October): 7.

27 NUWT Records. Box 176, Married Women Teachers. *Evening News*, 30 June 1933. *Daily Herald*, 19 July 1933. *Daily Sketch*, 29 December 1937.

28 Interview with Mrs Julia Maynard, 28 July 1989, who described such discussions among her teacher friends in London. She also described how they obtained birth control advice without being married.

29 Interview with Mrs Nan McMillan, 25 July 1986 and 29 July 1987. Even this solution meant women teachers had to forgo motherhood, a fact she recalled with anger.

30 Ibid.

31 C. Smith-Rosenburg (1985) *Disorderly Conduct: Visions of Gender in Victorian America*. New York: Knopf, pp.275–80. Jeffreys, *The Spinster and her Enemies*, ch.6. Weeks, *Sex, Politics and Society*, pp.116–17.

32 See Oram, *Women Teachers and Feminist Politics*, pp.189–91 for further details.

33 *TES*, 7 July 1914, p.113.

34 *News Chronicle*, 20 February 1930.

35 Mass-Observation Archive, University of Sussex. Miss Wall (pseudonym). Respondent no. 0188. Aged 32, lived Bishop Auckland. Monthly diary 1937. Miss Knight (pseudonym). Respondent no. 0102. Aged 35, elementary teacher, Cardiff. Monthly diary, November 1937.

36 Mass-Observation Archive. Miss A. Redford (pseudonym). Respondent no. 1659. Aged 23, secondary school teacher. Self-reports, 1939.

37 M. Clarke (1973) *A Short Life of Ninety Years* Edinburgh: A. and M. Huggins, p.17; also see p.30.

38 Interview with Mrs Nan McMillan, 29 July 1987.

39 Mass-Observation Archive. Miss Batchelor (pseudonym). Respondent no. 2975. Aged 33, elementary teacher, Thornaby. Directive Replies: Attitudes to Marriage, March 1944.

40 Mass-Observation Archive. Miss Gardner (pseudonym). Respondent no. 2475. Aged 58, training college lecturer, Norwich. Directive Replies: Attitudes to Marriage, March 1944.

41 Mass-Observation Archive. Miss Palmer (pseudonym). Respondent no. 1056. Aged 62, retired. Directive Replies: Attitudes to Marriage, March 1944.

42 Hadfield, *Psychology and Morals*, p.152. I have made this argument in A. Oram (1992) Repressed and thwarted, or bearer of the New World? The spinster in interwar feminist discourses. *Women's History Review* 1(3): 413–34.

43 M.E. Harding (1933) *The Way of All Women: A Psychological Interpretation*. London: Longman, pp.96–8.

44 Birkinshaw, *The Successful Teacher*, p.79.

45 Mass-Observation Archive. Miss Caine (pseudonym). Respondent no. 2984. Aged 34, Yorkshire teacher. Directive Replies: Attitudes to Marriage, March 1944.

46 AAM (January 1933) *Annual Report*, p.16.

47 *Daily Herald*, 5 September 1935.

48 Mass-Observation Archive. Miss MacDonald (pseudonym). Respondent no. 3415. Aged 31, schoolmistress, Slough. Directive Replies: Attitudes to Marriage, March 1944.

49 Royal Commission on Equal Pay (1946) *Report*. Cmd. 6937 pp.126–30. Birkinshaw, *The Successful Teacher*, p.68.

50 L. Hutton (1935) *The Single Woman and her Emotional Problems*. London: Bailliere, Tindall and Cox, pp.105, 106.
51 Mass-Observation Archive. Miss Smith (pseudonym). Respondent no. 1420. Aged 29, secondary schoolmistress, Kent. Self-reports, 1939.
52 Interview with Nan McMillan by Sue Bruley, 26 November 1976. I am grateful to Sue Bruley for giving me access to her interview material.
53 Hutton, *The Single Woman*, p.135.
54 NUWT Records. Box 124, papers.
55 *The Woman Teacher*, 15 January 1937, p.127. For further details see Oram, Women Teachers and Feminist Politics, pp.209–11. H. Kean (1990) *Deeds Not Words: The Lives of Suffragette Teachers*. London: Pluto Press, pp.118–20.

8 Pathways and subjectivities of Portuguese women teachers through life histories

Helena C. Araújo

If the subjective story is what the researcher is after, the life history approach becomes the most valid method.[1]

My aim in this chapter is to make visible the biographies of women teachers, which are so neglected in Portuguese social sciences and which have been traditionally excluded from the construction of a public discourse on schooling. Although in fact some published memoirs and autobiographies of Portuguese men teachers exist, it is much more difficult to find the voices of women teachers. To begin to redress this lack, in this chapter I provide a close reading of the lives of five Portuguese women teachers; following Liz Stanley, I attempt to 'speak the close detail of the fabric of women's lives'.[2] My explicit intention is to appreciate and value women teachers' lives and to build on feminist claims for 'the imperative right of women to have a "voice", their need to express their different experience, and the importance of uncovering suppressed and forgotten female texts.'[3] A feminist approach of this kind expands C. Wright Mills's notion of the 'sociological imagination' which, in his famous words, 'enables us to grasp history and biography and the relations between the two within society.'[4]

Historians and sociologists concerned with individualized pathways and subjectivities stress the need for scholars to concentrate on the lives of those who have been marginalized by the structures of power in society, those who are usually perceived as having common lives.[5] At the same time, it is important to emphasize that those who have been marginalized also need to be perceived as active subjects, who often challenge the oppressive representations and processes in which they are located, not only individually but also through their participation in social groups. As Stanley argues, biographical subjects are 'agents of their lives and not ... puppets [whose] thoughts and actions [are] determined.'[6] My intention in recording women teachers' life histories thus extends beyond merely recounting the main stages of their careers. Although the specific and detailed aspects of these women's professional development help us to understand the process of feminization in their lives, their life histories can also reveal the way they struggled daily to make sense of both their teaching activities and their family lives.

The hidden struggles

The professional lives of these Portuguese teachers started in a period of 'democratic instability' characterizing the republican years (1910–26). After the military coup of 28 May 1926, a period of political instability continued during the Military Dictatorship (1926–33), until the authoritarian regime of Salazar was able to gain hegemony over the political process within the Portuguese social formation. Portuguese women in these years lived in a society undergoing a slow process of industrialization in which a conservative Catholic Church supported by a large peasantry and rural bourgeoisie exercised great influence. In this society, the republicans expected the state to play a hegemonic role in modernizing society; as part of their concern with modernization the question of the education of women was frequently discussed. In 1926, only 27 per cent of girls were in primary school and in other sectors of the education system they represented a small minority. Women worked in factories or domestic service and those in 'non-manual' work were concentrated in a limited number of jobs, such as teaching. Ana Osório, a well known feminist of the time, stressed that the work situation of Portuguese women was worse than in other countries. She mentioned male resistance to opening up non-manual areas of work to women for fear of competition. In her view, the atmosphere of 'moral asphyxia' of Portuguese life[7] and the prejudices instilled by convent education contributed to a situation in which women lived 'as if they were incarcerated in a prison from which they can only escape by scaling the walls.'[8] After the military coup of 28 May 1926, women's legal rights were not immediately challenged. These rights changed mainly with the 1933 Constitution (the dictator Salazar was already in power) where the family was identified as a crucially important institution in which women were to be subordinate. Their access to citizenship was stated clearly as dependent 'upon their nature and the well-being of the family.'[9]

In her analysis of the ideologies and politics of Salazarism between 1926 and 1939, Filomena Mónica acknowledges the importance of studying resistances to the regime: 'If censorship, and the imposition of a rigid orthodoxy, after 1932, suffocated public debates, they could not suppress subterranean heresies. The problem is that we still know little of the hidden struggles that occurred during Salazarism'.[10] Explaining the ways that the transition from one political regime to another were experienced by women teachers in their workplaces can help uncover these hidden struggles: Was the new situation ignored? Was there a process of assimilation into the 'new order'? Did they develop various strategies to deal with an increasingly threatening situation for teachers' autonomy? The way in which women teachers confronted patriarchal relations also reveals hidden struggles. What was their knowledge of the changing legal situation of women? How did they contend with the renewed accent on their role in the family (more emphasized in the Estado Novo)? What was their opinion of, and attitude towards, the feminist movement? What meaning did they attach to their situation as women teachers in the public sphere, often working in remote villages, living alone with their children or leaving them behind with their families?

Through gathering these life histories, my own development as a feminist researcher took on a new meaning in what Le Grand calls an 'implicational heuristic', i.e. 'a way of finding, of discovering, which means to give birth to oneself, through the act of writing.'[11] Denzin has written in somewhat similar terms, stressing that 'when a writer writes a biography, he or she writes him or herself into the life of the subject written about.'[12] This process of giving birth to myself resulted from my search for meanings and words that could express the richness and deep feelings of these women teachers and the contradictions they lived. As Stanley states: ' "Doing biography" changes how you think about yourself, and this in turn changes how you understand the subject.'[13] In addition to recognizing their *voices*, I want to acknowledge the relationship between these teachers and myself: sometimes as close friendship arising out of curiosity, understanding, admiration and affection; and even, sometimes, as a kind of complicity between women.

The life histories of these women teachers yield detailed information about their lives as active participants in their workplaces, as well as spectators of a civil society which excluded them in many respects (such as with regard to the right to vote). It is through examining women's pathways and the contexts in which they developed that we gain some sense of 'the private nature of so much of women's lives.'[14] (By 'private' I mean what they did in the household, as well as what they did in the workplace.) My concern here is not to detail every aspect of their lives. Instead, Stanley's conception of the kaleidoscope or reflexive biography comes closer to capturing my approach: 'A reflexive biography rejects the "truth" in favour of "it all depends", on how you look and precisely what you look at and when you look at it. This is the "kaleidoscope" effect: you look and you see one fascinatingly complex pattern'.[15] I see the metaphor of the kaleidoscope presented by Stanley as crucial to an understanding of women's lives and to the writing of women's history. In the following discussion, the pathways and subjectivities of these women are described in a more detailed and systematic way, with my own analysis presented indented and unjustified in order to highlight the differences between these two kinds of discourse.

Career pathways and the context of professional and family lives

This chapter is based on my conversations with five Portuguese women teachers born between 1899 and 1910. To safeguard their anonymity, I have called them Luisa, Isaura, Ana, Teresa and Laura. It is now time to introduce them briefly. Luisa, Isaura and Laura started their professional lives before 28 May 1926; Ana and Teresa in the following years. Luisa, Teresa and Laura were 19 years of age when they entered teaching; Isaura was 22; Ana started when she was 26. They retired in their late sixties or early seventies. All of them married and had children, and later became grandmothers and even great-grandmothers. At the time of our meetings, all of them were widows. Generally, they praised their professional lives and defined themselves as having been very much involved in teaching. Each started her teaching career in a small village, initially as a relief teacher, and later in a permanent post. Only after some years were they finally able to come to teach in or near a town, which was generally considered to be a desirable step in the development of their professional careers.

All five women teachers shared the need to make a living. Although Isaura's parents were rich landowners, they had sixteen children and they were aware that the land would not provide a living for all of them. Therefore, the daughters needed an education to earn a living as well as the sons. Laura's situation was like Isaura's in that her parents also saw that the land would not be enough to provide for the future lives of their descendants. Teresa's father played a crucial role with regard to this question, pleading for Teresa's professional work against his wife's judgement since he supported the idea that women should be autonomous and work outside the household. Ana's parents wanted to provide all nine children with 'a position', which definitely meant to be able to get a certificate to enter the non-manual world of work.

As might be expected, these women teachers did not present a unified view of teaching. Teresa and Laura are probably the two who most clearly saw teaching as their vocation. Teresa quite often mentioned her ability to teach small children. This does not mean that she believed in a natural gift; instead, it was her early association with school life, through attending her sister's classes in the local primary school, as well as the talks and debates with her father, that she saw as explaining her facility as a teacher. Ana, on the other hand, emphasized that job opportunities for girls were scarce in her time: 'Three of my sisters became primary teachers, with me we were four.' Among the four sisters, only one sensed a vocation. Ana said: 'As a teacher I had no vocation, but a vocation is something that we could acquire later. I had no special inclination for children. . . . I could have been a civil servant or something similar. I went into teaching because I had no other opportunities.'

Isaura and Luisa went into teaching for different reasons. Isaura had thought about going to university. However, she already had a boyfriend and wanted to marry quickly, against the will of her family. A university course would delay marriage further whereas the college would provide her with a certificate and the possibility of making a living and thus of marrying almost immediately after the completion of the course. She acted accordingly. Luisa was admired within her family for her intellectual capacities. She was considered an 'exceptional child'. Therefore her family believed that she should go into teaching. However, what Luisa wanted most was to study, probably at a university, which would mean going to another town. Her parents refused: 'There were no other job opportunities for girls. We could become seamstresses or dressmakers. However, within a specific social situation, there was nothing else to choose other than teaching.'

> These life histories demonstrate that primary teaching was really one of the few opportunities for young women to lead an autonomous life in the non-manual world of work. The 'destiny' of a young woman to become a primary teacher, for women of these social groups, was already determined.
>
> Three interesting issues concerning this topic can be stressed. First, there is no uniform view of women teachers' vocation for teaching small children. Second, these women have a sense of themselves as continuing the work of women pioneers in teaching. Many of their friends did not work outside the household. They married, had children and a home, but no work outside. In contrast, these five women experienced an uncommon way of life (for their time). Third, they recognized that the opportunities for work outside the household were scarce and that this lack of opportunity influenced their 'choice' of teaching.

The first years of professional activity were not always easy. After her first teaching post in Oporto, Isaura went to Angola in 1923, with her husband, who was also a primary teacher. They remained there until 1925. She describes her marriage as 'disastrous'. She was able to get a divorce in 1929. Meanwhile, she received a teaching post as a relief teacher in the north east of the country in isolated and distant villages. These were comfortless places during the winter. She remembers that in one of these villages, she taught in the kitchen, with the pupils sitting around a great fire to warm them from the snow and cold outside. She also tells a story about herself and her daughter, during a cold night. She was in bed with her child and felt something dripping on them. The following day, her landlady informed her that it must have been the rats which inhabited the attic of the house. As Isaura commented, 'Our lives were similar to those of the gypsies.' They changed schools every year, sometimes twice a year; she always carried with her a palliasse to fill with straw in case the house lacked a mattress.

Things were not easy for Teresa or Ana either. Teresa got her first post in October 1929, at the age of 19, starting out as a teacher in a distant village, far from her family home. She changed schools to other villages in the following three years until 1932, when she got a tenured post in a larger village. It was there that she married. For Ana, the initial years after the end of college were difficult. She was not able to find a teaching post. She underlines that there were two main reasons for this: on the one hand, there were many unemployed teachers, and, on the other, she got a low mark on the final exam in the college. Therefore, between 1919 and 1927, she did not teach. In 1927 her family provided a house for a school under a programme intended to expand popular education. In exchange for providing a location, the property owner was allowed to choose the teacher. She was able to start teaching.

The other two women found that their first years in teaching were precarious but not painful. Luisa easily got a post in the town of her parents as a relief teacher for two years (1919–21). When this teaching post ended, she remained at home, because her father would not allow her to move out of town to teach. She married in 1923 and went to live in Lisbon with her husband. In 1930, she returned to teaching in order to teach her first child in primary school. Like Teresa, Laura easily found a teaching post in a village far from her family home. Until her marriage, she rented a room with a local family, where she was also able to get meals at a reasonable price. She has fond memories of the places she lived in during these first few years.

> The possibilities open to these women teachers were generally to start as relief teachers, usually in a distant village. Living conditions were precarious and difficult. Most of them had a sense of solitude. These first years of professional life were also those in which they started their married lives. Married life was articulated with their professional lives, but in one case, it had such an impact that it dictated the periods of teaching. In another case, the marriage was already breaking down painfully. For these teachers, their lives consisted of an attempt to reconcile their aspirations to an autonomous life (at least, in terms of making a living for themselves) through teaching, and the pressures to be good wives, mothers and respectable women.

In their frequent stays in remote villages, separated from husbands, some women teachers kept one or two of their children with them. To keep a child in the village could create a respectable image. Isaura always took her children with her. She stressed that having a child with her, especially during the period when she was going through her divorce, was vital for her respectability: 'I always had my daughter with me. My mother insisted that

I should have a child with me in the village. She was a kind of bodyguard.' In a similar way, for some years Ana, already married, lived alone with her older child in the village where she held her first post. Probably to have a child as 'a bodyguard' in the village was a successful strategy. Indeed, the teachers who lived in the villages alone with one or more of their children for several years had no complaints of being treated badly or of any unseemly attitude from the male inhabitants.

None the less, having their children with them in isolated villages also created difficulties for these teachers. For example, they needed to reconcile the rhythms of their babies' feeding and the school timetable. Teresa clearly remembers the stress of having to breastfeed her first child in order not to be late for school. Sometimes she would be in at 9 a.m., but on other days, she arrived there 15 minutes later:

> I used to breastfeed my first child at 9, thus he was able to wait three hours. At 12 o'clock, I returned to have lunch and again I breastfed him. The following was a common occurrence: when I was going to enter the school, under the school there was a shop, someone used invariably to ask: 'What time is it?' The reply was always the same: 'It is 9:10'. 'Ah! 10 minutes after 9!' I was furious. But I had no alternative. On the following day, I had to do the same thing, I had to breastfeed my baby before the classes started. 'What time is it?' 'Already 9:15?'

That the domestic and professional activities of these women teachers were deeply interwoven can also be seen in blurred definitions of private and public. It was a common practice among some of these teachers to bring their children into the classroom. They felt that, besides being good mothers, they needed to be their children's teachers as well. They would not trust their children to anyone else. When Teresa's older boy started primary school, she was forced to put him with another teacher, since she was teaching in a girls' school. However, he did not finish primary school with the level of knowledge she thought necessary. Therefore, she taught her second boy in the girls' school, against the law, and in danger of being reprimanded or punished. For Luisa, the interweaving of domestic and professional activities is even more evident since, having left teaching after her early experience, she returned when her older child started elementary school. She saw herself as best suited to teach her children and her return to teaching was justified for precisely that reason. She stopped teaching when her last child completed primary school and went back to teaching only when she needed to finance her older son's completion of his university course, against her husband's will. Luisa taught her older child in her class and her younger child, aged 2, sat at the other end of the classroom. Isaura took her child with her when she was teaching in both Lisbon and in remote villages:

My daughter was in the classroom. She did not interrupt . . . Sometimes, the inspector was in the corridor and came into the room. He
wanted to know if she behaved. She did. All my children were raised in
the schools where I taught. I never left them with anyone. When I was
in the village, I paid a local girl to look after them in the classroom. She
played with them or carried them in her arms. When the child wanted
to sleep, there was a small mattress available. I never failed in my duties.

Her concern for her own children combined with the pressure she was under,
as a single woman, to behave as a good mother may offer an explanation for
her concern to have the children constantly in her sight.

One of the most impressive features of the lives of women teachers,
illustrated by these life histories, is the interweaving of their
professional and domestic activities, in particular, childcare. The
collective representation of the main activity of women as mothers
probably made the teacher's responsibility for her children even
greater, having to move with them from village to village. From these
accounts it is clear that women teachers, like most women who
worked outside the household, had two workplaces. However, at
certain times of the day, domestic duties with their children conflicted
with their teaching responsibilities as they attempted to juggle their
professional activities and the needs of their children.

In the first years of these women's teaching careers, during the dictatorship, the emphasis in schools came increasingly to be focused on reading,
writing and arithmetic, a kind of 'return to basics'. In this context, the
importance of the pupils' examination at the end of primary schooling can
be better understood. All of the teachers mentioned their anxieties about
their pupils' success. On exam day, they accompanied their pupils to the
town or central village where the examination took place – sometimes this
meant going long distances. Ana has vivid memories of getting up at 4
o'clock in the morning to be in town before the examination would start.
She and her pupils rode the ten kilometres on horseback. Teresa's husband
drove her pupils to town for the exam. Given the fact that the children were
often very poor, teachers frequently paid the costs of feeding them for the
day and even the fees necessary to take the exam.

The visits of the inspector also represented an event in school life. These
visits were feared, especially at a time of increasing political control. At the
same time, the inspectors were perceived as embodying the potential
approval and legitimation of the work of the teacher. Teresa, for example,
did not strictly follow the teacher's duties established by the Estado Novo.
The first visit she had from a school inspector was when she had been in her
tenured post for some time. This inspector was feared because he was considered 'rigorous' and could be 'harmful':

He started to walk into the room, into the middle of pupils, slowly, and allowed me to calm down. Afterwards he looked at the black board where I had just written all the metric system, with the measures of height, volume . . . He looked at it and he liked it . . . I was more calm. He was very kind, he did not reprimand me. He sat at my desk, he was not bored, then he started to talk to me.

The second inspector's visit which Teresa mentioned occurred some years later. It was a Saturday and primary schools were supposed to dedicate some time to activities related to the nationalist youth organization, Mocidade Portuguesa, and to religion. The inspector first visited the boys' school, on the ground floor. Teresa could hear them starting prayers: 'I was on the first floor and I never prayed with my pupils. I was not going to pray this time just because the inspector was on the ground floor'. Teresa knew that there was a delicate balance to achieve. She started to talk to her pupils about solidarity. Afterwards she took the pupils out to the playground to play games and gymnastics, instead of the activities of the youth organization.

Although these women teachers taught under difficult and solitary conditions, their commitment to teaching did not suffer. Instead, there was a sense of professional pride which they built up and maintained, even when the social and professional conditions were neither stimulating nor encouraging. Among them, some who felt the political pressures of the authoritarian regime found the opportunity and the strategies necessary to maintain their own integrity in confronting problematic and complex situations.

Women teachers' subjectivities

Women teachers' life histories not only clarify teachers' involvement in schools and local communities, but also provide access to the meaning they attached to their work. It is to their subjectivities that I turn next.

I never had any intention of leaving the school and to stop teaching. Nor do I advise anyone to stop working. It maintains our autonomy. I have felt this all my life . . . I do not agree that women should be under the rule of their husbands. Many women had no other solution than to be submissive to a husband for economic reasons.

Here, Isaura speaks from the position of a woman who has been through divorce and who had to support herself as a single mother. While she was rearing her children and working in the village school, she clearly got the sense that men held power over women, like masters over servants. She also had to confront other people's pity for a woman who worked outside the household, as if this were a dishonour or a misfortune or even a breach of her duties as a mother.

This consciousness of the need for autonomy was not expressed in quite the same way by the other teachers, but a sense of their own autonomy was strengthened when these women teachers compared their lives to those of their acquaintances. They believed they were quite unique within their social groups as women working outside the household. Their sense of autonomy is expressed in their attitudes as well as their actions at specific turning points. Sometimes they were the strongest partners within their marriages in terms of responsibility and with regard to decisions that had to be taken. Isaura, Ana and Laura exemplify the case of single mothers, or of women living almost as if they were for lengthy periods. Luisa was probably the one who followed the most traditional pattern in managing family life. She left and re-entered teaching twice due to the needs of her children. A major turning point was her solitary decision, mentioned before, to finance the continuation of her eldest son's university course against her husband's will, which meant she had to return to teaching. In her turn, Teresa appears as the person in her family who held strong political beliefs with regard to the regime and who supported her brother, imprisoned by the political police. Her life conveys the impression that her influence in family life was central and decisive.

> None of these five women teachers appears to identify with the
> traditional 'middle class' (or even 'lower middle class') situation of
> women in Portuguese society. In fact they worked outside their homes.
> Their family lives (at least for the majority of them) apparently
> conformed to the ordinary conventions of social life. At the same
> time, their professional pathways were of active involvement, based
> on an understanding of the specific circumstances they were able to
> take advantage of in their workplaces.

An important theme in all the life histories of the five women teachers is the relationship that existed between them, as teachers, and the villages where they were located. Quite often, small villages were presented as 'backward' and 'primitive' places in which the woman teacher felt a sense of isolation. This feeling is explained mainly by the fact that they did not find people in the village who shared the same views and concerns. At the same time, some of these women teachers did know features of peasant culture, and spoke in a way as ethnographers of local life. Isaura, for instance, described her surprise the first time she went to church and saw the unique local clothes. Although she thought life in the village was 'primitive', she was also curious and attempted to cross the cultural gap by learning more about the life of the villagers.

Although they were curious about the culture of the villagers, at the same time the teachers stressed the need they felt to distance themselves from local life. Isaura, for instance, states that: 'I never went to the "slaughter of the pig". We must maintain a certain position, I had to keep myself in my rightful place. When people become so used to one another, they have difficulty in maintaining respect.' Ana also declared that she did not participate in the local celebrations:

> I did not participate in these festivities. However, I had very good relations with the peasants. They came to talk to me . . . In order to establish good relations, it is necessary to keep a certain distance . . . When I met them on the roads, they recognized me. In those times, people treated a woman teacher with great respect.

Although the women teachers did not involve themselves in public life, they understood the school to have a 'civilizing' mission through the pedagogic work carried out inside the classroom. However, they did not occupy the public space that the republican discourse envisaged for the role of the teacher. Even Teresa, who was probably closer to republican and 'New Education' ideals remained within the confines of the space of the school. None the less, the women teachers provided important services: 'They depended on me for everything during that year . . . if they needed a certificate, it was written by me . . . Whatever they needed to be written, I was always asked to do it.' In return, peasants would demonstrate their gratitude with gifts such as bread, wood or pork, and the teachers enjoyed the respect, prestige and legitimacy the village community granted to them. The teacher was praised for her knowledge and the power to confer a diploma for the world of work.

> The relationship of these women teachers to the rural community was not marked by open conflict. There were even clear demonstrations of gratitude from the peasants for their presence and practice in the village. Nevertheless, the relationship of the woman teacher to the rural community was complex. Although women teachers felt that they received the same treatment as men, issues of gender existed. Some of these women teachers stated the need for keeping their distance from the peasant community, in order to be heard with more attention. This can be interpreted as a strategy to deal with a situation in which their authority as women was tenuous. To have acquired knowledge through qualifications and training in state institutions as a woman was quite a recent innovation within the peasant community, too recent to gain a legitimacy by itself. These woman teachers frequently stressed the importance of the culture of the school – almost taking refuge within it – underlining their distance from the community.

The teachers were often confronted with the poor condition of buildings and lack of school materials. Irregular attendance was a further difficulty, which they addressed in different ways. Teresa, for instance, remembers that:

In one of my first years of teaching, I had to work with different classes in a small room which was adapted for the purpose. Some children had to sit on the floor. In the following year, in another school, there was again a room, in a building falling into ruins. Under the school room, there was a mare in a stable. The owner used to say that the mare already knew how to count!

All these teachers mentioned the difficulties they had with absentee pupils – although compulsory schooling was already legally in effect – and the tactics they adopted to attract and keep them in the classroom. Isaura argued with the inspector who came to visit her about the school timetable which she had organized according to the needs of her pupils' work: 'During the winter, children wanted school to be in the morning since the snow was still on the grass and the cattle could not reach it. During the hot summer, they asked for the classes to be held in the afternoon, because the fresh mornings were more tolerable for working in the fields'. She explained this to the school inspector, who insisted that this was not the official timetable and that she needed special authorization from the Minister for Instruction. However she chose to ignore this, since for her the only possible solution was to comply with the working demands of the local community.

Ana and Teresa were also confronted with pupils who, because of their poverty, did not attend school regularly. Sometimes Ana noticed that pupils hid when they saw her going to school across the fields. They used to work in the fields with older brothers or sisters; some were only 4 years old. She commented that she did not mark their absences: 'They were so frequently absent from school that I could not mark them in the school book, because, God help us, there would be more absences than presences. It was so difficult for us as teachers to bear such a situation!' Teresa was also confronted with pupils who did not attend school regularly:

> I had to adopt the right attitudes in order to obtain their school attendance. I was living in the village, and for that reason, I could establish good relationships with the families of my pupils and contribute to their understanding of the benefits of 'instruction'. It was necessary to attract them to the school, and make the school ambience enjoyable. Sometimes, they came to me crying since their mothers would not allow them to go to school. I organized a 'school excursion'. Nobody knew what this was. Some people were touched when I appeared with so many children around me.

Teresa established a relationship with peasant families on the basis of the importance of schooling. Several times she was confronted with the resistance of peasants to schooling. This resistance was even greater among girls, who were more often absent from school. Teresa also argued with the girls' parents. In one of these cases, the father, at the end of the conversation, finally accepted that Micas would return to school, with these words: 'She will go to school as a kindness to you.' Teresa pursued this kind of contact with the community. She extended school activities to include parties, excursions, singing and theatre, along the lines of the New Education, to stimulate the peasant children's interest in education.

Almost all of these teachers taught in both rural and urban settings and in general saw teaching in town as a desired step forward in their teaching career. However, this did not mean that urban pupils were considered less difficult to teach. Whereas Ana thought that peasant children's remoteness from the culture of the school presented a difficult challenge for the teacher, Isaura underlined the arduous character of teaching in town, particularly in poor urban districts: 'These places represent hunger, plague and war! . . . These people primarily need education. They needed education even more than "instruction" and I took every opportunity to guide them in the right direction.'

> Isaura's feeling of strangeness in the poor urban districts – but, at the same time, her acute sense of the strong social conflicts there – is translated in moral terms, revealing the pressure which she was under because of her former education, training and social upbringing. Probably the training in republican teacher colleges did not prepare teachers for the poor urban districts. Similarly, the lack of continuing teacher education during the Estado Novo could not help these teachers in their contact with poor urban populations.
>
> Many of the school activities of these women teachers, in old and inappropriate buildings, were guided by a sense of the need of peasant and poor children to have access to schooling. At the same time, they were confronted with peasant children's working in the fields and, consequently, with their absence from school. Sometimes they were successful in persuading peasant parents to send their children to school more regularly.

Different view of politics and the relationship of the teacher and the regime are revealed in the teachers' stories. It is quite clear from all their narratives that the events of 28 May 1926 were not experienced as bringing immediate change into schools. Teresa started to attend teachers college in that year. She was 16 then and hardly interested in political questions. She cannot remember anything abnormal happening. People neither talked about the recent political events, nor immediately felt the grip of censorship. Teresa remembered only a small incident in a class with a lecturer who took advantage of an answer she gave subtly to contest the growing influence of Catholicism in teachers' education.

Luisa was not teaching at the time of the military coup. Isaura had returned from Africa some time before the military coup took place but was too involved in the personal conflicts of her marriage to carefully examine the coup's possible implications for schools. Ana and Laura were living in remote villages and the coup did not represent a matter of great concern to them. Luisa remembered an event in 1934, the year the first elections of the Estado Novo were held. She was ordered to 'organize the elections' in the village (near Tomar):

> I had to call the population and explain what was going to happen, I had to promote the propaganda of the regime. I decided to call a meeting for a Thursday because I knew that nobody would come. Later I told the school inspector that nobody came except a man who suffered from incontinence and could not stay long. In the middle of the year 'they' closed my school and I was sent to a distant village, in the middle of nowhere.

Luisa saw this forced move as a punishment for her political attitude.

When Luisa returned to teaching for the second time, in 1942, many practices and teaching content had changed:

> When I returned to teaching, the Catholic prayers [suspended since the onset of the Republic] were again introduced. I did not agree with this. Thus, as there were other teachers in the school, when it was time for prayers, I would open the door of my classroom and let my pupils pray with the other class. With regard to the reading texts, I never selected those that included propaganda for Salazar and the political regime. I used to tell the pupils: we will read them later. However, I never returned to them.

Her distance from the political regime was also marked by her always declining to send telegrams or sign any letters of support for the regime. Luisa stressed that she always maintained a 'great distance' from the conservative regime.

Teresa, in her turn, after her first years in teaching and the experience of her brother being imprisoned by the political police, developed her own perspective on the regime. She underlined that she did not have a political consciousness during her first years of teaching: 'In the first years, what I wanted was to teach, I was very much concerned with the children . . . I did not read the newspapers at the time'. Her political awareness with regard to the regime developed over time. Teresa remembers the introduction of propaganda and religious texts in schoolbooks, as well as the nationalist emphasis. She did not agree with these political views, at least in some areas. Like Luisa, she did not give attention to the pro-regime propaganda texts included in the reading books and she never prayed in class. She even criticized the colonial policies of the regime.

For Laura and Ana, on the other hand, the issue of the relationship between the teacher and the political regime was not problematic. They were much too concerned with improving their pupils' ability to read, write and count and helping them complete primary school. They did not find either the time or the means to reflect on these political questions. Isaura was probably somewhere in the middle. She maintained some distance from the events or celebrations of the regime. For instance, she did not attend the demonstrations which the regime organized or send petitions and telegrams in support of it. Nevertheless, she always had to bear in mind that she needed her post in the primary school for the economic survival of herself and her family.

> The subjective perspectives of the five women teachers are not uniform regarding their political positioning towards the post-28 May 1926 regime. As civil servants of an authoritarian state and as women, there were many situations where conformity was imperative because they were employees and wished to keep their jobs. However, it is clear from some of their accounts that 'lip service' and more explicit stances of political distance and disagreement were taken when opportunities arose.

Conclusion

Life histories of women teachers who started their professional lives in the final period of the Republic or in the years of the Military Dictatorship (which gave away to the Estado Novo) illuminate the pathways they followed and the contexts in which they lived and worked. The analysis of these life histories reveals the private nature of their work, how much their life revolved around two workplaces – the household, where the responsibility for the domestic sphere largely fell on them, and the school. But their life histories also bring out their subjectivities. We have heard what these women said about their experience in the rural communities and the way it was shaped by social expectations and gender roles. All of the women felt that there was a delicate balance to be maintained: they felt their isolation in the rural community and the pressure of maintaining their 'respectability' as women living without men. In response to these pressures, they distanced themselves from villagers. They did not participate in peasants' daily activities or festivities, although they responded to peasant demands for their literacy services. We also heard about women teachers' strategies for dealing with pupils who had to work in the fields rather than attend school. They felt the need to negotiate between the importance that, as teachers, they attributed to schooling for children's future lives and the perceived needs of the peasant community.

The teachers had varying relationships to the political regime. Those most critical of the regime were aware of the constant political pressures which they had to confront in order to maintain their moral integrity. At the same time, it was crucial for four of them to maintain their teaching posts since they had no other job alternatives. Therefore, they often had to find strategies which allowed them to escape from what were defined as their duties as teachers within an authoritarian regime (such as Catholic prayers, the approval of the colonial policies of the regime or of its leaders, or even the support to be given to the great public marches or commemorations of Salazarism) without being expelled from teaching (or worse). Generally they valued their autonomy and independence as women working outside the household and believed teaching had a central meaning in their lives. Given the political context and the patriarchal relationships in which they were involved as women, they undertook 'hidden struggles'. Their work provided them with the means of maintaining their own independence. Finally their work also provided them with some means of influencing the communities where they taught.

Because of the openness, accessibility and friendship of these women teachers, I came to understand their ways of making sense of their own realities, their ways of knowing subjectively, and their professional pathways. In the future, it should be clear that studies of the development of mass schooling in Portugal need to take into consideration the active involvement of women teachers and to acknowledge that many of them had to deal with the complexity of reconciling the public and private domains in their lives, both as women and as professionals. In terms once again of Stanley's conception of a 'kaleidoscope', we can see how they were able to live their lives under great pressure, negotiating patriarchy, politics, religion, and local community views of education with a level of commitment which was impressive indeed.

Acknowledgement

Part of this research was financed by JNICT (Junta Nacional de Investigação Cientifica), Lisbon, Projet NORA.

Notes

1 K. Plummer (1983) *Documents of Life: An Introduction to the Problems and Literature of a Humanistic Method.* London: Allen and Unwin, p.102.
2 L. Stanley (1992) *The Auto/Biographical: The Theory and Practice of Feminist Auto/biography.* Manchester: Manchester University Press, p.160.
3 D. Sommer (1988) Not just a personal story: women's testimonies and the plural self, in B. Brodzki and C. Schenck (eds) *Life/lines: Theorizing Women's Autobiographies.* Ithaca, NY: Cornell University Press, p.136.
4 C. Wright Mills (1970) *The Sociological Imagination.* Harmondsworth: Penguin, p.12.
5 See, for instance, F. Ferrarotti (1983) *Histoire et histoires de vie.* Paris: Librairie

des Méridiens; Plummer, *Documents of Life*; P. Thompson (1978) *The Voice of the Past*. Oxford: Oxford University Press.

6 Stanley, *The Auto/Biographical*, p.219.
7 A.C. Osório (1918) *Em Tempo de Guerra*. Lisbon: Editora Ventura, p.19.
8 Ibid., p.111.
9 Quoted in E. Guimarães (1986) A Mulher Portuguesa na Legislação Civil. *Análise Social* 22(92–3): 567.
10 F. Mónica (1978) *Educação e Sociedade no Portugal de Salazar*. Lisbon: Presença, pp.11–12.
11 L. Le Grand (1988) Histoire de Vie de Groupe – à la recherche d'une 'lucidité methodologique'. *Societés – Revue des Sciences Humaines et Sociales* 18: 3.
12 N. Denzin (1989) *Interpretive Biography*. London: Sage, p.26.
13 Stanley, *The Auto/Biographical*, p.159.
14 M. Nelson (1992) Using oral case histories to reconstruct the experience of women teachers in Vermont, 1900–1950, in I. Goodson (ed.) *Studying Teachers' Lives*. London: Routledge, p.168.
15 Stanley, *The Auto/Biographical*, p.178.

9 'To do the next needed thing': Jeanes teachers in the Southern United States 1908–34

Valinda Littlefield

Writing in the mid-twentieth century, Carter G. Woodson and Horace Mann Bond saw only the limitations of African-American school teachers, especially in the South. 'One generation of Negro teachers after another have served for no higher purpose than to do what they are told to do,' Woodson wrote in the early 1930s.[1] Similarly, Bond felt that they lacked the power or inclination to alter the conditions of the race.[2] Because of such prevailing sentiments, and because some African-American women often deliberately shied away from publicity, the experiences of southern female educators, especially rural, have been neglected. Perhaps Bond and Woodson, two very insightful historians, looked for cataclysmic events similar to those occurring during that time such as the Russian Revolution, the First World War or strike activities by labour unions in the United States. However, the efforts of Jeanes teachers from 1908 to 1934 in teaching people how to preserve food, practise good hygiene and combat illiteracy, as well as coordinating and organizing the building of schools and raising funding, gradually altered the lives of an oppressed group. They often acted covertly and lived out the dictum, 'We are Not What We Seem'.[3]

In most respects, during the late nineteenth and early twentieth centuries, the social, political and economic climate for African-Americans in the South was worsening. Direct and open access to the political system for improvement of conditions became increasingly difficult for African-Americans. Beginning in 1890, the 'Mississippi Plan' created to eliminate Black voters was adopted by other southern states. Also in 1890, the Blair Bill, intended to reduce illiteracy among the southern poor by providing federal funds for education, failed to pass in the US Senate. In 1894 Congress repealed an 1870 Enforcement Act provision that would have provided federal marshals and election supervisors to ensure that election practices in local communities did not violate Blacks' right to vote. Reported lynching of

African-Americans, an often utilized method of deterring Black activism and advancement, averaged 103 per year from 1890 to 1900. Between 1889 and 1898, at least 15 of those lynched were women. In 1896 the Supreme Court gave credence to 'separate but equal' accommodations in the *Plessy v. Ferguson* case. In the Supreme Court's 1899 decision, *Cumming v. School Board of Richmond County, Georgia,* Blacks were denied the right to public secondary education.[4] The nationwide illiteracy rate among African-Americans was 44.5 per cent at a time when 90 per cent of the African-American population of approximately 9 million lived in the South.[5] Historian James D. Anderson noted that after 1900 the proportion of funding to Black schools dropped significantly and that from 1900 to 1920, although every southern state sharply increased tax appropriations for building schoolhouses, they provided virtually none of this funding for building of Black schools.[6] For the school year 1931–2, nine southern states spent an average of $15.14 per African-American child, as opposed to $49.30 to educate a white child. At that time the average expenditure for the nation was $81.36 per child.[7]

Within such a political, economic and social context, southern African-American female school teachers changed their pupils' daily lives. From a distance, their efforts seemed to sustain the status quo. Yet gradual change was within the realm of the possible although cataclysmic change was not. Throughout the late nineteenth and early twentieth centuries, most African-Americans viewed education as the salvation of the race and African-American communities expected members of a majority female teacher profession to provide a service to the race and to improve the status of community members.

The Jeanes teachers

Jeanes teachers were paid primarily from a fund established in 1907 by Anna T. Jeanes, a white Quaker woman interested in contributing to the education of African-Americans in rural areas.[8] The Jeanes Foundation was established with a donation of $1 million to 'encourage the rudimentary education of Colored people residing in rural districts' and the funding was administered by the General Education Board.[9] The Jeanes Teacher Program was modelled after the academic and social service work of Virginia Estelle Randolph, an African-American teacher at Mountain Road School in Henrico County, Virginia. Randolph became the first Jeanes teacher to be paid from the fund and her concern for the welfare of the entire community provided the base for the activities of future Jeanes teachers.[10] Prior to being asked to become the first, Randolph had improved her school and surrounding area, organized a 'Willing Workers Club', held fundraisers, and worked with local churches to improve the school as well as formed a

Patrons Improvement League, working mainly with community women to improve living conditions, especially sanitary, health and home conditions.

Sometimes referred to as Jeanes supervisors and sometimes simply as Jeanes teachers, their official southern title was Jeanes Supervising Industrial Teacher. The majority of the first group, 1908 to 1934, like Randolph, had previous teaching experience and were female. They were also normally rural born and attended or graduated from an industrial training school. For labour intensive work, they were paid an average of $45 per month for seven months and expected to encourage industrial education and community involvement in rural public schools.[11] County funds provided part of their salaries; however, county support was based on the ability to pay and county contributions therefore varied greatly over space and time.[12] For example, in 1933, due to the depression, North Carolina State Board of Education required that all Jeanes teachers work fulltime as teachers or principals and perform Jeanes work before and after school hours, on Saturdays, or during school vacations and that their salaries be paid by the Jeanes Fund or other donated funding.[13]

They were active throughout most southern states. By 1910, 129 Jeanes teachers worked in 130 counties in 13 southern states; by 1931 there were 329; by 1934, the figure dropped to 303 due to the depression; and by 1937, the figure increased to 426. Of the figure for 1934, 17 were men; 177 married or widowed females; and 109 unmarried females.[14] Virginia and North Carolina consistently employed the highest numbers of Jeanes teachers as compared to other southern states and received the lion's share of funding. In 1923, there were 56 Jeanes teachers employed in Virginia and 39 in North Carolina.[15] In 1930 Virginia employed 57 and North Carolina 43.[16] Although the Jeanes Fund funded the programme until 1968, by 1959 it made grants only to the States of Alabama, Mississippi, North Carolina and South Carolina. J.C. Dixon, Vice President and Executive Director of the Southern Education Board (SEB) hoped to discontinue the grants to North Carolina by the end of the 1959 fiscal year and noted that it was not possible to do so for the other states, without 'affecting unfavorably the status of supervision' of African-American schools.[17]

It is in the context of this indispensable support of education in the African-American community that the efforts of the women Jeanes teachers must be understood.[18] With few resources and strong convictions, they made tremendous sacrifices to provide an education for their communities' sons and daughters.[19] These women could not immediately change the 1896 *Plessy v. Ferguson* decision that segregation was not discriminatory, nor could they remove the disfranchisement of African-Americans. Yet Jeanes teachers clearly understood that a healthy and literate poor people were much more likely to survive and subvert oppression than an unhealthy and illiterate poor people. Thus they worked, often quietly, within the confines of the system to improve conditions. They constructed, reconstructed and maintained educational as well as social service systems in the face of gross inequality.

Dr James Hardy Dillard, President of the Anna T. Jeanes Fund 1908–31, felt that female workers should dominate an employee group which required intensive labour efforts and superb human relations skills. In a letter informing a county superintendent that money was available to him to hire a Jeanes teacher, N.C. Newbold, North Carolina State Supervisor of Negro Education, advised him that 'Dr. Dillard prefers that women be appointed for this work, though he does not make that a requirement necessary to secure the appropriation from the Jeanes Fund'.[20] The underlying perception of the administrators of the fund that women were better workers than men is evident in the employment records of the fund throughout the programme's existence.[21] In earlier correspondence to Newbold, Dillard wrote that with few exceptions he had not found 'a man on the list that measured up to the work which the women accomplish[ed]'.[22] Former students of Hampton and Tuskegee also dominated the first wave, from 1908 to 1934, of Jeanes teachers since the administrators of the funding stressed industrial education.[23]

The work of the first wave of Jeanes teachers required a tremendous amount of travel at a time when trains, horse and buggy and walking were the normal modes of transportation for the rural population and when transportation and communication methods were often unreliable. Good judgement skills were important assets for these women at a time when travel required that Jim Crow Laws, perceived or real, be factored into the transportation equation. Virginia Randolph hired a one-horse buggy and driver and paid for it out of her meagre salary. She later bought a horse and travelled alone. With 23 schools to visit, she usually left home at 6:30 a.m. and returned around 9 p.m.[24] Dillard remembered meeting a supervisor walking with her materials eight miles to keep an appointment because the gentleman who was to have provided transportation failed to appear.[25] Matilda Thompkins Harris of Camden County, Georgia, drove a horse named Sallie and used a buggy with fringes in the beginning of her Jeane's career. A granddaughter, Mrs Lula Harris Butler Robinson, noted that she sometimes accompanied her grandmother to the 'different schools and churches' and that 'Sallie seemed to know where to go'.[26] Sallie also served a dual purpose. In addition to providing transportation for the Jeanes teacher, Mrs Harris 'hitched Sallie up to a mill to grind cane' gathered by community members in order to teach children how to make syrup candy. She later purchased a T-Model but, like the buggy, it had no heat, forcing Mrs Harris to use a blanket for warmth in the winter. It did however provide a faster mode of transportation and allowed her to visit more schools and homes.[27]

Like transportation, limited correspondence methods also meant that Jeanes teachers relied on good personal judgement skills as suggested by a letter from Newbold to a county superintendent. He noted that he had received a telegram from Annie Holland, Gates County, North Carolina Jeanes teacher, requesting instructions about two students wishing to be examined – possibly for high school or county school admittance – and that he had been unsuccessful in reaching her by telephone. The letter to the superintendent was a result of failed communication attempts either by telephone or telegram as well.[28] Holland's options were to administer the exams or delay them until she received approval from Newbold. Ordinarily one step ahead of her employer in deciding on agendas and how they should be executed, her handling of a similar situation suggests that she administered the exams and sought approval afterwards. In correspondence to Newbold, Holland wrote 'I felt that you would be pleased if some of the girls would continue their gardens, so I had already begun to work up an interest.'[29] 'Work up an interest' in reality meant that Holland had informed the girls to continue their gardens, prior to her requesting advice from Newbold.

Jeanes teachers' job descriptions were so broad that they allowed for a considerable amount of freedom, flexibility and creativity. This often meant, however, that they were obliged to work around-the-clock hours and much of their 'overtime' labour was uncompensated. They were also responsible for creating public school support by providing encouragement mainly to local African-Americans and whites to give money and time, organizing and teaching in moonlight schools and organizing industrial education exhibits. Moonlight schools were evening school education, taught for two to four months, which provided illiterate adults with reading and writing instruction. A 1916 report to Newbold revealed that Holland organized two such schools in Gates County with six adults between the ages of 45 and 70 who were enrolled for three months. A Durham County supervisor reported that seven Moonlight schools were organized enrolling 65 adults between the ages of 35 and 60 for terms of two to four months and that subjects such as sewing and canning were taught in addition to reading and writing.[30] A supervisor in Chadbourn County wrote that 11 schools were organized with an enrolment of 225 students, the oldest being 73 years. The schools accepted anyone between the ages of 18 and 100 years and met two to three times a week normally from 7 p.m. to 9:30 p.m. After working during the day, Holland and other southern African-American educators laboured tirelessly at night to educate the parents and grandparents of their day students to improve the rural southern illiteracy rate.

Jeanes teachers visited schools to help and encourage teachers to teach sanitation, sewing, cooking, basket making, chair caning and mat making. They met with men and women in communities to form Improvement Leagues or Betterment Associations, whose purpose was to improve the 'living conditions among the colored people', and paint or whitewash schoolhouses, homes and outhouses. Responsibilities also included raising money to build better schoolhouses, and to lengthen the school terms with private payments; encouraging and organizing home and school gardens, tomato clubs and corn clubs; and generally to 'promote higher standards of living, integrity of character, honesty, and thrift among all people'.[31] Some teachers visited three to four schools once a week while others visited 20 to 30 schools on an average of once a month. Sometimes they spent a week at a particular school overseeing industrial training projects, assisting teachers with reading, writing, spelling and arithmetic instruction, and visiting homes and organizing clubs for school improvement. Although all of the first group of Jeanes teachers were considered industrial teachers, some women taught sewing, some cooking and some both sewing and cooking. A few taught washing and ironing. In 1918, at least two were trained nurses and taught the proper care for the sick and for children as well as good health and hygiene habits. Others were expert dressmakers, milliners, weavers and basket makers. The men mainly taught farming and gardening. Some gave instructions in carpentry and bricklaying and a few taught blacksmithing, shoemaking and repairing. Others included a painter and paper-handler, mattress maker, cook and tailor.[32]

As noted by historian Cynthia Neverdon-Morton, Jeanes teachers initially encountered resistance in some African-American communities. Parents objected to a curriculum that stressed industrial education and many felt that it was being forced on them by whites. Industrial education for African-Americans in many southern states took on a new thrust around 1914. State and county administrators attempted to unify and coordinate such work in all schools, especially secondary and higher education institutions, i.e. County Training Schools, Normal Schools. However, the first two decades of the twentieth century for North Carolina revealed tensions in putting such a policy as industrial education for African-Americans into practice. C.W. Smith, Jeanes teacher for Johnston County, noted that most teachers were unable to teach any industrial work.[33] A teacher in Anson County informed her superintendent that her county was not ready for industrial training.[34] In an interview with a former rural school teacher, Mrs S.P. Morton, she noted that the Jeanes teachers 'taught you how to skin branches off honeysuckle vines and then wrap and make into baskets, also cornshuck baskets, and how to cut out cardboard and sew pine cones on them'.[35] Different shaped, stylish hats were the result of the exercise with cardboard and pine cones. In addition to remembering what was taught, her memory also revealed tension between the community and the work of these teachers. 'Industrial work sometimes took precedence over academic', noted Morton.[36] However, by the second era of Jeanes teachers' work, around 1931, their attempts to balance industrial with academic education and their genuine concern for the betterment of the community eventually overcame the initial objections and normally endeared them to communities.[37]

Officially, Jeanes teachers were appointed by local county school boards, reported directly to the county superintendent and provided monthly written reports, sometimes directly, to the office of the State Supervisor of Negro Education. Informal as well as other formal lines of communication also occurred between the teachers and the office of the State Supervisor. Technically, Holland reported to Gates County Superintendent, T.W. Cotsen, but many of her duties were directed by N.C. Newbold. In addition to those Jeanes teacher duties previously stated, she was directed by Newbold to improve the quality of instruction in county group meetings, reading circles, study groups, extension courses, libraries, and summer schools, and to organize programmes dealing with health and industrial arts.[38] Such an arrangement meant that these women reported to two employers, the superintendent and the state agent. Personal characteristics of successful Jeanes teachers included patience, tact and persistence. These were important attributes often used by teachers within such a working environment.

Their work also demanded that the most tactful procedures be observed at all times in dealing with pupils and teachers, teachers and principals, teachers and committee members and teachers and community members. Occasionally, supervisors were dismissed, for 'the inability to harmonize with local workers', among other reasons.[39] All Jeanes teachers did not exhibit tactful traits and Holland was sometimes requested to intervene in such instances. In 1918 Newbold directed Holland to travel to Bertie County and convince Miss Jones to adapt to the community conditions and encourage members rather than 'pile down on them an insurmountable weight of pessimism and gloom'.[40] A Martin County Superintendent wrote that due to 'indiscretions in behavior and the exercise of a dictatorial spirit' his Jeanes teacher had lost the cooperation and confidence of many of the teachers and he had decided not to rehire her.[41] He had also decided not to immediately appoint a replacement because the teachers in the county respected her husband, a principal, and did not want to offend him. Whereas the Martin County Superintendent was sensitive to the African-American community and professionally handled his duties, other supervisors allowed the work of the Jeanes teachers to relieve them of most or all responsibilities of the Black school systems.

In the early years of the programme's operation, many superintendents paid little attention to the detailed work of the teachers unless whites in the community complained. One superintendent from Lincolnton, North Carolina, stated that he was well aware that he had not done 'anything for the colored schools in the way of supervising classroom work and improving standards, methods, etc., of teachers'.[42] Another from Catawaby County found 'his time all taken with administrative duties and therefore can give practically no time to the Negro schools in a supervisory capacity'.[43] Such statements reveal both the freedom teachers had and the neglect of the county superintendents. The climate in the public education system allowed superintendents to be very frank in their expressions. A superintendent in Snow Hill, North Carolina, wrote, 'I practically and almost completely turned the outside colored school work to her. This gave me more time for administering and supervising the white schools of the county and helped me in this way to make a greater success of them'.[44] A Gastonia superintendent said, 'They have relieved me so absolutely of all care and worry in regard to the colored schools that I have become absolutely dependent upon their help'.[45]

Within such local neglect and attitudes, Jeanes teachers identified the needs of a community and developed strategies to solve some of the problems, often working within the existing social order.[46] For example, many rural schools lacked basic equipment as evident by a letter from Jeanes teacher Annie E.B. White in Bertie County to Newbold. She started working 1909 and by 1913 had organized Betterment Clubs and provided 'water-pails, drinking cups, wash basins, towels, soap shode's, curtains, lamps, clocks, balls, locks for school doors, desk, black boards, maps, pictures, tools and song books'.[47] White could have petitioned the school board for such basic needs, but probably to no avail. Recognizing the need as well as the problem of an entrenched Jim Crow system with specific attitudes about the needs of African-Americans, whites and others sought innovative methods to often bypass the system. Within the first decade of the programme's existence, for every dollar of cost, approximately $2.50 was raised by Jeanes teachers for school improvements.[48] For every dollar paid by the counties, approximately $5.00 was raised for improvements. And in 1922 southern Jeanes teachers visited 7,850 county schools and raised $428,528 for school buildings and improvements.[49]

Health and sanitation

In order to improve the educational system, Jeanes teachers addressed basic concerns such as health issues of the rural population. Most counties could not afford a health nurse and few institutions were organized to care for Blacks and/or the poor, which was primarily a community responsibility in the rural South. In addition, many African-Americans could not afford private medical care and some did not trust white providers. Health issues were often tied to the standard of living, social and environmental problems and the duties of the Jeanes teachers encompassed the task of providing information and lessons of health and sanitation in the schools and homes. Especially since one of the Jeanes teachers' duties was to increase attendance, it became essential to address health issues in order for children to attend school on a regular basis.

Their efforts attracted the attention of local white organizational leaders, especially health officials. The North Carolina State Board of Health and the American Red Cross recognized the organizational and networking skills of the supervisors. An agreement in 1917 between Dr L.B. McBrayer, North

Carolina State Board of Health, and Newbold stipulated that the State Board of Health provide an additional month's salary for Jeanes teachers. This agreement required that the supervisors dedicate 'definite time to health work' by devoting a part of each month to duties dealing with health issues. Newbold felt that 'very effective service' could be rendered by addressing church and lodge meetings on Saturdays and Sundays.[50] Mrs Mary S. Gray of Martin County assisted a Red Cross physician in vaccinating 300 of the 400–500 Blacks against typhoid fever. After a storm damaged the county, she canvassed the town 'collecting many useful things' and noted that the Red Cross helped every family who had suffered loss in the storm with clothes, food supplies and furniture.[51]

Jeanes teachers' role in addressing the needs of an economic deprived group required that in health education they, like nurses and other health officials, acquaint themselves with information on the disease, its symptoms, cure and prevention. In addition, they raised funding for those unable to afford treatment, as well as funds to hire county welfare workers and nurses.[52] They obtained cooperation of county and city physicians, arranged public meetings with the State Board of Health and local physicians and community members, arranged instruction on sanitation in public schools and homes, secured medical inspection of school children for all diseases, kept records and oversaw the building and installation of sanitary privies at schools and homes.

They also addressed other needs of communities. Jeanes teachers delivered food and clothes to the poor; organized farm meetings to keep farmers abreast of new agricultural findings and techniques; convinced mayors to improve transportation; placed orphan children in orphanages; secured county aid for families; organized community committees to handle needy cases; visited homes and schools with welfare agents; and worked with welfare workers in securing help for slow learners or mentally handicapped children.

Home-Makers' Clubs

Home-Makers' Clubs served as a vehicle for Jeanes teachers to effect social and economic change. Holland's assignment from Newbold in 1916 was to oversee the 44 supervisors who were organizing Home-Makers' Clubs.[53] A student and parent organization, its members grew and preserved foods such as peaches, apples, corn, beans and tomatoes, and raised mainly poultry and pork. The principal duties of Jeanes teachers in establishing Home-Makers' Clubs were to encourage home gardens, home sanitation, cooking and sewing. Each club consisted of 10–20 members and 10 or more clubs were organized and maintained by a Jeanes teacher. A person in each club acted as sub-leader and helped in the absence of the teacher. By the beginning of 1916,

Home-Makers' Clubs were established in 31 counties as compared to 22 counties for the previous year. Some Home-Makers' Club work was performed during the regular school term but major emphasis was placed on this work during the summer months when teachers were able to spend more time in the homes and community. Also, summer was the most productive time for raising and preserving produce as evident in a 1915 report of Jeanes teachers in North Carolina. During the summer, they were instrumental in a total of 175,645 quarts of vegetables and fruits canned, 19,771 glasses of jelly and pickles preserved, and in raising $6,639.25 from sales of vegetables, fruit and poultry.[54] Such an effort was a tremendous accomplishment considering that most rural Black women spent long and exhausting hours working on farms and serving as domestics for whites and maintaining their own homes.[55]

Home-Makers' Clubs had more far-reaching aims than simply providing encouragement to community members to grow gardens and preserve food.[56] These clubs actively attempted to improve the conditions of African-American communities. African-American teachers often took on such responsibilities as health and hygiene issues through agencies such as the Home-Makers' Clubs which allowed them to stay in direct touch with the home life of the students in the communities. In order to get the children to attend schools regularly, they often had to address issues in the home, such as helping parents provide health care, food, clothing, shoes and other basics. Visiting community homes also provided an opportunity for teachers to convince parents to allow students to secure additional education. For example, Mrs L.B. Yancy, of Vance County, visited 40 homes during the month of May and made it a point to visit homes of children who completed the seventh grade. Her main goal was to 'get the parents to see the importance of sending them to high school somewhere'.[57] Somewhere is the operative word, for most would have to attend school in the city or another county which meant arranging travel or lodging accommodation. Many Jeanes teachers were instrumental in making such arrangements.

Home-Makers' Clubs and Betterment Associations were female organizations for community improvements. One supervisor reported that a Betterment Association had been organized and that they were working to improve schools, churches, and were 'looking after the poor of the neighborhood'. After community members saw the results of the efforts of the Organization, others 'decided to clean church yard, cemetery, and scrub church'.[58] In addition to supporting education and assisting with the provision of health services, the efforts of Jeanes teachers in Home-Makers' Clubs provided material support to the community. The annual reports of the North Carolina clubs show progress in Jeanes teachers' organizing and fundraising abilities. In 1916, $9,778.92 was raised by selling vegetables, fruit, other canned goods and poultry compared to $1,396.26 raised in 1914.[59] Preserved products saved community members money by providing a source of food that was less expensive than in stores.

Jeanes teachers and the Rosenwald Fund

Jeanes teachers' success enticed funding from other philanthropists such as the John F. Slater Fund and the Rosenwald Fund, and increased funding from the General Education Board.[60] Julius Rosenwald, President of Sears, Roebuck and Company, provided the funding for a rural school building programme. Rosenwald contracts stipulated that African-American community members match or exceed the amount requested from the fund; required the approval and cooperation of the state and county school authorities; and that all property (land, equipment) be deeded to the local school system. The Rosenwald programme stressed industrial education and community members agreed to promote industrial education. Most schools had an industrial room for the boys and a kitchen for the girls. The first Rosenwald school was built in 1913 in Alabama. By the 1930s, over 5,300 buildings had been constructed in 15 southern states.

A 1920 North Carolina press release noted that 'The best rural school houses for colored children are the Rosenwald school buildings'.[61] Blacks as well as whites were aware of this fact and the construction of Rosenwald schools probably required the most intensive fundraising efforts, public relations and organizational skills of Jeanes teachers. In a North Carolina 'State School Facts' newsletter, it was noted that there were 36 Jeanes teachers and one state-wide worker working in 37 counties and their efficiency could be seen in the improvement of schoolhouses in their respective counties. With one exception all the counties had at least one modern Rosenwald school, secured by Jeanes teachers' fundraising drives.[62] The relentless efforts of women such as Mrs Carrie L. Battle, Jeanes teacher, Edgecome County is an example. In 1924, Newbold noted that Superintendent R.E. Sentelle of Edgecome County had sent in his fifteenth application for Rosenwald building aid. The Rosenwald Fund would contribute $10,700 and the total cost of the buildings would be approximately $50,000. Recognizing the person responsible for such a feat, Newbold noted that Mrs Battle had 'raised and deposited $7,500 in a local bank'.[63] In addition, she had raised $425 for ranges to be placed in five of the schools and that she had raised well over $8,000 that year.[64] During that same year, another Jeanes teacher, Mrs M.C. Falkner, Guilford County, reported the construction of two six-room buildings. Other teachers reported the construction of one or more smaller schools. Mrs Katie M. Hart, Hertford County, reported that between $3,000 and $4,000 had been raised for Rosenwald schools. Mrs C.F. Rich, Nash County, reported that they had begun their building programme with four Rosenwald school projects to be completed by the next school term.[65]

Money was not the only support secured by the teachers. A Jeanes teacher, Miss Elizabeth Harris, informed Newbold that at a parent–teacher meeting, crowded school district parents and teachers pledged $3,000 worth of lumber and other substantial help. She had given them the 'State Plans for Public Schoolhouses' and they were working accordingly. Rosenwald provided states with designs, detailed blueprints and specifications for these schools.[66] Mrs Mary S. Wynn, Craven County, reported that 'Mr. I.J. Cooper, colored,' promised to give two acres of land on which to build Mt Sinai Rosenwald School and that 'Mr. & Mrs. M.K. Everett, colored,' gave the site for Everett school.[67] In addition to raising funding for the buildings, Jeanes teachers also raised funds for such items as kitchen equipment. A 1924 report reveals that funding in the amount of $5,996.50 was raised for 47 Rosenwald kitchens during 1923. Funding raised ranged from $15 to almost $2,000 per county.[68] The efforts for and success of the Rosenwald Program were largely a result of the work and planning skills of the Jeanes teachers.

Conclusion

Social work, industrial education training and the establishments of such organizations as Home-Makers' Clubs by early educators such as Jeanes teachers should not be viewed as an example of middle class women trying to impose their views and values on an oppressed group. These rural women were regarded as middle class by the Black community because of their profession; most were not born into middle class families and such status could be removed by the community as easily as assigned. Their ability to develop organizations by working at the grassroots level reveals that they understood the day-to-day workings of their communities.[69] Successful Jeanes teachers, born and raised in counties similar to the ones in which they taught, took the time and initiative to understand the concerns, regulations and rules of their communities. For example, it is evident that Mrs P.L. Byrd, Vance County, North Carolina Jeanes teacher, understood her community's parents' working schedules. She was able to get 60–100 children to attend a 'Community Play Day' on Saturdays. Byrd actively involved the teacher of the school which meant less chance of tensions between teacher and supervisor. She also used this day to hold 'parents' meetings after the games'.[70] Such working relationship with the community possibly helped to convince several community citizens to mortgage their property and borrow $3,500 for building a school. Byrd noted that 'they had to do this as it is hard to raise money at this time of year. The parents have pledged this money and will pay those who borrowed the money in November'.[71]

Jeanes teachers produced results in agencies like the Home-Makers' Clubs because they knew how to grow produce and had received training in preservation of food. They also rolled up their sleeves and worked with people from all class levels. A Jeanes teacher described her role as learning to do the 'next needed thing' and that they were called upon to 'Improve my soil, add my account at the commissary, feed my children, take me to the hospital, bury my mother, write my son, read this letter, mend my steps, find a minister or justice of the peace to get me married, show me how to build a sanitary privy'.[72] First generation rural African-American school teachers, who had grown up under many of the conditions that they were trying to improve, had a better understanding of as well as sympathy or empathy for community members. They used their experiences to enable them to show and convince people how to improve their living conditions. Jeanes teachers were a vital force in many rural communities and their records reveal a rich history of agency and community service through the experiences of southern African-American women during the early decades of the Jim Crow era.

Notes

1 C.G. Woodson (1933) *Mis-Education of the Negro*. Washington, DC: Associated Publishers, p.23.

2 H.M. Bond (1934) *The Education of the Negro in the American Social Order*. New York: Prentice-Hall, pp.167–283.

3 R. Kelley (1993) 'We are not what we seem': rethinking Black working-class opposition in the Jim Crow South. *Journal of American History*. June: 75–112.

4 J.D. Anderson (1988) *The Education of Blacks in the South, 1860–1935*. Chapel Hill, NC: University of North Carolina Press, pp.192–3. Lynching would continue after 1900 despite attempts to pass legislation to make the practice illegal and despite relentless efforts to bring attention to the problem by such African-Americans as Ida Wells Barnett. In 1952 for the first time in 71 years of documentation, the Tuskegee Institute reported that there was no known lynching of African-Americans. See also T. Cowan and J. McQuire (1994) *Time Lines of African-American History: 500 Years of Black Achievement*. New York: Berkley.

5 NASC Interim History Writing Committee (1979) *The Jeanes Story: A Chapter in the History of American Education, 1908–1968*. Georgia: Southern Education Foundation, pp.109–91. Over 60 per cent of the US African-American population lived in Georgia, Mississippi, Alabama, the Carolinas and Louisiana.

6 Anderson, *The Education of Blacks*, p.156.

7 See D.T. Blose and A. Caliver (1935) *Statistics of the Education of Negroes, 1929–30 and 1931–32*. U.S. Office of Education Bulletin No. 13.

8 Miss Anna T. Jeanes was born 7 April 1822, the youngest of ten children. She never married, was the longest survivor of her family and inherited a small fortune. She also gave money to Hampton Institute, Tuskegee Institute and the General Education Board.

9 The General Education Board (GEB) established in 1902 and composed of business people to 'provide funds and to follow up and give effect to the work of the propagandists'. The Southern Education Board (SEB), established at the same time, served as 'an investigating and "preaching" board for carrying on a propaganda of education', Anderson, *The Education of Blacks*, p.85. Jeanes's funding was provided for Delaware, Maryland, Virginia, W. Virginia, North

Carolina, South Carolina, Georgia, Florida, Alabama, Mississippi, Louisiana, Texas, Arkansas, Missouri, Kentucky and Tennessee.

10 Virginia Randolph was born in Richmond, Virginia, 8 June 1874, the second oldest of four children. She started school aged 6 and at 8 worked for a Mrs Powell in the morning and evenings before and after school. See L.G.E. Jones (1937) *The Jeanes Teacher in the United States, 1908–1933*. Chapel Hill, NC: University of North Carolina Press, p.23. See also Minutes of the Meeting of the Jeanes Funds, 1907, Hampton Archives, Virginia; L. Harlan (1958) *Separate and Unequal: Public School Campaigns and Racism in the Southern Seaboard States 1901–1915*. Chapel Hill, NC: University of North Carolina Press, pp.86–7.

11 N.C. Newbold to R.G. Kizer, Salisbury County School Superintendent, 20 May 1916, North Carolina Division of Negro Education Records (NCDNE).

12 N.C. Newbold to Dr E.C. Brooks, 19 November 1919, Box 221, Folder 2122, GEB Records, Rockefeller Archives, Tarrytown, New York. North Carolina Jeanes teachers received funding from the Jeanes Fund, North Carolina State Board of Health and the Smith-Lever Fund.

13 Jones, *The Jeanes Teacher*, p.117.

14 Ibid., pp.72–3.

15 Jeanes Work, Year Ending 30 June 1925 Report, Series 1, Box 221, Folder 2122, GEB Records.

16 See Education of Negroes in North Carolina, 1914–1925–1939, Box 115, Folder 1045, GEB Records.

17 The SEB consisted of the Peabody, Slater, Jeanes and Randolph Funds. See J.C. Dixon to Lindsley F. Kimball, 6 October 1959, Box 222, Folder 2124, GEB Records.

18 There were a small number of male Jeanes teachers, less than 2 per cent, during the existence of the programme, 1908–68.

19 See Report of N.C. Newbold, March 1914, Division of Negro Education Records.

20 Newbold to R.G. Kizer, Salisbury County School Superintendent, 20 May 1916, NCDNE Records.

21 See *The Jeanes Story: A Chapter in the History of American Education, 1908–1968*, prepared by the NASC Interim History Writing Committee for a 'Roll Call of Workers', for all states, pp.109–91. Special thanks to Dr Susie W. Wheeler, former Jeanes teacher, and member of the writing committee for bringing this manuscript to my attention.

22 Dillard to Newbold, 14 August 1914, NCDNE Records.

23 See Education of Negroes in North Carolina 1914–1925–1939, Box 115, Folder 1045, GEB Records.

24 Jones, *The Jeanes Teacher*, p.46.

25 J.H. Dillard (1923) School help in the open country. *Opportunity* 1(3).

26 Interview with Mrs Lulu Harris Butler Robinson by author, Raleigh, North Carolina, 6 June 1995.

27 Ibid.

28 N.C. Newbold to N.W. Britton, Winton, North Carolina, 30 June 1922, General Correspondence, September 1920-August 1921 Folder, NCDNE Records.

29 Holland to Newbold, 5 September 1914, NCDNE Records.

30 See 11 April 1916 Report of Jeanes Teachers, N.C. Newbold Correspondence, Division of Negro Education Records.

31 Informational and explanatory letter about Industrial Work in Public schools of the State, J.Y. Joyner, c. 1913, Box 1, Folder 1913, Miscellaneous Reports and Outlines, NCDNE Records.

32 See Supervising Industrial Teachers, February 1918, Box 222, Folder 2125, GEB Records.

33 Jeanes Teachers Reports 1913, Correspondence Box 1, NCDNE Records.

34 W.C. Bivens to N.C. Newbold, 20 April 1918, Director's Correspondence, Box 3, Folder B, NCDNE Records. Although the superintendent was writing to Newbold to dismiss the supervisor because he felt that she was unable to solicit the support of the community, it is evident that the community and the teacher were unable to come to a compromise concerning industrial education.

35 Interview by author with Mrs S.P. Morton, 27 July 1992. Mrs Morton served as a supervisor for Home Economic Education and the School Lunch Program in the Virginia system for '29 years and one month'.

36 Ibid.

37 C. Neverdon-Morton (1989) *Afro-American Women of the South and the Advancement of the Race, 1895–1925*. Knoxville, TN: University of Tennessee Press, p.93. Such actions of a supervisor in Wake County also earned respect. Mrs P.L. Byrd, Jeanes Teacher of Fuquay, extended the term for seventh graders with money won at an industrial exhibit at the State Fair. See Monthly Progress Report, 6 April 1924, Box 119, Folder 1076 for North Carolina, GEB Records. In the same report, another teacher, Mrs Mary S. Gray of Martin County, reported that the County Teachers' Association purchased a roadster for her use and she noted that she had been able to get more work done and to find some weak places in teaching.

38 See N.C. Newbold Correspondence, 1913–14, NCDNE Records.

39 In a 9 March 1910 report, James H. Dillard, President and General Agent of the Jeanes Fund, stated that we have 148 extension and supervising teachers and organizers. During this session . . . five have been dismissed . . . two by superintendents in Lafayette Parish, Louisiana, and in Glynn County, Georgia 'because of inability to harmonize with local workers', Jeanes Fund, Box 2, Hampton Archives, Virginia.

40 Newbold to Holland, 4 January 1918, NCDNE Records. Newbold informed Holland that Miss Jones was offering unsolicited advice to teachers such as informing them that they should not build fires in the schools; rather, the men in the neighbourhood should be responsible for such tasks. Newbold also instructed Holland to meet with a superintendent and Jeanes teacher in Hertford County and help plan a two-day teachers' meeting; visit a Jeanes teacher in Beaufort County and convince her to spend more time with the 'country folks and country schools' and visit a new supervisor in Person County and help her get started with her work.

41 Asa J. Manning, Superintendent of Martin County Schools to Newbold, 15 June 1916, Jeanes Teachers, Box 2, Lenoir-Wilson Counties' Folder, NCDNE Records.

42 Unnamed superintendent to Holland, 17 June 1926, NCDNE Records.

43 J.A. Capps to Holland, 21 June 1926, NCDNE Records.

44 H.P. Robertson to Holland, 16 June 1926, NCDNE Records.

45 F.P. Hall to Holland, 28 June 1926, NCDNE Records.

46 C. Neverdon-Morton, *Afro-American Women*. For further discussion on responses of southern Black women to community problems, see pp.233–6.

47 Annie E.B. White to Newbold, 12 June 1913, Jeanes Teachers Reports 1913, Director's Correspondence, Box 1, NCDNE Records.

48 The Jeanes Supervising Industrial Teachers: Some Things they helped to do Last School Year, 1916–1917, North Carolina, Box 115, Folder 144, GEB Records. In 1917, NC Jeanes teachers raised approximately $25,000 (cash, material and labour); the Jeanes Fund paid salaries of $6,550; the counties paid salaries of $5,197.88.

49 Dillard, School help in the open country.

50 The State Board of Health also assigned Mrs Florence C. Williams to travel and work with the various Jeanes teachers to assist in organizing health clubs, etc. It was suggested that the Improvement Leagues in the county already established by Jeanes teachers appoint Health Committees. See Newbold Correspondence, Box 3, Miscellaneous Reports, Division of Negro Education Records. See also circular from Newbold to County Supervising Teachers, 1 October 1917, Division of Negro Education Records.

51 Mrs Mary S. Gray, Martin County to N.C. Newbold, 'Progress Letter', 5 June 1924, Box 119, Folder 1076, GEB Records.

52 January 1928 Summary Report of Jeanes Supervisors, North Carolina, NCDNE Records.

53 Newbold to Holland, 10 April 1916. NCDNE Records.

54 Home-Makers' Club Work, Box 113, Folder 1028, GEB Records.

55 See Chapter 3, 'Black Women Workers', in Neverdon-Morton, *Afro-American Women of the South*; T.W. Hunter (1995) Domination and resistance: the politics of wage household labor in New South Atlanta, in D.C. Hine, W. King and L. Reed (eds) *We Specialize in the Wholly Impossible*. New York: Carlson.

56 See Summary of Reports, 1 July 1915–30 June 1916, NCDNE Records.

57 See North Carolina Progress Letter, 5 June 1924, Box 119, Folder 1076, GEB Records.

58 See Monthly Progress Report, January 1914, Statement of Bessie L. Fogg of Beaufort County, NCDNE Records.

59 See Home-Makers' Clubs Summary, Box 16, Folder NC 236.2, GEB Records.

60 T.W. Hanchett (1988) The Rosenwald schools and Black education in North Carolina. *North Carolina Historical Review* 65(4): 395.

61 See Press Release, November 1920, on the condition of education in North Carolina, Box 118, Folder 1072, GEB Records.

62 See Box 119, Folder 1076, GEB Records.

63 See Monthly Progress Report, 6 March 1924, Box 119, Folder 1076, GEB Records.

64 Ibid.

65 See Monthly Progress Report, 6 May 1924, Box 119, Folder 1076, GEB Records.

66 Miss Elizabeth Harris to Newbold, 5 April 1916, Director's Correspondence, Box 3, Folder Home-Makers' Clubs, NCDNE Records.

67 See Progress Report, 6 May 1924, Box 119, Folder 1076, GEB Records.

68 Holland to W.F. Credle, 11 September 1925, Correspondence of the Supervisor of Rosenwald Schools Fund, Box 2, Division of Negro Education Records. Edgecombe County raised $565, Mecklenburg $418, Sampson $500, Warren $678 and Durham County $1,908.

69 D.M. Pinderhughes (1987) *Race and Ethnicity in Chicago Politics*. Urbana, IL: University of Illinois Press, ch.7.

70 Mrs P.L. Byrd, Progress Letter, 5 June 1924, Box 119, Folder 1076 for North Carolina, GEB Records. Holland always advocated involving the teacher in whatever activities a Jeanes teacher planned as well as travelling to homes in the company of the community teacher.

71 Ibid.

72 Committee, *The Jeanes Story*.

Kate Rousmaniere

Margaret Haley is one of the most popular and popularized icons of American teachers' history, heralded as a radical school reformer, labour activist, and feminist. In the first three decades of the twentieth century, Haley led the Chicago Teachers' Federation to be the first teachers' labour union in American history and in so doing, she changed the shape of US educational politics forever. To educational historians and teacher activists, the outlines of Haley's life and work are well known. From the moment this Irish American elementary teacher joined the newly founded Chicago Teachers' Federation in 1898, she led it into the heart of urban school politics by challenging corporate tax deductions to city school finances and raising federation membership to over half of all Chicago teachers, most of them women. Until her death in 1939, Haley led federation battles for increased teacher salaries, pensions and tenure laws, and she initiated investigations into teachers' working conditions and school funding. Haley also developed the federation as a professional support for teachers when she introduced representative teacher councils into Chicago schools, after school classes for teachers on progressive education, and a monthly news and network bulletin. Haley negotiated an unprecedented affiliation between teachers and the Chicago Federation of Labor, and led her organization to become Local 1 of the newly formed American Federation of Teachers. Haley worked at the national level too, traversing the country to promote political activism among the nation's predominately female teaching force, and pressuring the powerful, administrator dominated National Education Association (NEA) to include the representation of women teachers. She was the first woman and elementary school teacher to speak from the floor of the NEA, and she organized a successful campaign to elect Chicago school superintendent Ella Flagg Young to be the first woman president of that organization.

An early critic of what she called the 'factoryization' of education, Haley fought not only for teachers' rights as workers but also for teachers' authority to shape the classroom into a caring and supportive environment for children. Echoing John Dewey's faith in the school as a potential agent of social change, Haley believed that the classroom teacher could be the centre of humanitarian reform. If the school could not 'bring joy to the work of the world', she argued, then 'joy must go out of its own life, and work in the school as in the factory will become drudgery.'[1] This progressive vision reached outside the school as Haley promoted child labour laws, direct primaries, women's suffrage and labour rights. But her vision was not to be. Her work was opposed by an emerging coalition of school reformers and business interests intent on creating a centralized school administration, detaching teachers from their previous community and working class base, and thwarting any affiliation of teachers with organized labour. By the mid-1930s the federation was all but defunct, and Haley's power had evaporated.

In her work with the federation, Margaret Haley covered a wide range of political playing fields, linking teachers with labour, the feminist reform movement, municipal reform and progressive education and because of this, her allegiances were often at odds with one another. For all her notoriety as a progressive activist, she expressed profound ambivalence about some of the causes she held most dear, revealing a dynamic tension between her own class, gender, ethnic and political identities. She was often frustrated with the passive and provincial attitudes of the teachers whom she defended, yet she also feared that an activist national union like the American Federation of Teachers would minimize her own local authority. She criticized the Chicago Federation of Labor for being male dominated and derogatory to women workers, although she also belittled the social reform work of upper class feminists like Jane Addams. Although she spoke the rhetoric of democratic leadership, in practice Haley was more of a labour bureaucrat who managed a densely hierarchical organization that was under persistent attack from the outside.

Haley's often contradictory political responses evolved from her own complex identity as a woman, a teacher, a labour union activist and a working class Irish American, and those four 'sides' of her identity did not always coexist harmoniously. Like all teachers, Haley encompassed in her life and work a range of social and political identities, but she always identified as a teacher first, and the identity of teacher permeated all aspects of her life and work so that her commitment to both labour and feminist issues was often inconsistent. In her efforts to negotiate the male dominated labour movement and the middle class dominated women's movement, Haley epitomized in her very person broader conflicts of class and gender politics within the occupation of teaching.

This chapter is a preliminary outline of a new biography of Margaret Haley that broadens our understanding beyond her public achievements with the federation. Drawing on the biographical approach of 'life history' that focuses on the subject's own interpretation of her experience, I pay less attention to what Haley did and more to who she was, attending to the fault lines and inconsistencies of her life as much as her successes. My object is to understand how Haley developed and negotiated her political identity as a teacher union leader.

Rethinking teachers' biography

Part of the problem facing a biographer of Haley is that both her contemporaries and historians enshrined her as a kind of heroic icon of political activism. In her day, this former elementary school teacher was nationally famous among women activists, social reformers and industrial unionists. She was often described by her peers as a heroic, swaggering and eloquent figure who linked all corners of progressive thought and who persistently fought for social justice. Her contemporary Carl Sandburg described her as a dynamo of integrity who 'flung her clenched fist into the faces of contractors, school land lease holders, tax dodgers and their politicians, fixers, go-betweens and stool pigeons' and never had her enemies 'been able to smutch her once in the eyes of decent men and women of this town who do their own thinking.'[2] Such descriptions have been hard for historians to resist, and Haley is usually described as a militant unionist, a radical feminist and a teacher leader. The famous 'lady labor slugger' is described as both domineering and demure, both industrial unionist and professional teacher, and yet always a cohesive and self-confident whole, a seamless web of radicalism.[3] She appears to us as a highly tuned legislative machine, a skilled and assertive political mediator, for whom ambiguity and contradictions were an unknown quantity.

Haley herself furthered this image of a modern day Joan of Arc. That she titled her autobiography 'Battleground' is telling. It is classic labour autobiography that is essentially a litany of public accomplishments and political thunderstorms with barely a shadow of self-reflection or personal conflict. She self-consciously presented herself as a valiant block of energy forging against injustice in much the same way she must have seen her male counterparts organize their public lives. To some extent, the biographer in search of Haley's life history has to work against Haley's own presentation of herself.

The biographer also has to struggle with clarifying the unique political identity of urban teachers, an identity that does not fold easily into common historical categories of class or gender activism. Like her less famous sisters in the teaching force, Haley embodied in her very work simultaneous positionings in multiple power relations. In late nineteenth century Chicago, up to one-third of all teachers were daughters of the Irish immigrant working class, yet they held white collar jobs with both economic security and high social status. Women teachers worked in a feminized labour force with explicit gendered and classed prescriptions for behaviour, yet they also shared their days in relatively hetero-social environments in interactive relationships with men and women staff, parents, school officials and community members from a variety of class and cultural backgrounds. Their daily working relations were both highly structured under a male dominated school hierarchy, and communal as they spent their days in social inter-actions with women colleagues and children. Teachers' occupational identity thus shared components of the industrial proletariat, feminized social service work and white collar professionals and they engaged in a range of alliances and conflict across class and gendered social spheres. The biographer of any teacher needs to understand the complex work of teachers by drawing on a combination of insights and sources in labour, feminist and ethnic studies.[4]

For Haley, the complex dynamics of being a teacher were intensified by her work as a political leader. From her office in the heart of Chicago's business district, Haley interacted with powerful men from the labour movement, city government and the legal system, as well as middle class women reformers, leaders of Chicago's ethnic communities, and power brokers in the Roman Catholic clergy, industry and the Illinois state house. As she expanded her work nationally, Haley's work took on broader proportions with larger political repercussions. She literally took the complicated class and gender identity of the woman teacher out of the schoolhouse and into the public political world.

Being a teacher like Margaret Haley meant inhabiting a variety of social contexts, and writing a biography of a teacher like Margaret Haley means exploring the different social contexts of her life history and the way those different contexts were played out in the meaningful moments of her life.[5] Margaret Haley becomes more of a three dimensional person when we look less at what she did and more at how she lived, the way she followed certain scripts and adapted others at different political moments. By attending to Haley's perspective of her life and not simply her accomplishments, she emerges less as a labour leader, feminist or educational professional pure and simple, and more as herself, complete with contradictions. The biographical question is not the extent to which Haley was a feminist or a unionist, but what aspects of her multipositionality shaped her decision making at different moments in time, and how she perceived and experienced her work and politics? The point of analysis begins where Haley stood, and not where prior categories would position her.[6]

The education of Margaret Haley

In her own brief recollections of her childhood, Haley emphasized her early education in labour activism and progressive politics. According to this account, it was her working class Irish immigrant father, a member of the Knights of Labor, who taught his eldest daughter an innate distrust of monopoly capitalism and a faith in the power of the democratic state to control the unbridled interests of profit.[7] When her father went bankrupt, these early lessons of economic injustice were cemented in her mind. Moving to Chicago and observing the Haymarket riot and the economic inequities of an industrial city, Haley became more convinced of the necessity of reforming the political economy of the modern industrial state. She joined a community of Chicago social reformers who believed that in the industrial wars of the late nineteenth century, the 'barbarians have come from above', and that it was the responsibility of state agencies like the public school to create a systematic and paternalistic civic apparatus.[8]

But in the shadows of Haley's account of her early political education, we can see that gender, too, shaped her emerging view of the world. Haley was 10 when her older brother drowned, and this left her the eldest in a family of seven children. She recounted that the most defining moment of her life was at age 16 when her father declared bankruptcy and she was 'catapulted' into the workforce to support her family. Thus it was the death of one male, and the financial catastrophe of another, that offered Haley the avenue for escape from a traditional nineteenth century woman's life. Her mother had already encouraged her career by enrolling her in a local parochial school and, later, teacher training. Like other immigrant Irish women, Elizabeth Haley saw teaching as a viable means of employment for her daughter, and possibly as the best avenue to escape her own life pattern of marriage and motherhood.[9] Teaching also offered Haley the opportunity to leave her small town and join the wave of young people moving to Chicago, and it offered intellectual stimulation at teacher training schools and summer institutes. However stereotyped teaching was as a feminized occupation, it offered a young rural immigrant's daughter a life of unprecedented independence. These gendered lessons of the limitations and possibilities of women's lives further informed the way that she thought about the occupation of teaching.

Haley's identity as a second generation Irish Catholic also contributed to her developing political identity as both a reformer and a teacher. By the turn of the century, first and second generation Irish American women saw a career in school teaching as almost part of the natural life line. Local parishes and dioceses supported female education as a counter to the Protestant based public school system, and Irish American women who suffered ethnic discrimination in other white collar jobs benefited from the job patronage system in Irish dominated civil service and governmental structures. In late nineteenth century Chicago, which housed the fourth largest Irish population in the United States, the Irish American presence in local politics furthered Haley's sense that teaching was not only a possible career option, but also a welcoming one.[10]

The political and cultural community of Irish Catholics in education also influenced Haley's vision for a progressive welfare state. Her first notions of the school as an agency of social reform were developed in Catholic summer schools for teachers where she learned not only progressive child centred pedagogy but also the importance of intellectual clarity, charity and social reform.[11] Throughout her career, she would draw on both those spiritual and reform principles and on actual Irish Catholic connections in Chicago, weaving a web of support that stretched from the state house to the local parish. Her Catholic links crossed otherwise impervious class and gender lines, as she entered the halls of industrial unions and the offices of high ranking city officials, holding her Irish Catholic identity as a reference. Her ethnic and religious identity was thus far more than who she was as an individual; it also played a significant role in shaping what she worked for and how she worked.

Haley's active political life began in her late thirties after she had been a classroom teacher for 16 years. Until then, she was in many real and symbolic ways silent and preoccupied with family. As a young Chicago teacher, Haley brought her entire family to the city, taking care of her ageing parents and helping her younger siblings to secure civil service jobs. When her sister Jennie's husband was diagnosed with cancer soon after the birth of their first child, the two sisters joined the Women's Catholic Order of Foresters, an organization devoted to the distribution of insurance and pensions to women. It was here that Haley entered the political world, perhaps because age had given her the confidence to act, perhaps because she worked on behalf of her sister, or perhaps because her years in the classroom had taught her both rhetorical skills and an impatience with clogged bureaucracy. She entered politics with an explosion: she had only recently joined the Foresters when she charged the leader of the organization with illegally holding her position for life. It was not just the legal aspects that bothered Haley, but the traditional hierarchical structure of the organization that she believed repressed democratic practices. In the Foresters organization as in schools, Haley complained, formalities 'paralysed' and 'hypnotized' otherwise intelligent people so that they lost the spirit of the cause and acted 'as if they belonged to the nobility'.[12]

Ironically, Haley's enemy here was Elizabeth Rogers, one of the most beloved women officials in the Knights of Labor, but who Haley saw only as an autocrat. When Haley was threatened with expulsion for her challenge of Rogers, she asked three priests to the convention stage to defend her integrity and support her argument against the life rule policy. Haley agreed to apologize for previously insulting Rogers, and she did so in her soon to be characteristic manner saying: 'I'm sorry I offended anybody. *Even if* what I said was true, I should not have said it.' This statement set off another tumult: Elizabeth Rogers was furious, the priests scolded Haley, and the whole convention was set into hysterical motion. Having made her point, Haley left the organization and began her work with the newly founded teachers' federation.

To the biographer, Haley's experience with the Foresters is more than a minor political skirmish unrelated to her later work with Chicago teachers.

The Foresters battle marks her emerging political style: here she first displayed her penchant for dramatics, her skill at legal argument and her tactical reliance on Catholic male authority. Here also she displayed her complex political affiliations. Knowing that she was assured a voice in an all women's organization, she felt completely justified in criticizing that organization for its political flaws and in dramatically attacking its renowned leader who was beloved by labour and women alike. From the beginning of her political career, then, Haley crossed political loyalties.

Gendered politics, teachers' politics

Haley's tendency to develop multiple commitments and to juggle her affiliations to address her cause is most clear in her work with organized women's social reform. Haley's belief in the responsibility of the state to protect women workers aligned her with prominent women's reform organizations of the day. Denied a formal political voice through suffrage, progressive era women took part in a broad network of social reform work using quasi-governmental, rationalized and scientific welfare agencies. The political culture of Chicago's middle class women reformers at the turn of the century centred around the notion of 'municipal housekeeping' – a city-wide agenda which implied not just social betterment, but also the institutionalization of a publicly financed welfare structure, modelled on the ideal caring home and community. Municipal housekeeping placed the interests of the family and community as central to the interests of the state, and the school was included in the social equation of the state as a large home. As one prominent proponent of municipal housekeeping expressed it: 'Woman's place is Home . . . But Home is not contained within the four walls of the individual house. Home is the community. The city full of people is the Family. The public school is the real Nursery. And badly do the Home and Family need the mother.'[13] School issues as they related to poor urban children – compulsory enrolment, curriculum, school building maintenance and school health – were a critical part of Chicago women reformers' programmes.[14]

In her work with the federation, Haley loosely adopted the notion of municipal housekeeping, but inserted teachers at the exact centre of the entire reform movement. When Haley argued that 'the cause of the teacher is the cause of the people and vice versa, and their common cause is that of the children', she meant, literally, that teachers' interests should be at the first priority of municipal reform.[15] Satisfied teachers would improve the schools and thereby improve the city as a whole. In adopting the rhetoric of municipal housekeeping, Haley made the tactical move of emphasizing gender over labour politics. As a woman activist, Haley had a far better chance of political success by echoing the rhetoric of municipal housekeeping rather than that of the specific interests of labour unions. Throughout her career, Haley struggled to balance the public image of municipal housekeeping with specific labour interests by claiming that salaries, pensions, and improved working conditions were not benefits for a special interest group but a matter of government responsibility.[16]

Haley's philosophical equation of teacher benefits as civic benefits unravelled in actual city politics and with none other than her friend Jane Addams. When Addams became a member of the Chicago Board of Education, the two women found themselves in conflicting tactical positions. Addams saw her job on the board as one of appeasing opposing factions, and Haley's federation was one of those factions. The Chicago business community pressured Addams to see teachers as a special interest group which had no more right than any other special interest to dictate the policy of the Board of Education. Meanwhile, Haley tried to convince her that the federation did not promote special interests, but rather, the crucial elements of the social reform cause that the two women shared.[17] When Addams sided against the teachers on a number of decisions about school management and the teachers' pension, Haley was ruthless in her criticism. She charged Addams with the very accusations used on her: that she was privileging her own special interests of maintaining political connections for Hull House: 'You pay too dear for your forty playgrounds, or forty times forty playgrounds, when you trade them off for the fundamental rights that the teachers have.'[18]

This conflict between Haley and Addams gives the biographer insight into Haley's character as well as her tactics. Single minded and egocentric, she was incapable of seeing any cause as more important than her own, and was convinced that she alone carried the burden of educating the world to the importance of that cause. But she believed her self-sacrifice was justified because of the colossal significance of her movement which was not merely local city politics, but a righteous battle to prevent the school, 'the last institution of democracy' from 'becoming a prey to the dominant spirit of greed, commercialism, autocracy and all the attendant evils.'[19] By making teachers central to civic reform, Haley saw any compromise of teachers' interests as an abdication to the entire social reform agenda. If teachers were not central to the political cause, then the cause was simply wrong.

Labour politics, teachers' politics

Haley found organized labour to be similarly inadequate in its commitment to teachers. On the surface, Haley's affiliation of the Teachers' Federation with the Chicago Federation of Labor (CFL) in 1902, and as a founding member of the American Federation of Teachers in 1916 identify her as a strong labour activist. She served on major legislative committees of the CFL, and supported the mayoral candidacy of her friend and the president of the CFL, the popular John Fitzpatrick. Under the conservative city Loeb Law that prohibited teachers from being members of labour unions, Haley was forced to withdraw her Teachers' Federation from the CFL, and this story has traditionally been described as a critical turning point in US teacher politics, forcing teachers toward a professional model of organization rather than an industrial labour one.[20]

But Haley's feelings about the CFL were far more ambiguous than she publicly expressed. Her first encounter with the labour organization was observing a fixed election, exposing its powerful leader, and expelling him from the federation. She retold the story in her autobiography with characteristic bravado. As one of the few women in the voting room she hitched up her skirts and jumped onto a table to give the men a lecture about politics and values. In private, however, Haley seemed less confident. She worried about the chaotic organization of the CFL and the troubles it had with cooperating with outside agencies. 'That CF of L is turbulent, disorganized . . . no co-ordination, full of suspicion of one another, hatred, discord, self-seeking, coarse, crude, and almost anarchistical,' she wrote privately, and she feared that it was 'rushing on to self-destruction.' She worried doubly that her concerns about the CFL organization would be misunderstood as opposition to labour in general.[21]

Haley also had doubts about the AFT even though her political actions consistently supported the idea of a nationwide teachers' organization. In practice, such an organization threatened to undermine some of her own control and made her a reluctant and often hostile unionist. She was wary of the male leadership of the AFT, and felt particularly uncomfortable with the politically radical Jewish men who ran the powerful New York local union branch and edited the AFT newspaper. But even locally and with women, Haley jealously guarded her power. In 1928, a new AFT local to Chicago elementary teachers was organized, and Haley refused to either join her own elementary teachers with them or to shut down the federation. A woman AFT member from Chicago gave her analysis of Haley's political limitations in this matter. Her 'greatest crime of all' was

> keeping the members of her organization away from associating with other teachers and organizations that are striving to realize larger ideals of education and a larger personal life . . . Leaders may come and leaders may go, but the movement lives on. I hardly think Margaret has ever thought of what her scheme of 'going it alone' is doing to her membership. We can not live in isolation and really grow – neither can we afford to lose the desire of cooperation.[22]

The references to the Teachers' Federation members' lack of a 'larger personal life' seems to refer to Haley's commitment to segregated politics of forefronting women in education, and particularly within her organization.

Yet as we have seen, her commitment to gender politics was circumscribed by her interests as a teacher, interests which also conflicted partially with those of the organized labour movement. Thus as a labour activist, Haley's gender identification often crisscrossed and opposed her labour identification, so that she balanced her reliance on industrial labour organizations with her suspicions that they might not come through for women, and for teachers. In a similar way, she suspiciously eyed the middle class women's reform movement for its commitment to teachers.

Civic politics, teachers' politics

The federation battle for tax reform offers yet another perspective on Haley's complicated negotiations of labour, gender and teachers' politics. In late 1899 the Chicago Board of Education told teachers that a financial shortfall meant that they could not give them a promised raise. Haley began an investigation of the Board of Education finances and found that the city taxation office was under assessing a number of major utilities companies. The federation sued, and won the money which eventually went to teachers' salaries. The federation won national attention for this campaign, in part because the case touched the interest of political lobbying groups outside of education, especially tax and municipal reformers. Characteristically, Haley promoted the fight as one that would serve both teachers' needs specifically and the broader interests of the city at large. She billed the tax struggle as 'the people's victory', as much as it was the teachers' victory.[23] And indeed, much of the nation did see the teachers' tax struggle this way. The topic of tax reform for schools hit a powerful double chord that attracted both economically minded business men and social reformers concerned with women and children. To many Chicagoans, the federation campaign against 'tax dodging' was much more than interest group politics or women's politics but an agenda that cut a wide path across a number of political agendas.[24] The problem Haley faced was that the specificity of the teachers' cause was often subsumed under these broader platforms.

In the popular press, the teachers' claim for their promised salary increase was transformed into a flamboyant battle between the sexes where prim and proper schoolmarms took on cigar smoking bureaucrats. Essentially, teachers' labour claims were ignored and their gender identity highlighted. A popular Chicago daily encapsulated this image:

> Mandamus Proceedings were brought by the teachers
> Against the incorporate Tax-dodging Creatures
> 'No, no,' say the ladies, 'you can not flim flam us,
> We'll keep up the fighting, though every man damn us.'[25]

Even federation supporters saw the image of women elementary teachers monitoring the government as far more engaging an issue than the specific cause of teachers' low pay. A male lawyer friend of Haley's wrote to her:

> How cheerful it is to know that we men have such efficient women in the public service to prod us to the full limit of our duty. I would have given three dollars and sixteen cents to have seen those fellows squirm when that meek (!) and quiet Haley got wound up and shotting [sic] off her hot shot at the many million dollar corporations. It must have been fun.[26]

Other reports of the tax fight stripped away both gender implications and the teachers' case, focusing solely on the issue of municipal waste and corruption. This emphasis on government watchdogging reinforced the popular belief that the teachers had no self-interest, and that this was a cause larger than themselves. Like the traditional view that women taught school because they loved children and not for money, some supporters of the federation saw Haley's group as self-sacrificing angels for civic reform. The Archdiocese of Chicago approvingly described the teachers' victory as a moral one and not one of self-interested teachers or suffragists.[27] The Bishop of Peoria wrote that the federation had successfully avoided partisan politics while still inspiring teachers with 'new courage, a higher moral earnestness and a nobler pride in their vocation.'[28] The importance of Haley's work was not that she had fought for an improvement in teachers' working conditions or for a voice for women teachers, but that she had forced city officials to do their civic duty correctly. Other groups, particularly tax reform associations dominated by men, asked Haley to speak to them about tax reform, and not about the teachers' cause. The federation tax fight was thus divested of its specificity and became merely an agency of tax reform – albeit an unusual one because it was led by women.

Middle class women's reform groups also approved of the Teachers' Federation tax struggle but they deviated away from teachers' interests into the more amorphous areas of social reform. As the Chicago tax fight gained national notoriety, Haley became wildly popular among women's groups to whom she had become less of a teacher activist and more of an icon of women's social reform. A mother of six in Wisconsin invited Haley to speak to the County Fair where she had recently founded an Educational Department. Wouldn't Haley come to speak 'on taxation and on schools and on teaching? . . . I think our young people need more enlightenment of these subjects and we can get along with less horse racing.'[29] Haley herself sometimes suspected the way that the tax fight was broadened to leave teachers' interests behind. When the Cleveland chapter of the Women's Christian Temperance Union (WCTU) invited Haley to speak to their group, claiming that their city too, 'needs this lesson', Haley refused the invitation after she discovered that the group was not particularly popular among teachers. Instead, she sought an audience with the Cleveland Board of Education and a teachers' institute.[30] Certainly Haley was not above mixing causes to promote her own. When the suffrage leader Susan B. Anthony argued that the federation was supporting all women's best interest, Haley made sure to publicize the support.[31] Haley's struggle was to maintain the popular image of broad social reform while addressing the specific needs of an overworked and underpaid female teaching staff.

Personal politics, teachers' politics

In her personal life, too, Haley challenges any preconceived identity or affiliation. While she stood on the margins of the political women's movement, Haley lived and worked in a vibrant community of women teachers. For over 15 years she shared the leadership of the Teachers' Federation with her friend Catharine Goggin. Much has been hypothesized about this relationship, particularly because the two shared a home together for some years. Haley and Goggin did work very closely together, and they were clearly intimate friends. But each also lived with a variety of other friends, and spent much of their work and vacation times apart. Furthermore, whoever Haley led her private life with, she clearly enjoyed the company and camaraderie of powerful men with whom she shared the political talk of the state house and city hall. Whatever Haley's sexual identity, her personal identity was intimately involved with her work with teachers: she lived and breathed her work, she rarely left it behind and rarely wrote of anything else. Those whose work she disrespected, including many women, were of no interest to her.

As a teacher, too, Haley's identity and loyalties were complicated. Although she always identified herself as a teacher, she herself rarely spoke of her 16 years in the classroom, and in her relationships with teachers she was often condescending about their day-to-day concerns and critical of what she perceived to be their political apathy. In her writings and speeches, she was a torrent of enthusiasm, physically reaching out to teachers to fight for better working conditions and improved schools, but she was often domineering, single minded, self-centred and so long winded that colleagues audibly groaned when she began to talk at the end of a long meeting. For all her talk about democracy, she was at times obnoxious, condescending, autocratic and distant. Her strong personality could alienate her from other women who interpreted her zealous political cause as rude and insensitive. She described herself as inheriting family traits of obstinacy and confrontation – characteristics which friends sometimes advised her to moderate. At one critical political moment, her lawyer sternly advised her to watch her step and 'not let your delight in contest invite you into a conflict, before you have grown large enough to win'.[32]

But for all her energy and independence, Haley never ventured into radical politics and she avoided any affiliation with such contemporary figures as Eugene Debs or Charlotte Perkins Gilman, both of whose socialist ideologies matched with Haley's political vision. For all her faith in the government as a social mediator and her criticism of privilege, Haley was not a member of the Socialist Party, and she veered wide of any other leftist organization. And while she threw her energy into the woman suffrage movement, she was devoid of any race consciousness and avoided the topic of African-American students and teachers altogether.[33] She was a pacifist during the First World War, but probably only because of her Irish hatred for England and not out of any philosophical pacifist principles.

The intensity and immediacy of Haley's focus on teachers allowed her to flirt with mainstream progressive groups and avoid taking political or intellectual risks into the left. Nor was she one to question her own motives. Unlike her middle class peers in the women's reform movement, Haley had little formal education beyond teacher training, and she was not inclined by character or class background to reflect on her personal philosophy or behaviour. While Jane Addams spent much of her young life in self-doubt, 'weary of myself and sick of asking what I am and what I ought to be', Haley spent the same years preparing to become a teacher and reading Catholic reform tracts and the economic platforms of Henry George.[34] Her interests were the concrete, legal and financial concerns of teachers, and she shaped her own independent political platform on those concerns, unfettered by affiliations, loyalties, or even specific principles. This allowed her to be somewhat of a pit bull in her leadership, single mindedly driven toward results.

Conclusion

A life history of Margaret Haley suggests that she was a more complicated and conflicted woman than prior portraits have described. She was a woman who wrestled not only with her own personal history and character, but also with the opposing pressures of the political world around her. As a woman teacher union activist in the progressive era, Haley did not fit into standard categories of the American left. Standing at the centre of often conflicting reform movements, Haley symbolized both a synthesis of the politics of education, labour and women's social reform and epitomized the persistent contradictions and disagreements of those movements.

Notes

1 R. Reid (ed.) (1982) *Battleground: The Autobiography of Margaret Haley*. Urbana, IL: University of Illinois Press, p.286.

2 C. Sandberg (1915) Margaret Haley, *Reed's Mirror*, December.

3 Examples of these perspectives of Haley can be found in J. Nolan (1995) A Patrick Henry in the classroom: Margaret Haley and the Chicago Teachers' Federation. *Éire-Ireland* 30: 104–17; C. Collins (1984) Regaining the past for the present: the

legacy of the Chicago Teachers' Federation. *History of Education Review* 13: 43–55; M. McCormack (1994) Margaret A. Haley, 1861–1939: a timeless mentor for teachers as leaders, in R.A. Martusewicz and W.M. Reynolds (eds) *Inside Out: Contemporary Critical Perspectives in Education*. New York: St Martin's Press; D. Tyack (1974) *The One Best System*. Cambridge, MA: Harvard University Press, pp.257–67. The fullest biographical study of Haley is in Reid's edited version of Haley's autobiography, *Battleground*. Examples of a more nuanced and critical view of Haley can be found in L. Weiner (1996) Teachers, unions, and school reform: examining Margaret Haley's vision. *Educational Foundations* 10; W. Urban (1982) *Why Teachers Organized*. Detroit, IL: Wayne State University Press.

4 Studies that take on this type of interdisciplinary perspective on teachers and other women workers include E. Lewis (1993) Invoking concepts, problematizing identities: the life of Charles N. Hunter and the implications for the study of gender and labor. *Labor History* 34: 292–308; A. Kessler-Harris (1993) Treating the male as 'Other': re-defining the parameters of labor history. *Labor History* 34: 190–204; E. Faue (1993) Gender and the reconstruction of labor history, an introduction. *Labor History* 34: 169–77; D.M. Copelman (1996) *London's Women Teachers: Gender, Class and Feminism, 1870–1930*. London: Routledge; S. Middleton (1993) *Educating Feminists: Life-Histories and Pedagogy*. New York: Teachers College Press.

5 Middleton, *Educating Feminists*, p.9; S. Middleton (1994) Schooling and radicalisation: life histories of New Zealand feminist teachers, in L. Stone (ed.) *The Education Feminism Reader*. New York: Routledge, pp.279–99; M.C. Bateson (1990) *Composing a Life*. New York: Plume. See also R. Quantz (1992) Interpretive method in historical research: ethnohistory reconsidered, and The complex vision of female teachers and the failure of unionization in the 1930s: an oral history, both in R. Altenbaugh (ed.) (1992) *The Teacher's Voice: A Social History of Teaching in Twentieth Century America*. London: Falmer Press.

6 I am drawing loosely on feminist standpoint theory as articulated in D.E. Smith (1987) *The Everyday World as Problematic: A Feminist Sociology*. Boston, MA: Northwestern University Press; N.C.M. Hartstock (1983) *Money, Sex and Power: Toward a Feminist Historical Materialism*. New York: Longman, pp.231–51.

7 M. Murphy (1979) Progress of the poverty of philosophy: two generations of labor reform politics: Michael and Margaret Haley. Paper delivered at Knights of Labor Centennial Symposium, Chicago, 17–19 May.

8 Henry Demerest Lloyd quoted in J.L. Thomas (1983) *Alternative America: Henry George, Edward Bellamy, Henry Demarest Lloyd, and the Adversary Tradition*. Cambridge, MA: Belknap Press, p.302. See also A. Feffer (1993) *The Chicago Pragmatists and American Progressivism*. Ithaca, NY: Cornell University Press, esp. pp.179–93, 208–11.

9 J.A. Nolan (1994) Irish-American teachers and the struggle over American urban public education 1890–1920: a preliminary look, unpublished paper; C.G. Heilbrun (1979) *Reinventing Womanhood*. New York: Norton, pp.16–17.

10 H. Diner (1983) *Erin's Daughters in America: Irish Immigrant Women in the Nineteenth Century*. Baltimore, MD: Johns Hopkins University Press.

11 Reid, *Battleground*, p.28.

12 Margaret Haley Autobiography (Chicago version) p.633, Chicago Teachers' Federation Archives, Chicago Historical Society [hereafter, CTF Archives].

13 Rheta Childe Dorr quoted (p.632) in P. Baker (1984) The domestication of politics: women and American political society, 1780–1920. *American Historical Review* 89: 620–47.
14 Baker, ibid., pp.620–47; M.A. Flanagan (1990) Gender and urban political reform: the City Club and the Woman's City Club of Chicago in the Progressive Era. *American Historical Review* 95: 1032–50; K.K. Sklar (1996) *Florence Kelley and the Nation's Work: The Rise of Women's Political Culture, 1830–1900.* New Haven, CT: Yale University Press.
15 Margaret Haley, 3 August 1901, Box 36, Folder 1, CTF Archives.
16 W. Graebner (1980) *A History of Retirement: The Meaning and Function of an American Institution, 1885–1978.* New Haven, CT: Yale, pp.88–119; T. Skopol (1992) *Protecting Soldiers and Mothers: The Political Origins of Social Policy in the United States.* Cambridge, MA: Harvard University Press.
17 Margaret Haley to Jane Addams, 4 May 1906, Anita McCormick Blaine papers, Box 281, Wisconsin Historical Society, Madison Wisconsin.
18 Margaret Haley Autobiography (Seattle version) p.200, CTF Archives.
19 Margaret Haley to Jane Addams, 4 May 1906.
20 M. Murphy (1990) *Blackboard Unions: The AFT and the NEA, 1900–1980.* Ithaca, NY: Cornell University Press, pp.82–3.
21 Undated, unsigned handwritten fragment by Margaret Haley, Box 37, Folder Jan.–June 1903, CTF Archives.
22 Jennie A. Wilcox to 'dear friend', 29 July 1928. Box 2, Series 6, Folder 3, AFT Archives, Walter Reuther Library, Wayne State University.
23 *The School Weekly* 7(18) 3 May 1901.
24 M. Flanagan (1987) *Charter Reform in Chicago.* Carbondale, IL: Southern Illinois University Press, pp.41–2.
25 *Chicago Journal* 18 October 1900.
26 Letter to Margaret Haley and and Catharine Goggin from Josiah Cratty, 23 March 1901, Box 36, Folder Jan.–May 1901, CTF Archives.
27 *The New World* 4 May 1901, p.1.
28 J.L. Spalding, Bishop of Peoria, to Katharine [*sic*] Goggin, 11 November 1901. Box 36, Folder 3, CTF Archives.
29 Letter to Margaret Haley from A.J. Phillips, 20 March 1903, Box 37, Folder Jan.–July 1903, CTF Archives.
30 Letter to Margaret Haley from Sarah M. Perkins, 23 November 1901, Box 36, Folder Sept.–Dec. 1901, CTF Archives; Letter to Margaret Haley from Edward W. Bemis, 4 December 1901, Box 36, 1901–02, Folder Sept.–Dec. 1901, CTF Archives.
31 Handwritten copy of letter from Susan B. Anthony to Margaret Haley, July 1903, CTF Archives.
32 Letter to Margaret Haley from Isaiah Greenacre, 4 December 1902, CTF Archives.
33 For recent investigations of Irish Americans and race see N. Ignatiev (1995) *How the Irish Became White.* New York: Routledge; D.R. Roediger (1991) *The Wages of Whiteness: Race and the Making of the American Working Class.* New York: Verso.
34 J. Addams (1981) *Twenty Years at Hull House.* New York: Signet, p.68.

Index

Mónica, Filomena, 114–15
Morton, Mrs S.P., 135
motherhood, and attitudes to marriage, 96–7
municipal housekeeping, and Margaret
    Haley, 153–4
Murphy, John, 15

narratives of women teachers
    Californian, 47–56
        depictions of 'the first school', 53–4
    and class, 52–3
    and race, 48–52
    and relationships with the 'subject', 54–5
National Education Association (NEA), 147
National Union of Women Teachers
    (NUWT), 106, 108
Neal, Clare, 108
Neverdon-Morton, Cynthia, 135
New Zealand
    changing government policies, 92
    childcare issues, 90–2
    dress of teachers, 82
    early childhood education, 77, 82, 86–8
    Education in Change, 84
    Education and the Equality of the Sexes
        (conference on), 89–90
    Maori students, 80, 83–4
    mixed-ability teaching, 84–5
    and multicultural schools, 84
    novel of teaching in, 11
    photographs of women teachers, 61–3,
        75–6, 92–3
    progressive education, 5, 75–93
        and discipline, 77–9, 85–7
        and feminism, 5, 76–7, 88–92
    protest movements and neo-progressivism,
        79–81
    and school uniforms, 83
    youth culture in secondary schools, 82–3
    see also Maori women
Newbold, N.C., 133, 134, 136, 137, 138,
    140
nineteenth century
    African-American teachers in California,
        48–52
    Canadian women teachers, 27–9, 30,
        31–3
    concepts of women teachers, 3–4, 16–21
novels, written by former teachers, 10–11

O'Brien, Mary, 28
oral history
    California women teachers, 49, 50–6
    Canadian women teachers, 34–6, 37
    and Maori women teachers, 62, 63
    teachers, memory and, 3–4, 9–21
Oram, Alison, 5
Ormsby, Margaret A., 34
Orr, Helen, 91

parents, nineteenth-century, and women
    teachers, 27–8
Passerini, Luisa, 12, 13
Payne, William, 51
Phipps, Emily, 108
photographs, of New Zealand women
    teachers, 61–3, 75–6, 92–3
physicists, women at Canadian universities,
    34, 35, 36
Pihama, Leonie, 66
playcentres, and progressive education in
    New Zealand, 86–8
Pogue, Grace Canon, 52–4, 57
Portuguese women teachers, 5, 113–28
    and absentee pupils, 123–4
    and childcare, 118–20
    and marriage, 117, 122
    and the political regime, 114–15, 125–7
    and pupils' examinations, 120
    in remote villages, 117–20, 122–4
    and school inspectors, 120–1
    subjectivities, 121–7
    and teaching as a vocation, 116–17
    in urban schools, 124–5
postcolonial theory, 2
poststructuralism, and feminist theory, 2, 4,
    44, 45
power
    Foucault on 'capillary' power, 78, 81–2,
        93
    and gender relationships, in *Women Who
        Taught*, 1–2
Prentice, Alison, 4
    and Theobald, Marjorie, *Women Who
        Taught*, 1–2
primary schools
    married women teachers in, 98
    and progressive education in New
        Zealand, 76, 77, 78, 86
Prince, Margaret, 48, 49, 50–2
professional identity, women teachers and
    marriage, 98
professionalism, and Canadian women
    teachers, 28, 36
progressive education, in New Zealand, 5,
    75–93
protest movements, and neo-progressivism in
    New Zealand, 79–81
psychology, and female sexuality, 97, 105–6,
    108

race
    and Californian women teachers, 48–52
    and feminist theory, 46–7
    see also African-Americans
radical feminists
    and progressive education in New
        Zealand, 76
    and sexuality, 88–9